Recalling
The Call

"The 80's Most Underrated Rock 'N Roll Band!"

By: Knoel C. Honn

Exotic Okie Productions 2021

In loving memory of:
Michael Been 1950 – 2010

&

Celebrating 40 years of The Call!

Michael Been

Photo courtesy of Pat Johnson

Introduction:

Why me? Why am I writing this book? It's pretty simple... friendship, good music, and Michael's words resonate with me. They make me think. I'm not a very "religious" person. I don't subscribe to typical, organized religion. For me it's more individual, personal, and spiritual. Michael has said, on occasion, he considers himself to be a Christian, but not in the typical sense. He didn't believe that his beliefs are for everyone. His music reflects how he feels and his truths. The Call's music strikes a chord with me that is powerful, emotional, spiritual, and beautiful. Sadly, I never knew Michael personally, but through his music and words, somehow, I did. I got to know him through his friends, his "family", his heart through his message. I am fortunate to know Scott, Dicky, Jim, Greg, and Steve... and Michael, through them and the music. I truly value my friendship with these great guys. Michael was a powerful craftsman of words and **The Call** a band with a message that still needs told. That still resonates. That is timeless. It was time someone dug deeper and told their tale. Ladies and Gentlemen...

My friends.

"The Call"

Contents:

Chapter One:

In the beginning...

Every band has its beginning, its spark, what breathed life into it. The Call began with deep-seated roots in Oklahoma. Michael Been and Scott Musick grew up in Oklahoma, with Michael in Oklahoma City and Scott in Tulsa. Oklahoma has birthed many talented musicians. Not yet knowing Michael, Scott attends Tulsa Edison High School at the same time as Dwight Twilley, Phil Seymour and Jamie Oldaker. Dwight and Phil went on to form the Dwight Twilley Band. Jamie Oldaker started out in The Rogues 5, also playing drums. Eventually, Jamie goes on to play for Eric Clapton, Bob Seger, and The Tractors (also an Okie band lead by Steve Ripley).

In high school, Scott became a student teacher for local drum instructor, Paul McGhee. During this time, he taught student, Phil Seymour, and met part-time student Jaime Oldaker. He also worked with David Teegarden Sr., a fellow student teacher. All of these musicians went on to become professional drummers, with prestigious careers.

Michael Been's roots were about 2 hours west of Scott Musick in Oklahoma City. Eventually Michael moved to the Chicago, Illinois area and later to California in 1972.

Fellow Okies, Michael and Scott had no idea that fate would eventually bring them together in Santa Cruz, California, along with guitarist, Tom Ferrier, as Airtight. Bassist Greg Freeman would soon join them, becoming Motion Pictures, and eventually The Call.

Michael, in a ten to twelve year period, cut his teeth performing with several bands, cultivating his unique sound and perspective. Michael formed his first band in high school, The Chessman, and later The Saints. Next, he joined Aorta in 1970. These were followed by Lovecraft, Fine Wine and The Original Haze (which also featured Scott Musick on drums).

Michael Been on stage in the late 1960's playing in his band The Saints.   Photo courtesy Pam Wilson Wetzel.

Michael and Scott also played with Barry McGuire in the 70's. After The Original Haze, The Michael Been Band Is Airtight was formed which quickly became Airtight. From Airtight, they became Motion Pictures and finally, The Call emerges.

The Call's initial path to discovery was via fellow Okie and Edison High School alum Phil Seymour. Phil Seymour phoned Scott Musick, to ask if he could enlist Motion Pictures / The Call as his backup band. Seymour and Dwight Twilley had found success with their 1975 hit single, "I'm On Fire," with Leon Russell's Shelter Records Label and The Church Studio in Tulsa, Oklahoma. Denny Cordell (Leon's partner in Shelter Records), set The Call in motion to record their first record in England, thanks to Phil Seymour.

Call it destiny or perhaps fate that would bring The Call together in California, even with roots firmly planted in Oklahoma. Oklahoma roots, that would influence the band for the next twenty years. From a more spiritual "Bible Belt" morality to "Another Hot Oklahoma Night," the roots found in two young Okies were inescapable. Scott as with Dwight Twilley, Phil Seymour, Jamie Oldaker, and David Teegarden Sr., would eventually find his way back to Oklahoma. Michael would continue to work on the road with his son's band B.R.M.C., until his untimely death in 2010.   Even though Oklahoma was a part of their soul, The Call's self titled, 1982 debut album, on Mercury / Polygram, came about via California and a trip to England.

When asked by the record label, "If given the chance to work with anyone *who would it be*?" As long time admirers, The Call said, "Garth Hudson of The Band. As fate would have it, the label rep knew Garth Hudson and invited him to the studio. This began a relationship with Garth that resulted in their first two studio albums. Garth also toured with The Call for a couple of tours and appeared in their music video for "The Walls Came Down" off of 1983's *Modern Romans* album.

MOTION PICTURES

Above: Enjoying their trip to England at Stonehenge.
Below: In Oxfordshire, England to record their first album with Greg Freeman, Garth Hudson, Michael Been, Tom Ferrier and Scott Musick at The Manor in 1981.

The early days of The Call

Tom Ferrier, Greg Freeman, Michael Been & Scott Musick – Circa 1982

Pictures used with permission from The Call

The Call's self-titled debut album, in 1982, caught the attention of the critics, calling them "uncompromising," "apocalyptic," "bristling," and "urgent." The Philadelphia Daily News said, "The Call will soon be heard and celebrated 'round the world as the best new rock band of the '80's." Ironically, The Call's first demos were rejected by nearly every major American label. Ultimately, they ended up in England with English producers eager to produce the passionate new band. The self titled first album was produced by Hugh Padgham, who is known for working with David Bowie and the Police, among others. In the early 80's, many people thought The Call were an English band.

The Call continued on with 1983's *Modern Romans* and 1984's *Scene Beyond Dreams*. The band continued to get good reviews and praise from critics and peers, alike. Billboard, Musician, Melody Maker, and New Musical Express magazines cite The Call's depth of material and their passion of performance. "Rock 'N Roll is a vehicle to express the emotions you are not allowed to use in everyday life," says Michael Been about their songs. "The Walls Came Down" (written as an answer to Ronald Reagan's anti-Soviet saber-rattling) is nothing, if not full of emotion.

In 1984, after *Scene Beyond Dreams,* The Call became embroiled in legal disputes with its label and management. The unexpected benefit of this, according to Michael, was that the band had extra time to work on songs and put together what some view as their main stream breakthrough album, 1986's *Reconciled.* The album exemplified The Call's unflinching commitment to its unique and uncompromising music.

****

"I suppose I could have written cheesy pop songs for movie soundtracks and hit radio. When I was young that's what I wanted to do. But when I sat down to write, only these songs would come. I guess the band is called The Call for a reason." – Michael Been

****

Michael proves the band's relevance is just as much there today, as ever… "We're good at rhetoric of freedom in America, but our track record is less than stellar. And at a time when more and more Christians are becoming involved in politics, it's shameful that much of our activism ignores or even scapegoats the weak, the outcast, the widows and the imprisoned – the very ones Christ says are the 'least of these, my brothers.'"

Stepping back to the 70's... When did The Call really begin to manifest? I would say the core of the band really began to develop in Airtight. Airtight being Michael and Scott, with Dale Ockerman, and eventually Dicky Dirt. Dale Ockerman brought Dicky into the band. Greg Freeman was a roadie / tech at this point.

When did Airtight officially begin? According to Ockerman, late '76 or '77 to the best of his recollection. "I walked into the Crow's Nest and Airtight was playing. Mike was on piano and Scott was there. I can't remember anyone else. There was a Telecaster on stage, I played lead guitar, had a great time and joined on the spot." "I think at one point Tommy Spurlock played a couple of Santa Cruz gigs..."

"I have a lot of love for Scott and Michael. Ultimately, Airtight just didn't work out. I felt Michael wasn't being true to himself. Michael was conflicted and had inner turmoil at times. Airtight had a record deal that ended up dead in the water. Great Songs. Bad recordings. Scott, Mike and I did the recording, which sucked, at Studio 55, where Streisand was recording, Richard Perry's studio. The partnership was obviously eroding... We had 2 songs in the can and Mike wanted a release date and they "released us."

"Mike and I had very different tastes in music as well. I'm not a big fan of new wave [the direction things seemed to be going even then.] …anymore than I liked disco. I do like grunge, blues and funk… The big deal to me was really R & B, blues and funk [at the time], so I got bored and left the band in '78."

Like often happens in music with growth and growing pains, comes conflict and ultimately change. The partings of ways, and the good with the bad. Dale seems to look back fondly at the good times.

Many years later, as The Call was nearing the end of it's heyday in 1999/2000, Dale Ockerman rejoined them once again briefly, to do some shows bringing back the classic Airtight-days lineup to The Call.

As Ockerman left and Airtight gave birth to Motion Pictures and The Call, Dale joined other bands enjoying his own career with groups like the Doobie Brothers.

Ultimately even though Airtight didn't work out, one thing is for certain as the funkier grooves gave way to the "new wave post punk" vibes. If there hadn't been Airtight, if Dale hadn't introduced Michael and Scott to Dicky, if songs like "Say the Word" hadn't led to "The Walls Came Down"… There would be no The Call.

Interestingly, The Call could have let themselves be influenced by other forces too, such as the label and become the labels' vision for the band. Lucky for us, Michael and band held fast and made the right decisions, giving us what we came to know and love.

Other concepts for the band and first album included:

Names suggested by the record label.

What if The Call were *Foil Matrix, Silicon Fuse, Armageddon's Child or Cobalt Flash*?

The simplicity of the first album art and concept made an impact on me. The cover art and concept they chose simply said: we are The Call.

Above is some of the proposed album art and a concept for the direction of the first album. Artist Unknown.

Consider... War Weary World by *Armageddon's Child* on the *"On the Edge of Obsession"* album. The band could have gone so many different directions. Thankfully they delivered and didn't fall victim to the "80's".

Four other album concepts for the first album follow.

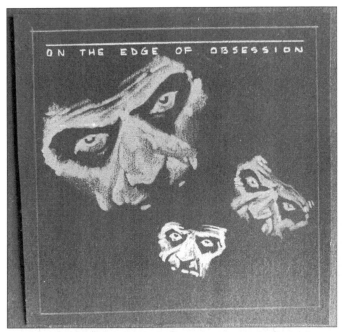

ON THE EDGE OF OBSESSION

Courtesy Greg Freeman – Concept Artist Unknown

WAR WEARY WORLD

"Andy Warhol
Style Portraits

Courtesy Greg Freeman – Concept Artist Unknown

Chapter Two:
Behind the Music

Michael Kenneth Been – vocalist, lyricist, guitarist and bassist. Born in Oklahoma City, Oklahoma March 17th, 1950, Michael later moved to Park Forest, south of Chicago, Illinois. It was here that Michael went to high school and started his first band. Michael moved to Chicago at age 16 and eventually joined the band Aorta, for their second album *Aorta 2,* in 1970, at the age of 20. Michael then joined the band Lovecraft, which was formerly the rock band H.P. Lovecraft. In the mid 70's, Michael moved to Santa Cruz, California, playing in the band Fine Wine with former Moby Grape members, Jerry Miller and Bob Mosley. Eventually, Been would play with Jerry Miller in the band The Original Haze, which also had future The Call drummer Scott Musick on drums. Michael played bass for 2nd Chapter of Acts on their first two albums in 1974 and 1975; also, on Barry McGuire's 1974 release, *Lighten Up.*

Eventually, Michael Been and Scott Musick join forces with Dale Ockerman to form The Michael Been Band Is Airtight, which became Airtight. After Ockerman left the group, Been, Musick, Ferrier, and Freeman formed Motion Pictures, which became The Call.

Michael said of growing up in Oklahoma that the only real entertainment came from a radio speaker.

Michael's first sight of Elvis on TV really had an effect on him and it changed his life. By age 7, Michael began frequently performing on local television and radio. Music has been Michael's passion and profession ever since.

In the mid 60's, Michael met Wood Mason, Jimmy Rignall, and Dana Cole. They formed The Chessmen and began playing together in late 1964 and early 1965. As freshmen at Rich East High School in Park Forest, Illinois, they played high school dances and sock hops. According to Wood Mason, somewhere along the way, they changed the name of the band to The Saints. Mason said, "I don't recall the exact reason for our change to The Saints, but during that time we lost Rignall and Cole. We gained Bill Tollefson and Bill Austin. We played as a quartet for a short time. Michael felt we needed a dedicated singer, as he was singing pretty much every song. Mark Gallagher came on board and we were a five piece until the winter of 1968 when we broke up." The Saints played in the greater Chicago area, even playing fraternity and Halloween parties at Perdue University around 1967.

According to high school friend Pam Wetzel, "Michael and the guys were very talented and popular, and made quite a name for themselves performing around the Chicago area for about four years."

Michael did also experiment, for a short period of time, with comedy in Chicago. He placed first in the Illinois state competition, besting his friend John Belushi, who placed second. Ultimately, it was music, not comedy that brought Michael out to California.

Michael's love of music, performing, and his dedicated hard work paid off, leading to the start of a professional career in music at the age of 18, just out of high school.

Scott Musick – drummer and vocals. Born June 8th, 1952 in Tulsa, Oklahoma, Scott grew up in a musical environment. He started playing as a young kid. His dad was a musician, playing drums, guitar, and trumpet. His older brother sang in local bands. Scott played in the jazz band at school and then began drumming for a rock band. He attended Edison High School with fellow musicians Dwight Twilley and Phil Seymour, who went on to record on Leon Russell's *Shelter Records* label, at Church Studio, in Tulsa. Seymour would eventually help connect Scott and The Call with Denny Cordell.

After high school, Scott moved to Los Angeles. He played in a couple of bands and ended up in Las Vegas with a club band. After 6 months or so, he moved back to Tulsa, which resulted in him running into a friend from California. He was then steered back to California with the suggestion of looking up a guy named Michael Been, whom he was told had a great voice. Scott returned to California and tracked down Been, which resulted in them playing in several bands together, and settling down in Santa Cruz, California in 1976.

The irony was not lost on them that they were both from Oklahoma. Years later the two discovered that their grandfathers had been best friends in college and worked at the same pharmacy in Tulsa, Oklahoma.

****

Above Photo: Scott - bottom left drummer with high school mate
Phil Seymour - top left above Scott. Tulsa, OK

Thomas Walter Ferrier – guitar, aka Dicky Dirt, born July 7th, 1948. Growing up in California, Tom recalls at about the age of 7, "I got a walkie-talkie for Christmas and I would pretend to have this radio show and play all my favorite music. After I got my first guitar, it became an obsession pretty quickly." Tom eventually gigged around in different bands in California. Back then, surf music was the rage, but Tom preferred playing in blues-based bands. Recalling his start with The Call, "It was a fluke, really, that we got together. Scott and Michael were in a band and their guitarist didn't show up for a gig one night. Someone called and asked if I would sit in. We played so naturally together - everything just clicked."

Motion Pictures / The Call (used with permission)

Greg (Gregory) Freeman – bass guitar. Born October 1956 in Watsonville, California.

Greg grew up in the east San Francisco Bay area, in the San Ramon Valley. He went to high school in Danville and attended UC Santa Cruz from 1974 until 1978. Greg started playing bass around 1975, and from 1977 until 1979, played in a 60's cover band called The Waybacks, that played at UCSC and at parties around the Santa Cruz area. Greg was also a DJ at the UCSC campus radio station KZSC. He was strongly influenced by 60's rock music, like the Grateful Dead, Jefferson Airplane, Moby Grape, Sly and the Family Stone, Bob Dylan and The Band. Eventually, he became obsessed with punk rock and new wave music from bands like The Ramones, Television, Talking Heads, Joy Division, The Cure, Wire, and many more.

In 1979, Greg was still in The Waybacks when he started playing with Michael, Scott, and Dicky in what eventually became The Call. "I think it's safe to say that I learned on the job, since I had no real professional music experience at all when I joined the group, and very little unprofessional experience, for that matter. I played on the first two The Call albums, *The Call* and *Modern Romans*, and left the band in 1983."

Greg was also the unofficial band historian / record keeper in the early years.

Steve Huddleston – keyboard. Born October 10th. A fellow "Okie," Steve had known Scott through mutual friends since the early 70's. Steve recalls, "Scott was living in the Santa Cruz Mountains and played with several bands - The Original Haze, Airtight and Motion Pictures. Michael was in all of those bands, playing bass, as I recall. I was from Enid, Oklahoma, but was living in Colorado in those years, and I travelled to California frequently to hear Scott and Michael play. Those bands were fantastic. "

"Sometime in the late 70's, I had heard that they had a new band, so I went out to see them. I think it was the [early] lineup with Michael, Scott, Greg, and Tom. The whole sound was very new wave. Denny Cordell was managing them and it was obvious that big things were coming. So, I decided to move out there and help any way I could. I volunteered for roadie work and soon found myself as Scott's drum-setup guy. After some time, Michael wanted me to be his guitar tech, which I did. That was a busy job, because he played very aggressively and broke a LOT of strings. "

"I owned a Fender Rhodes electric piano and told Michael before one rehearsal that I was going to bring it and sit in with them. He didn't say no and apparently, they liked it, because he had me trade it for a synthesizer. For a while we would set up the synth, but

I wouldn't get up on stage till the last number, which was "The Walls Came Down." (Note: Michael had written a song years earlier called "Say the Word," which had the little hook lick which he incorporated into "The Walls Came Down").

"As time went on, I eventually became 'full-time,' sort of. I left when my wife got pregnant in early '83."

****

Steve playing with Scott in Tulsa – 2015
Photo copyright Knoel Honn 2015

Eric Garth Hudson – Born August 2nd, 1937, in Windsor, Ontario, Canada. Garth (as you probably know) is an amazing multi-instrumentalist, playing organ, keyboard, and saxophone for The Band.

Hudson played on The Call's first three albums and toured with them in the early years of the band. He contributed his undeniably unique sound to the first two albums, resulting in a sound and experience that The Call and the fans will never forget.

Hudson, in Musician magazine said, "I thought the writing was excellent. I liked the melodies and all the little things they put in. They're all strong players - both in arrangements and improvisation. They felt good; the songs had something to do with what's going on. The words had a cause which was important, because I'm concerned about the state of America. I'd rather be representative of the fighters than the wimp-rockers." Hudson toured with The Call in 1982 and '83 when they supported both Peter Gabriel and Simple Minds.

Joe Read – played bass for The Call for a short period of time, from 1983 to 1985, replacing Greg Freeman after his departure. Joe recorded on the album *Scene Beyond Dreams* and played live with The Call during this time. Joe also played with other artists, such as Tulsa's Phil Seymour, Strapps, Code Blue, and Carla Olson and The Textones.

Jim Goodwin – keyboard and vocals. Born in Eugene, Oregon in 1958. Jim came to The Call in a time of transition with record labels, in line-up and sound. Jim studied piano for a year at the age of 10. Then, at age 13, he started piano lessons again, because he was inspired by his cousin, who was learning piano and composition. He played in his cousin's band two years later, while in high school in Portland. After high school, Jim went to Paris, France and studied saxophone for a year (1977/78), then came back to play with his cousin in San Francisco, where he continued to study sax and piano (1978/79). After a year, Jim followed a girl to New York City and played in bands until he was hired by John Cale (Velvet Underground) to record an album for A&M Records and go on tour (1980). Jim eventually got offered a gig with Sparks, in Los Angeles in 1982, and did a tour, an album, and another tour, before hooking up with The Call in 1983.

Jim helped develop the keyboard sound The Call is known for, on albums such as *Reconciled, Into the Woods* and *Let the Day Begin*. Jim has the rare, shared writing credits with Michael Been on songs such as the track, "I Still Believe." Jim has continued working in music, writing songs and commercial scores for independent films, and created themes most notably for Sunny Delight, ABC Primetime, and Miller Beer.

Ralph Patlan – guitar. Ralph joined The Call for a brief period in the 90's as a second guitar player (after being Dicky's guitar tech), during the period of time Jim Goodwin was not playing keyboard with the band, to fill out the sound and make up for the lack of keyboard.

Scott Musick playing the drums 1970's.
Courtesy Scott Musick and The Call.

Photos used by permission: Dan Russell and The Call

Robert Levon Been – Son of Michael and Carol Been. Born August 22nd, 1978 in Felton, California. Robert, a member of the band Black Rebel Motorcycle Club, recorded on his father's 1994 solo album, *On the Verge of a Nervous Breakthrough*. After Michael's passing (August 19, 2010) at the Pukkelpop festival in Belgium, Robert filled in for his dad (paying tribute) with The Call at two shows in 2013. Robert is also featured on the subsequent live album recorded at the Troubadour tribute show, *The Call: A Tribute to Michael Been*.

Dan Russell – Friend & Manager from 1988 to Late 90's

Dan's credits include promoter, producer, collaborator, manager, video / film supervisor and so much more. He worked with Mark Heard, U2, Black Rebel Motorcycle Club, Sam Phillips, Andy Pratt, Bruce Cockburn, Switchfoot, Robin Lane, The Vigilantes of Love, Ramona Silver, Rachel Taylor, The Violet Burning and of course The Call. Dan first met Michael after a show in 1983. For almost two decades, Dan worked with Michael Been and The Call. Dan went on the road for an extended period with The Call on the *Let The Day Begin* tour. Dan once said, "The Call offers a balanced perspective of spirituality."

****

Dan Russell and Michael Been lower left on previous page.

Chapter Three:

Who are The Call?

Where did The Call and their unique sound come from? The Call, at their core, is Michael Been, Scott Musick, and Tom Ferrier. Their sound was a once in a lifetime universal alignment that was meant to happen evolving from Michael's passionate lyrics and vocals, Scott's driving drums, and Dicky's blues-inspired guitar.

"In strong voice through 17 songs and a generous encore, Been held nothing back, bringing a biting rock brilliance to the group's semi-acoustic lineup. He's also a spiritual, anthemic songwriter who flows easily between the searing and the soaring, and the night's set offered strong evidence that The Call, unsung or not, may well be the closest thing America has ever had to its own U2. No wonder Bono, Peter Gabriel and Bruce Cockburn are Call fans." - Chicago Tribune, Lou Carloza - June 1998

"This critically acclaimed band counts Peter Gabriel, Robbie Robertson, and Jim Kerr among its biggest fans. So what are you waiting for? This is a Call well worth heeding." - Rolling Stone

Even through all of their personnel changes, from the fated pairing with The Band's Garth Hudson and Steve Huddleston on keyboards, Greg Freeman's pounding bass-playing, to Joe Read, and eventually, Michael taking over bass duties, and Jim Goodwin stepping in on keyboards after Garth and Steve's departure, the core of The Call, its heart and soul, always remained Michael, Scott, and Tom.

Photo by Joe Piccorossi 1982 Destin, FL
Used with permission R. George Inness III

Michael has said that one of the most important things to have happened in 1985 is that the group solidified into a "cohesive unit of players struggling toward a common end." "That's something I've wanted since I was 16 years old, when I heard The Band for the first time," says Been. "When that happens - that chemistry between people - it's incredibly satisfying." Culminating in bassist/vocalist Been, drummer Scott Musick, keyboard player Jim Goodwin, and guitarist Tom Ferrier as integral parts of a whole - a whole which is greater than the sum of its parts. "We've been through hell and high water together." "To know that we've done this together is what makes it all worthwhile."

During this transition, Garth Hudson stepped away due to other commitments, but his colleague, Robbie Robertson, stepped in and played guitar on "The Morning." Michael also guested on two tracks for Peter Gabriel and four tracks on Simple Minds: *Once Upon A Time*.

This newly solidified and more streamlined band lineup opened for Simple Minds on their spring 1986 tour of the U.S. and Canada. Building on their previous successes and coming out of conflict with their previous label and management, The Call embarked on a five year high with *Reconciled, Into the Woods, Let the Day Begin,* and *Red Moon*, their most successful period.

Despite their growing popularity, Michael still kept things in check and remained down to earth in his commitment to his music and message. "We were never impressed by fashion, or the latest haircut or the newest trend," said Michael, "With us, it was always the music. The music is everything. The cult of personality and celebrity that surrounds rock 'n roll and the modern pop culture in general, never really interested us. I would say that if it got to a point where music was just a function of making money, and we had to play a song we didn't believe in, or present ourselves in a way that wasn't true to us, I don't think we'd do it anymore. I'd get into another line of work because that's not why I play music. Don't get me wrong, we would love to be able to do a song that everyone loved and have it be a big hit. We'd rather have a hit record than not have one, but I don't think it's in our nature to fake it or try and create something out of nothing."

True to form and his word, Michael referred to his compositions as "...basically love songs. I'm talking about the love between us all. I think it gets down to what love demands of us. Unconditional love and acceptance - where you love not only what is lovable in a person, but you also love their weaknesses as well as their strengths, their failures as much as their success, and their ugliness as well as their beauty - to me this is true love, God's love. And I'm not even sure it's humanly possible. I'm still working on that one."

Some argue that Michael's *Reconciled* and post-*Reconciled* songwriting carried a more forgiving, less confronting tone than much of the material on their earlier efforts. Still, Michael marches forward with passion and intensity.

Into the Woods changes the game again and is played and sung entirely by the group. "That was intentional," said Michael. "We wanted it to be just the band this time. We also made an effort to incorporate different styles of playing that we learned over the years. I can hear blues, soul, gospel, folk, country, of course rock and roll, and even classical influence, but it still sounds like The Call."

Another first on *Into the Woods* is "In the River," featuring a rare vocal co-lead by Scott, who also co-wrote the song with Michael. *Into the Woods* is viewed by many to be a very intense, compelling, and spiritual album.

Let the Day Begin was again a transition, both musically and from Elektra to MCA records. Elektra didn't like the album and asked them to start over. MCA liked the record, but a few weeks after the label picked up the band, record executives changed and again, they had issues with the release. The single, "Let the Day Begin," performed really well and the label had to scramble to have more copies of the record pressed and failed to give the album the proper support.

In 1990, *Red Moon* was also released on MCA, but the band had problems once again, due to the label insisting on releasing the wrong song as a single, because Bono was singing backing vocals on the track. While the album was a solid, well-liked album, it suffered due to lack of support and being dropped by the label.

After this period, the band did other projects, such as Michael's two solo efforts, *Light Sleeper* and *On the Verge of a Nervous Breakthrough*. Jim took a break to spend time being a husband and father. During this period (in the mid 90's), The Call was again stripped down to the original core three - Michael, Scott, and Tom - only periodically playing with others, such as Ralph Patlan.

Eventually, the band regrouped with Jim to release *To Heaven and Back*, some greatest hits collections, and the *Live Under the Red Moon* album, recorded in 1990.

Live Under the Red Moon proved to be the last album released (in 2000), bringing twenty years of The Call to a close, until the tribute album release in 2014 with Robert Been on vocals.

****

"Why did The Call have so many problems with record labels and deals falling through? Because, making it in rock 'n roll is just random luck. There are so many good bands out there. You have to have the right stuff, at the right time, and LUCK!" – Tom Ferrier

****

"With all of the problems that we did have, we survived 25 years because we worked well together. It was easy for us to play together and make good music. We were survivalists and the loveable losers. We never quite got there, but we really did it well." – Tom Ferrier

****

"What I really remember, and like talking about, is the albums and what went into making them. Each experience was so different. I remember when Jim and Peter came into the studio for Reconciled. It was very exciting." – Tom Ferrier - Oct 18th, 2020

****

The Chessmen

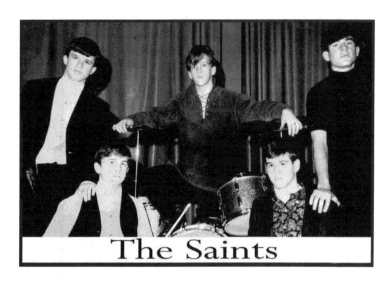

This page: Saints promotional photos circa 1967

Michael	Bill	Mark	Bill	Wood
Been	Austin	Gallagher	Tollefson	Mason

Chessmen (previous page) circa 1965 – used with permission.

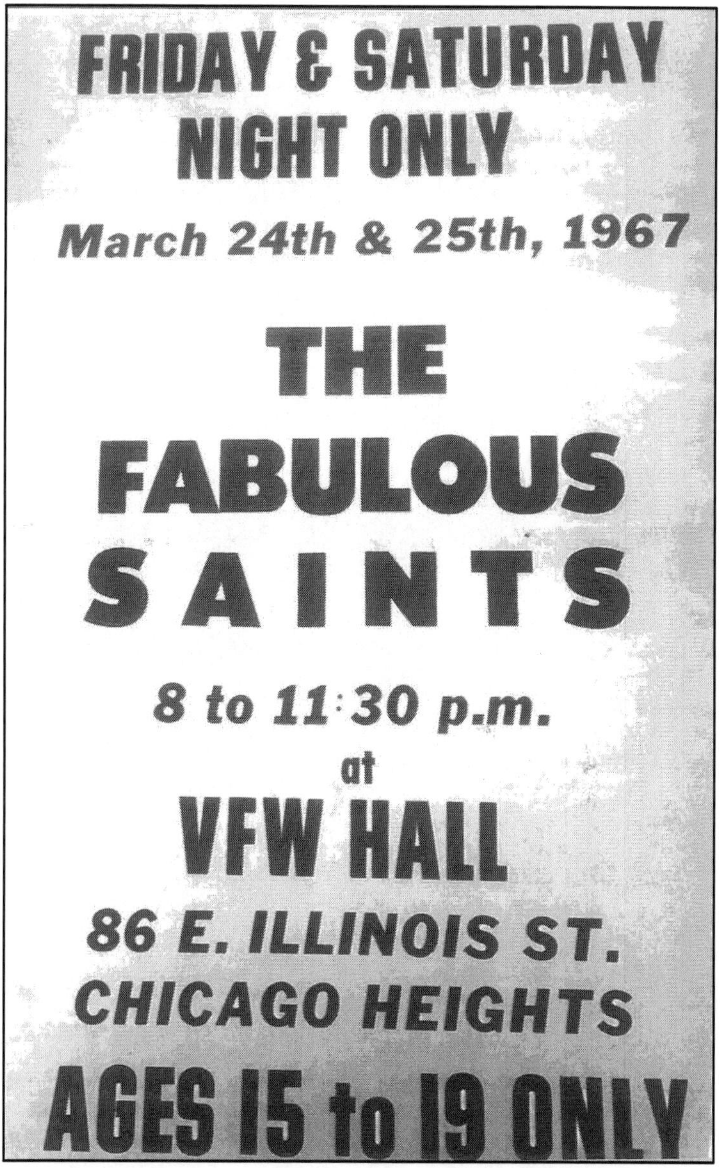

FRIDAY & SATURDAY
NIGHT ONLY

March 24th & 25th, 1967

THE
FABULOUS
SAINTS

8 to 11:30 p.m.
at
VFW HALL
86 E. ILLINOIS ST.
CHICAGO HEIGHTS
AGES 15 to 19 ONLY

Michael's high school band The Saints - 1967

A rare original 45 from Michael's high school band:

The Saints

****

Show poster and 45 RPM single

Courtesy high school friend Pam Wilson Wetzel

Photos courtesy Pam Wilson Wetzel

Michael Been – mid 1960's – near Chicago, Illinois

Michael Been & The Saints – mid 1960's

Courtesy Pam Wilson Wetzel

Michael Been & The Saints – mid 1960's

Michael and high school band mates:

The Saints

The Call - Cabaret - San Jose, CA mid 80's

Cabaret photos courtesy Paul Goeltz – Photographer

Dicky Dirt – Cabaret – San Jose, CA

Michael and Jim Goodwin – Cabaret – San Jose, CA

Photos courtesy Paul Goeltz - Photographer

Michael Been – Cabaret – San Jose, CA

Cabaret – San Jose, CA - Paul Goeltz - Photographer

Cabaret – San Jose, CA - Paul Goeltz - Photographer

Michael Been – Cabaret – San Jose, CA
Courtesy of - Paul Goeltz – Photographer

Michael Been – Cabaret – San Jose, CA
Courtesy of - Paul Goeltz – Photographer

Chapter Four:

Michael's Pre-Call Timeline

Aorta – Aorta 2 album – Michael joins 1969/1970
Michael on bass, backing vocals and co-writes songs
Aorta 2 was recorded and released on L.A. label Happy
Tiger Records.

Lovecraft (Formerly H.P. Lovecraft) 1969/1970
was formed / joined by Jim Donlinger and Michael from
Aorta with Marty Grebb from the Exceptions. They
released the album *Valley of the Moon*. Interestingly,
Lovecraft went on the road during this time, in support
of Leon Russell.

[During this era Michael records and tours with the 2nd
Chapter of Acts on 1974's *With Footnotes* and 1975's *In
the Volume of the Book.* He also works with Barry
McGuire on 1974's *Lighten Up*]

Fine Wine – Releases the self titled album *Fine Wine*
which finally came out in 1976. This band was formed
with former Moby Grape members Jerry Miller and Bob
Mosley.

The Original Haze (Late 70's) comes from Fine Wine.
Scott Musick joins Michael as a member of The Original
Haze, which leads to The Michael Been Band is Airtight.

"The Call"

Timeline – Late 1970's to Present

The Michael Been Band is Airtight

Airtight (with Dale Ockerman)(Tom aka "Dicky" joins)

Motion Pictures & Phil Seymour Band – 1979/1980

Motion Pictures (The Call) (Vs. 1) - 1980

Michael Been, Scott Musick, Tom Ferrier, Greg Freeman

The Call (Vs. 2) – 1981 (Officially becomes The Call)

Michael Been, Scott Musick, Tom Ferrier, Greg Freeman, Steve Huddleston, Garth Hudson

The Call (Vs. 3) – 1983/1984

Michael Been, Scott Musick, Tom Ferrier, Joe Read, Jim Goodwin.

The Call (Vs. 4) – 1985/1986

Michael Been, Scott Musick, Tom Ferrier, Jim Goodwin

The Call (Vs. 5) - 1991

Michael Been, Scott Musick, Tom Ferrier

The Call (Vs. 6) – 1991/92

Michael Been, Scott Musick, Tom Ferrier, Ralph Patlan

The Call (Vs. 7) - 1997

Michael Been, Scott Musick, Tom Ferrier

The Call (Vs. 8) - 1998

Michael Been, Scott Musick, Tom Ferrier, Jim Goodwin

The Call (Vs. 9) – April 18th & 19th, 2013

Robert Been, Scott Musick, Tom Ferrier, Jim Goodwin

The Call (Vs. 10) - April 22nd, 2017 New Orleans

Scott Musick, Tom Ferrier, Jim Goodwin

With Guest Vocalists: Michael Divita (of Alarm 58),

Ray Ganucheau and J.D. Buhl (R.I.P. J.D. Buhl 2017)

1979		
MONDAY	**TUESDAY**	**WEDNESDAY**
NOTES		
3	4	5
		BWE LAGUNE (SEYMOUR)
10	11	12
STARWOOD (SEYMOUR)	FLIPPERS (MOTION ACTORS)	BUZZCOCKS IN L.A.
17	18	19
CROW'S NEST (M.P.)		
24	25	26
31 HI-CO. (MOTION PICTURES)	Christmas Day	[TO S.C.]

Greg Freeman's personal calendar for Motion Pictures and Phil Seymour dates. December 1979. Several dates in December are designated as Phil Seymour shows and

		DECEMBER
THURSDAY	**FRIDAY**	**SAT./SUN.**
		1 SAT.
		2 SUN.
6	7	8 SAT.
	NUGGET (SEYMOUR)	9 SUN. ROSEMARY @ 5 PM.
13	14 BUZZWORKS IN SANTA CRUZ	15 SAT. HONG KONG (SEYMOUR) Chanukah
		16 SUN. [TO S.C.]
20	21	22 SAT.
	"HUMAN FLY'S" RADIO SHOW 3-6 PM	[TO SAN RAMON] 23 SUN.
27	28	29 SAT.
		30 SUN.

others, as simply Motion Pictures shows. It appears that December 15th, they did a show at Hong Kong Café with Phil Seymour, then back to Santa Cruz the following day.

1980		
MONDAY	TUESDAY	WEDNESDAY
HIGH COUNTRY (MOTION PICTURE) *[crossed out]* MASON ST. BASH *[crossed out]*	1 PRACTICE ~8:30 PM New Year's Day	2 DR. MULE 10:15 AM S.C. MED CLINIC
7 MADAME WONG'S [MOTION PIX]	8 WHISKY [MOTION PIX]	9
14	15	16 CROW'S NEST *[crossed out]*
21 CROW'S NEST	22 RADIO SHED ~3-4 PM	23
28	29	30

Greg Freeman's January 1980 personal calendar for Motion Pictures and Phil Seymour dates. Several dates in January are designated as Phil Seymour shows and

THURSDAY	FRIDAY	SAT./SUN.
3 3:45 PM DR. WINDSOR [DENTIST]	4 2:30 PM REHEARSAL WAMBACKS /SHELLIES JONES' / SISIS	5 SAT. HOLLYWOOD RECORD SWAP MEET (?) 8 PM [TO L.A.] 6 SUN. BLACKIE'S [SEYMOUR]
10 WITH SKEY [PHIL]	11	12 SAT. HONG KONG [PHIL] 13 SUN. [TO S.C.]
17	18	19 SAT. 20 SUN.
~~FRAX/N.Y.~~ ? ~~[SETTING PAD]~~	WAMBACKS (W) SHELLIES	
24	25 DAD A.M. [TO LONDON]	26 SAT. ARRIVE LONDON 11:45 AM 27 SUN.
31 OLYMPIC STUDIO 7-2	NOTES	

others, again as simply Motion Pictures shows. On January 25th, they flew to London the first time and January 31st, they went to Olympic Studio.

1980		
MONDAY	**TUESDAY**	**WEDNESDAY**
NOTES		
4	5 OLYMPIC STUDIO	6
11	12 JOHN PEEL RADIO 1 10-12PM P.I.L. ON OLYMPIC O.G.W.T. STUDIO 11:30 PM Lincoln's Birthday	13
18	19	20
Washington's Birthday		Ash Wednesday
25	26 GREYHOUND, FULHAM PALACE ROAD	27 SOUTHAMPTON UNIVERSITY

Greg Freeman's February 1980, personal calendar for Motion Pictures. The first two weeks of February 1980 are spent at Olympic Studio.

THURSDAY	FRIDAY	SAT./SUN.
	1	2 SAT.
	OLYMPIC STUDIO 7PM	3 SUN.
7	8	9 SAT.
	→	10 SUN.
14	15	16 SAT.
	→	17 SUN.
21 / 11.15 AM DENTIST APPT. SLITS FOXY VENUE OPEN?	22 RAMONES @ ELECTRIC BALL FOXY VENUE OPEN?	23 SAT. HIGH w/ JAKS WYCOMBE RAMONES @ ELECTRIC BALL / 24 SUN. PRETENDERS IN BIRMINGHAM
28 BOURNEMOUTH STATESIDE, DORSET [STONEHENGE IN AFTERNOON]	29 ASTON UNIVERSITY, BIRMINGHAM	

The next two weeks appears to be shows, with a visit to Stonehenge on February 28th.

Photos courtesy Greg Freeman collection.

Release Timeline

The Call **(LP)** – 1982

Modern Romans **(LP)** – 1983

"The Walls Came Down" (Single) - 1983

Scene Beyond Dreams **(LP)** – 1984

Reconciled **(LP)** – 1986

"Everywhere I Go" (Single) – 1986

"I Still Believe (Great Design)" (Single) - 1986

Into the Woods **(LP)** – 1987

"I Don't Wanna" (Single) - 1987

(Michael – Film) The Last Temptation of Christ - 1988

Let the Day Begin **(LP)** – 1989

"Let the Day Begin" (Single) – 1989

"You Run" (Single) - 1989

Red Moon **(LP)** – 1990

"What's Happened to You" (Single) - 1990

The Walls Came Down: The Best of the Mercury Years **(LP)** – 1991

(Michael Been) *Light Sleeper Soundtrack* **(LP)** – 1992

(Michael Been) ***On the Verge of a Nervous Breakthrough*** **(LP)** – 1994

The Best of The Call **(LP)** – 1997

To Heaven and Back **(LP)** – 1998

Love is Everywhere **(EP)** – 1998

Live Under the Red Moon **(LP)** – 2000

20th Century Masters – The Millennium Collection: The Best of The Call **(LP)** – 2000

The Call - A Tribute to Michael Been featuring Robert Levon Been (BRMC) **(LP)** – 2014

(Scott Musick) *Americana Gold* - 2016

The Call – Collected **(LP)** – 2019

Timeline of Significant Events:

The Call / Motion Pictures is born – 1980

Recording in England – 1981

The Call meets Garth Hudson – 1981

The Call 1st Album released – 1982

Jim joins band forming the basis for their best known hits lineup – 1984

Scott Musick and Michael Been fills in, playing drums and guitar for The Band – 1985

"Let the Day Begin" hits #1 on U.S. Charts – 1989

"Let the Day Begin" is used by Al Gore during his Presidential campaign – 2000

OKPOP Exhibit "Another Hot Oklahoma Night" – 2009

"Another Hot Oklahoma Night" book Released featuring The Call and other Oklahoma Bands and Oklahoma music history. – 2009

Michael's passing - 2010

The Tribute shows at Slims and The Troubadour – 2013

March On! New Orleans Show at Siberia – 2017

Leon Russell Monument Benefit Show Cain's Ballroom - (Tulsa, OK) – Featuring Tom Ferrier and Scott Musick doing a set including some The Call material. - 2018

The Call Collected is released on CD and a numbered 1000 limited release on orange colored vinyl.

"Another Hot Oklahoma Night" – A book on Oklahoma music history inspired by The Call Song "Oklahoma". Produced by Oklahoma History Society & the OKPOP Museum - Tulsa, OK.   Permission: Jeff Moore / OKPOP

The OKPOP Museum in Tulsa, OK

"Tales from the road." Journal outtakes from Steve Huddleston, summer 1983 on his final tour with The Call.

May 12, 1983 – With Greg, Scott and Tim. We stopped at a Café' on the East side of the road where Scott got a chicken fried steak with "Campbell's soup poured on." It was BAD.

May 14, 1983 – HoJo. There was a girl there (at the gig) with hardly any top on. The club was the "Metrone." I roomed with Max.

May 16, 1983 – Drove to NYC. Photo Session with Musician magazine. Greg, Dicky and I were recognized in a restaurant by Candy and Julie, cute girls. [Then] we went bar hopping in Greenwich Village with Tim, Greg and Dicky. Saw CBGB's. We met Joe Ruffalo at an Italian restaurant and ate snails. I sat next to Joe.

May 17, 1983 – Drove with Max and Garth to New Haven, CT. Played at "Toad's Place."

May 18, 1983 – Drove with Max and Garth to Boston. I roomed with Max and Garth. Went looking for food. No luck. Then I ended up at the motel with Scott. We ate seafood. It was great. Played the "Paradise Club." Garth and I went out for a midnight snack and got lost. We couldn't find food anywhere. We finally settled for some horrible sandwiches at a 7-11 type place. It was bad.

May 19, 1983 – Drove with Joe and Garth to NYC. With Garth navigating we went through Central Park to Taft Hotel. Times Square. I roomed with Max. We went to Studio 54 and I snuck in a bottle inside my coat. We were on the guest list and went to the head of the line. I [finally] walked back to the hotel. Stopped at a deli for a ham and cheese sandwich and cheesecake and was attacked by Scott outside the hotel. He squashed my cheesecake!

May 20, 1983 – Got up and went to MTV with Greg and Max. Played Gig. Candy and Julie were there right in front. Garth played his butt off. Rick Danko visited afterwards. Martin Scorsese also. Nice folks.

May 21, 1983 – Drove with Greg and Scott to Hartford. Roomed with Max. At sound check Max decided his guitar was broken. Garth left and it was hard to play without him.

May 22, 1983 – Drove with Max and Dicky to Atlantic City. Ate at a HoJo with Dicky while Max slept in the car. We played at "Blondies" which was a dive club. It had a small stage but we played great.

May 23, 1983 – Drove to Syracuse, NY with Greg. Tim, Dicky and Scott were in the other car. Max went to NY to talk to Scorsese. A great trip! We played the "Lost Horizon"... I banged my head on the stage lights.

May 25, 1983 – Drove to Rochester with Dicky, Scott and Max. He [Max] told me how great a musician I was. Told me how great Greg was too. We played the "Casablanca." Dicky fell through a hole in the stage and hurt his back. There were lots of people there.

May 26, 1983 – Drove to Buffalo. Picked up Dicky from the chiropractor. I roomed with Greg. We ate "Thanksgiving Food" at sound-check. Disco upstairs. Scott dragged me up there.

May 27, 1983 – I was woken up early by Scott who hadn't slept all night because Dicky was with some girl making a bunch of racket. Since Dicky had been moaning about his hurt back... He couldn't drive, couldn't carry anything... (but apparently he could still screw!) So we declared Dicky to be in the "dog house." (We treated him like crap and made him do everything).

May 31, 1983 - Drove with Tim, Scott and Joe to Cleveland.

June 1, 1983 – Drove with Tim, Scott and Greg to Kendalville, IN. The hotel had a batting cage in the back. A good day.

June 2, 1983 – Drove to Chicago. I was pulled over by a Chicago cop but he let me off.

June 3, 1983 – Scott told Max that Greg was leaving the band. Then I got the "Spanish Inquisition." Played at a club with poles sticking up through the stage. I got real drunk. Scott and I wrestled afterwards. I [finally] made up my mind that I was leaving the band.

June 4, 1983 – Drove to Nashville with Max, Dicky and Scott. Max told me he wanted me to play on the next album even if I was going to quit.

June 8, 1983 – Drove with Tim, Scott and Greg to Jacksonville. Nice Drive. Drove through Georgia swamps. Ate a great catfish dinner with blackberry cobbler. We had the night off. We went to Bennigans and drank a bit. A few people recognized us.

June 10, 1983 – Drove with Tim, Scott and Greg to St. Petersburg. We ate at a motel restaurant. It was bad. We played at the "Rocking Crown." It had a tiny stage. Scott, Greg and I went to White Castle afterwards.

June 11, 1983 – Drove to Ft. Lauderdale with Greg, Scott and Tim. Played at "Summers." The waitresses all had skimpy swimsuits. The club was on the beach. There was a lot of people at the gig.

June 12, 1983 – Got up early and drove with Max and Dicky to Daytona Beach. We stopped at a restaurant on the freeway and saw the other guys car so we went in and ate breakfast. Max slept in the car. In Daytona we saw an airplane towing a banner that said, "THE CALL." We stayed at the Plaza Hotel which was overrun with drunk "high school students." We played at 4 in the afternoon to like a 1000 high school kids. There was a fight in the hotel afterwards between our crew and some high-schoolers.

June 13, 1983 – Drove with Scott and Greg to Destin, Florida. Greg was driving and we ran out of gas! Arrived in Destin to find that our equipment van was broken down 200 miles away. On the advice of Joe Ruffalo we borrowed the opening bands equipment. Playing was bad.

June 14, 1983 – Drove with Scott and Greg to Pensacola and toured Ft. Pickens. Ate oysters. Drove on to Birmingham. We arrived at the Hilton and then went out to a disco with Scott and Greg. They played "Time of your Life" and it cleared the dance floor! We laughed and laughed. We played the Bell Theater at the college.

June 17, 1983 – Drove with Greg and Scott to Little Rock. We played at the fairgrounds in the stock building. There was an autograph signing in a sporting goods store.

June 19, 1983 – Oklahoma City. We played a basement club. Girls kept taking their clothes off. My Tulsa friends were there. It was one of the better gigs.

"And that's all there was."

[Steve left the band and worked for an airline as a pilot for the next 30 + years. He decided road life wasn't for him. Steve and his wife just had a baby. Soon after Steve departed, Greg also left the band, as did Garth Hudson. Joe Read briefly joined and played bass at this point. Jim Goodwin joined on keyboard. Joe Read left and Michael took over on bass, creating the classic 4-piece lineup most people remember.]

****

Several of the dates reflected in Steve's journal are also documented in the following pages of Greg Freeman's personal tour calendar from 1983.

****

	Sunday	Monday	Tuesday	Wednesday
Mental health, like dandruff, crops up when you least expect it. — ROBIN WORTHINGTON				**1** (KENDAL-VILLE, INDIAN~~A~~) ~~INDIAN~~
	5 (TO ATLANTA) —→	**6**	**7** (DECATUR) "RUMORS" ATLANTA	**8** (to JACKSONVILLE)
	12 "PLAZA HOTEL" DAYTONA ~~BEACH~~	**13** DESTIN	**14** D/o (HILTON) (BIRMING-HAM)	**15** "BELL THEATRE" BIRMINGHAM U. OF ALABAMA
	19 "THE BOWERY" OKLAHOMA CITY, ~~NORMAN~~, OK	**20** ("THE NIGHT LIFE (X-CLUB FOOT)) D/o (AUSTIN)	**21** "6TH ST. LIVE" AUSTIN	**22** "NUMBER?" HOUSTON
	26 D/o (IN AMARILLO)	**27** "GRAHAM CENTRAL" ALBUQUERQUE N.M.	**28** "ROXY" ROCK-2" LUBBOCK, TEXAS	**29** D/o CARLSBAD, N.M.

Greg Freeman's June 1983, personal calendar for The Call. This was a couple of months before the end of Greg's time with The Call. They played and / or traveled to dates most of the month, with only a few days off.

			1983
2	**3**	**4** "CANTRELL'S"	
") CHICAGO, IL.	INDIANAPOLIS	NASHVILLE, TENN.	
9	**10**	**11**	
"PLAY GROUND SOUTH" JACKSONVILLE	"ROCKIN' CROWN" TAMPA	"SUMMERS" (AT THE BEACH) FT. LAUDERDALE	
16	**17**	**18**	
"MADISON HOUSE" MEMPHIS	"HALL OF INDUSTRY" LITTLE ROCK	D/O (TULSA)	
23	**24**	**25** BILLY- BOB'S FT. WORTH W/T. SPURLOCK	
"DADDY'S" SAN ANTONIO	"TANGO" DALLAS	(DALLAS)	
30 "PAN-AM. CENTER" LAS CRUCES N.M.			
Thursday	Friday	Saturday	

JUNE

Most notable to me is a day off in Tulsa, OK on the 18th, and the show the next day, in Oklahoma City on the 19th of June 1983, Michael & Scott's hometowns.

Courtesy Greg Freeman collection.

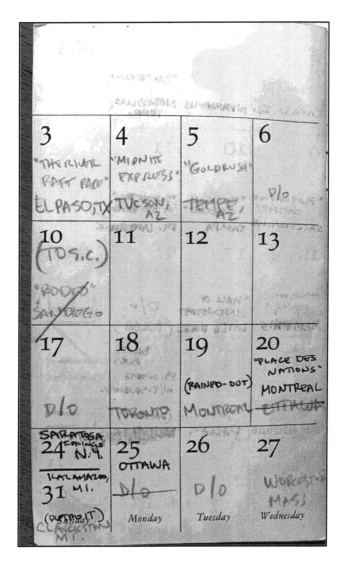

Greg Freeman's July 1983, personal calendar for The Call. This was nearing the end of Greg's time with them.

1 BLOW-OFF "ROCKY'S" ODESSA,TX MAGIC MT. L.A.	2 EL.PASO D/O	1983
7	8	9
"COUNTRY CLUB" RESEDA	"MAGIC MOUNTAIN" VALENCIA	"GOLDEN BEAR" HUNTINGTON BEACH
14	15	16 "AGORA" HARTFORD, CONN.
(TO ALLENTOWN)	ALLENTOWN, PA.	
21 D/O	22 "GARDEN STATE PARKWAY" HOMEDEL, N.J.	23 "MANN'S MUSIC THEATRE" PHILA.
28 D/O (QUEENS) *Thursday*	29 FOREST HILLS, N.Y. *Friday*	30 COLUMBIA MD. *Saturday*

JULY

They played dates and / or traveled 20 days this month.
Courtesy Greg Freeman Collection.

Other events of note:

Michael Been recorded with Bruce Cockburn on *Nothing but a Burning Light,* recorded and released in 1991. Michael played bass on 4 tracks.

****

Michael played with Mark Heard in 1992 on *Satellite Sky* released on Dan Russell and Mark Heard's Fingerprint Records. Michael played bass guitar and Jim Goodwin played horns.

****

In 1994, Michael, along with Dan Russell, and many others, contributed to a Mark Heard tribute album after Mark's untimely passing in 1992 at the age of 40.

****

In or around 2000, Dale Ockerman briefly rejoins the band for the classic Airtight lineup for a limited run of The Call shows.

The Pat Johnson – Photo Sessions

Pat Johnson did several spectacular photo shoots of The Call in the mid to late 1980's. Images that were used for promotional purposes for Michael, The Call, and Harry Dean Stanton with The Call.

Michael Been and Harry Dean Stanton

Photo courtesy: Pat Johnson

Courtesy Pat Johnson

Courtesy Pat Johnson

Courtesy Pat Johnson

Courtesy Pat Johnson

Photos courtesy Pat Johnson

Pat Johnson is a very accomplished photographer that has worked with musicians such as Jerry Garcia, David Bowie, Tom Petty, Jeff Beck, Fleetwood Mac, Ringo Starr, Frank Zappa, Brian Wilson, Freddy Mercury and hundreds of others over his career. Pat recalled working with The Call, fondly. You can see more of Pat's work at: patjohnson.com/rock

Chapter Five:

The Interviews

So what would a book about The Call be without comments and stories from their musical friends and former band-mates? Friends like Jim Kerr of Simple Minds, Peter Gabriel, Bruce Cockburn, Dan Russell (former manager), Greg Freeman (Original Bass Player) or Steve Huddleston (Keyboards 81 – 83).

Aug 20th, 2020 I spoke with Jim Kerr of Simple Minds.

I asked Jim to reminisce about his friendship with Michael Been and their time on the road and in the studio with The Call.

Jim Kerr: "I was just talking about The Call a couple of weeks ago, to my younger brother. He's about ten years younger than me and had only recently heard of The Call. He called me on a Sunday night. He knew a little about them, but not any great pearls. Not any depth. He was wanting my antidotes, how we met and all of that. So we talked about The Call and then talked about how a few years ago, Simple Minds recorded The Call's "Let the Day Begin." (Also) recently, we have recorded "The Walls Came Down" and there is a good chance it will feature on the new album we have coming next year (2021). I say good chance, because you never know with record companies. But you know, we hope everyone loves it. It's appropriate timing because, you know, it's probably more relevant now."

In reference to meeting Michael and Scott, Jim said, "I think the first time I ever heard of Oklahoma (was) "The Grapes of Wrath" and stuff. It's relevant (today) because in some ways we talk about immigrants and people leaving homes and trying to find a living and some salvation elsewhere. All over the world. So much of The Call's songs seemed to be about that. Being 'Sanctuary' and well, you don't need me to tell you... but it's better than ever. It really is more relevant (now)."

(How Simple Minds and The Call came together.)

"I guess it was fate that brought us together. It was 1982, or probably 1983, we were touring America for our album, *New Gold Dreams*. It was a breakthrough album outside of America. We finally managed to get some radio play and had a hit album and it was very rewarding. But, with America we still had to roll up our sleeves and we had quite an extensive tour organized at colleges and stuff like that. And, I guess, Simple Minds and The Call were kind of thrown together. I don't recall knowing the band until we turned up to play together. I assume maybe we had the same agency, or something, at the time. Although we weren't getting any major radio play, we were making a name for ourselves in college radio and kind of grass roots and all of that. At that time, The Call comes out... 1982. 1983. They had a few songs that stood out. Let's call them college anthems. And so, I could imagine why that would be a pretty good bill (together). They had a bit of a hot-shot manager for awhile. I guess they (originally) put us together. So um, meeting the guys... was really impressive. They always got a great reaction as the opening band. A lot of times, the opening band is just tolerated, but (with them) it didn't seem like that all. At the end of their set, they always had people jumpin' up and down and... which we loved. We loved that. With The Call, there was an intensity. Particularly, an intensity and it created an appeal for us. They were into it. There was something else about The Call, in the sense that Michael and the guys... You'll probably laugh when I tell you, you should laugh. For us to meet people from Oklahoma ... That was exotic!"

(Both.. Laughter)

"Because, I'll tell you why... Because, us coming from Glasgow, Scotland, to meet someone from Oklahoma... I mean, we had been to Paris or cultural capitals... but, um, we had done all of that. We are all so in to Americana…. music, movies, books... and we never really came across of a lot of Americana before. We would meet people from New York or LA, but to meet people from Oklahoma. I think you know what I am saying…You know, 'The Salt of the Earth.' That was exotic and impressive… and unusual. I remember the first time Michael made his way to speak to me. I was on the tour bus. We had played a couple of gigs together, but hadn't really had a chat. I think it was somewhere like Arizona or something…I was on the bus. We had done our sound check and Michael came over and wanted to talk about how he really liked *New Gold Dreams* and it was apparent that he really knew it and was into it… The thing that really hit me about him was… first of all, and I say this in a positive way… He was someone that was older than me…. What age would he be now?"

(70.)

"Alright so he was 10 years older. So he wasn't old enough to be your dad or anything, but he was older. So watching him on stage … He was a guy that was older and wiser. So we started talking and we hit it off … and right away we were kindred spirits. We hit it off right away and I knew there was something there. Often, we didn't get the chance to hang out so much; we'd do a show and go on to the next place. Eventually, one of the things was… the rest of the guys… I mean, I'm a Scotsman that doesn't drink alcohol. You know, it's fuckin' unheard of! So, I didn't go out, but the guys would go out and you know they would meet Scotty, Jim, and Michael, and get tainted. You know they would get hammered and hung out in each other's worlds, and you know they might smoke a bit. I especially remember that Jim, the keyboard player, was hilarious. He's fuckin' hilarious."

(KH: Yeah he's a funny guy.)

"Yeah he's fucking hilarious. So, our guys, they love the guys in The Call. We always got the sense from Michael and the guys that they were the 'real deal.' What I mean is... The irony is, with Michael and the guys, what I admire, is with British bands, and bands like us, there was still a bit of "pause." With Michael there was no 'pause.' There was nothing pausey about The Call. They were just the real fuckin' deal. And that was very impressive. And so I know they had a few problems with their record label and they went quiet for a bit, but then when we came back a few years later, after this time we kind of had a break through with our album and MTV and stuff... we did another tour together and by that time we were close and we looked up to Michael. He was the big brother. He had stories to tell, and things to say, and he was impressive. So yeah, he was a big brother and so much to the extent that I found Michael, In equal measures, both inspiring and intimidating. Intimidating, in the sense that there was no fuckin' bullshit. The rest of us, you know, we were still looking in the fuckin' mirror too much. Michael just didn't do that. He was from a different era and he was cut from a different cloth. He was really inspiring. He wasn't intimidating in the sense you didn't want to be around him, in fact, to the contrary. [Michael] he made you want to up your game, and be a better person as much as an artist. And you know this was the 80's and it had its share of bullshit. Every era has its bullshit. So, um, Michael was great to be around, especially in America. America was still new to us... Also, I used to feel slightly awkward, because The Call should have been bigger than what they were. In a fair world... I mean don't get me wrong... What the guys did achieve was great. I mean fuckin' hell they were great! They were one of the greatest bands. What they achieved was great, but in terms of success and all of that stuff, they were worthy of so much more, in my book. I mean, with all of the politics with the record company and MTV and all of that stuff... I mean, I just felt we should have been opening for them."

"With Peter Gabriel, and again as fate would have it, we were finishing our album in New York... our *Once Upon A Time* album. The Call were also wrapping up some recording. So, you know, the connection that The Call had opened up for Peter (Gabriel) and knew him and they looked up to him so much... so we all ended up in the same place, at the same time, which was great. So, we were hanging out with Michael and he came to us and we were so happy to get him on a couple of tracks, and likewise, I did something with the guys (The Call). Peter was very insistent on Michael and I coming over (when we were finished) to, I think it was the Power Plant station, and we did two songs. I mean god, what two songs, 'In Your Eyes,' a great song, and uh 'Red Rain.' Peter and I really got along with Michael, and even though Peter was older than Michael, you could see who the daddy was. Peter looked up to Michael. Michael had a 'strength.' Um... (For me) Peter was a legend. One of the first shows I saw was Genesis with Peter Gabriel, and he always had that thing, but when we were in the room, it was Peter who was looking up to Michael. You know he was a preacher. That is my recollection ..."

"My only regret, is the last time I spoke to Michael would have been the late 90's, and Simple Minds were in a tough period, you know. We didn't know if we were going to call it a day or what, and I remember speaking to Michael, and we were talking about a couple of songs we were really excited about, and we had the notion... um, we spoke to him (Michael) about the notion of coming over and working with him. We were enthusiastic and he was enthusiastic, but it didn't happen and yeah I regret that."

(KH: Sometimes life happens and gets in the way of things.)

"Sure, yeah, yeah. Kind of like you, we talk about The Call a lot and we kind of carry their legacy. You know we still play their song and people fuckin' love it! The song is great! When you cover a song, you cover it because it's fun. We took a more in depth approach and we really feel the song. (We) really connect with the values of the song, so we really did want to do it. When I sing the words... When I sing the words to 'Let the Day Begin,' and I sing it a lot... Hundreds of times. I still get this feeling. I still get the hairs on the back of the neck. The words are so relevant, so beautiful, so humane; there are some lines that make me want to well up. I mean, all in the one song. I mean, Jesus, that's saying something. Then, at the same time, it's a song that the whole place can jump up and down to."

"So, anyway, going back to 1982 or 1983, that's nearly 40 years ago, we still carry the legacy of the band and Michael's lyrics. And... there's no other [band] like that, that we do that with."

(KH: It's always bothered me that that they didn't get more recognition. That people often don't know (remember) who they are. Currently, something I am attempting to do, since Scott and Michael are from Oklahoma - I am working on getting them inducted

into the Oklahoma Music Hall of Fame. I can't believe that they are not already in there. When I found out, I felt like now was the time to do something about it.)

"Well, hats off to you. That's great! *Because of course, they should be in any hall of fame.* They should be. That's a glitch. That's an error. I know there is so much great music to come out of Oklahoma, but if you are talking about a specific period... In music, you got to be talking about a specific period. It's historical, you know, the 80's! I mean the guys (The Call)... I'm sure it is an error, there."

Thank you, Jim Kerr, obviously a fan and longtime friend of Michael Been, and The Call.

****

Peter Gabriel Interview – Monday September 21, 2020

Peter, when talking to Jim Kerr (of Simple Minds) last month he talked fondly of a memory involving you, he (Jim Kerr), and Michael Been, in the studio together, in New York. I believe at the Power Plant. You worked on "In Your Eyes" and "Red Rain" together. Can you tell me about (that)?

"I had been introduced to The Call by Peter Philbin, who I had become friends with after meeting [him] during some interviews. He had become an A and R man for CBS and introduced Springsteen to the label, amongst others. He [Peter Philbin] was very enthusiastic about the quality of the writing and Michael's extraordinary voice, and I was convinced the first time he played their music to me."

"On the *So* record, I was looking for a blend of unusual voices to reinforce the choruses - which I had with Michael and Jim..."

In the early 80's, you were quoted referring to The Call as the next big thing or future of rock music, can you elaborate as to why you felt so strongly about The Call and their music / message?

"What I loved was the passion in Michael's voice and lyrics. He could bring the emotional intensity up and down in an almost operatic way. I am not sure the production and arrangements lifted the songs as far as they might have gone. I don't think they were as unusual as Michael's contribution, although, the intensity was really compelling for me."

What do you recall about being on the road with The Call?

"I remember the band being fairly easy-going and convivial. I remember how mean some acts had been to Genesis when we were supporting, so, I would always work to give the support act all the opportunities we could, like a good sound check, and I would go out every night to introduce them to my fans. Michael was always charming, but you could feel the turbulence he carried internally."

Peter's last remark about Michael, for me, really brings to light the two sides of Michael and why he was such a powerful songwriter.

Greg Freeman - 2016

Greg was The Call's original bass player and band historian for about four years, from Motion Pictures in 1979, to playing with The Call through August 1983.

In the first of several interviews with former band members, I checked in with Greg Freeman. Greg kept great notes and calendars of shows, travel, and recordings.

Greg Freeman Interview - August, 2020

"So, I started out with them [The Call] the summer of 1978, as a roadie for Airtight. I think I was making, like, $10.00 a gig. Then, in the summer of 1979, Michael wanted to switch things up and switched to guitar. So, he asked me if I wanted to play bass for Airtight. Then, in September of 1979, Phil Seymour reached out to Scott and was looking for a backup band. He was working on a solo record deal with Denny Cordell. We ended up being Phil Seymour's band, playing live shows in late 1979. During that period, we were playing at The Crow's Nest and someone held up the payphone while Airtight / Motion Pictures was playing and Denny Cordell heard us over the phone. He said, 'Man those guys are good.' So, Denny decided to bank roll us to make our own record. So we went to cut an album."

"We did some work for Phil (Seymour) and some demos as 'Michael Been Band is Airtight.' Then, 1980 rolls around and January of 1980, we end up going to England. We go there to record on Denny's dime. So in six months' time, I go from joining the band, to flying to England to record an album. We were there for six weeks, at Olympic Studios, which is pretty historic. So, we finished up recording but, Michael wasn't happy with how it came out, so the end of February we went back to Santa Cruz (CA). In California, we decided to record again with (British Sound Engineer) Andy Johns. We started working with him on try number two. This is still with Denny Cordell paying for it. On his dime. So, we start on the Andy Johns sessions and he is an amazing engineer. He was in his 'Hollywood Cowboy' phase... cocaine and women... you know. He literally had a 3 or 4 inch square mirror on the console so he could do blow right off of the console. He had different rooms there... like a hot tub room. We would work until 1:00 a.m. or so, and he would go find some girl and go off in the hot tub room for awhile. Then, maybe around 2 or 3 a.m., he would come out and say, 'Okay guys! Come on! Let's get back to it!' Anyway, he was a character. Then Scott, Michael and all of us would go to his bungalow and there were bullet holes where he had shot his gun off inside... (Laughter) So, anyway, we recorded with Andy for a couple of weeks and nothing really happened with that, either. So, then we went to Cherokee Studio - also in Hollywood and we got an engineer (Ed Sacker) and Mark Miller and tried to rework the Andy Johns Sessions. That is when Garth Hudson came into the picture. Someone asked Michael who he would like to work with, given the chance, and he said Garth Hudson and they said, 'okay,' they happened to know him. So, a couple of days later Garth shows up with his insane keyboard rig, which was super-cool and amazing."

"The rest of 1980 not much else happened. Going on into 1981, we were kind of in limbo. Then, finally, we went to England again (this time w/Garth) to work with Hugh Padgham, and recorded what would become the first Call record. This was at The Manor in Oxfordshire and also at Island Studio. The Manor was owned by Virgin Records. You could stay there and record there. It was in the middle of nowhere, out in the countryside."

(This location proved to be quite the environment they needed, even though things got crazy at times.)

"So, we were in the studio in London with Hugh Padgham and we hadn't been there long. Scott was already getting a bit stir-crazy. We were in the control room and had just cut a song. We were listening to the playback and I made some offhand comment about it. I didn't mean anything by it. I was just being a clown and Scott was like 'Arrrggg!' and just lunges at me and tackled me in the control room. He wrestles me to the floor and bit me through my pant leg. I mean, teeth marks on my thigh. I was, like, 'What the fuck??' (Laughter)... I mean, we were surrounded with, like, a million dollars worth of recording equipment and he literally started a 'bar fight' with me. So, occasionally yeah, we had to blow off some steam."

"So, we finished the recording for the first album and then had a long wait for the album to come out. So, that's when we finally came up with the name "The Call"... sometime late 1981. We were playing small bar shows. The first record I have in my notes of being billed as The Call was January 21st, 1982. In February, we had our first official show as The Call, announcing our new band name and the album release. Then, in the summer of 1982, we recorded *Modern Romans*. We recorded it, finished it, and a few weeks later, went back to mix it. Then, we were right back to doing shows the Fall of 1982. Then, the album came out and in 1983 we toured a ton. We did the Simple Minds dates and others. Then, my tour of duty ended in August of 1983. That stretch of shows we did was hard on me. Steve Huddleston and I left the band at [about] the same time, in August of 1983. Then they got Joe Read, I think, for the Peter Gabriel stuff and he was on *Scene Beyond Dreams* with Jim Goodwin, because Garth had left."

"My last show, which was at the Greek Theater in L.A... Well the very next day, they had try-outs for bass players at SIR in L.A. and I was there (on location) for some reason, and I could hear through the wall the different guys come in and play 'The Walls Came Down' or something. I was hearing the bass players mess up and I was like, 'Oh, he isn't playing that right' and it was funny."

"Dave Jerden, (Record Producer and Primary Engineer) who worked on *Scene Beyond Dreams,* he and I worked on a remix of 'Destination,' from *Modern Romans,* for a 12" version extended mix. I don't think it ever came out and I have the acetate of it. I would say it is probably pretty rare. There could be one other copy, but this is probably the only one now."

"I also remember introducing Michael to Joy Division. He really liked them and they seemed to be a big inspiration to him. I was younger (than the other guys) and really into independent music and the new British stuff. He would ask me, 'What's going on Greg?' He was really interested in what was new. He was really open to knowing new music and what was going on. Yeah, Michael really liked DEVO, and he thought those guys were really great players. He was really open to all kinds of stuff [music]."

"Going back to why he asked me to join the band... I think because I was a younger guy, and kind of up on all of the current shit, he thought I would be a good addition to the band, at the time."

[A funny story about Dicky Dirt.]

"We were at The Manor [In England] recording [the first album] and Dicky Dirt [Tom] taped a picture of Adam Ant to the wall and lit it on fire [No one remembers why, because Dicky liked Adam Ant]. I know I have a photo of that somewhere. So there was Dicky, burning Adam Ant in the control room. That was the dumb stuff we would do when we were bored out of our minds, just standing around, waiting."

Dicky Dirt lighting Adam Ant on fire in the control room.

Jim Goodwin Interview Oct 10th, 2020

Jim, when you first joined the band, how did that occur? How did you first hook up with the band? Was it initially to record (*Scene Beyond Dreams*) or to tour? There was a lot of change and transition going on during this period and you were right in the middle of all of it.

"I had a friend who auditioned to play bass for The Call on their upcoming tour with Peter Gabriel in Europe, and he mentioned that they needed a keyboard player and gave me the number of the management company. I called, and the girl who answered said they were looking for a keyboardist and would pass on my info. It turned out they weren't looking for a keyboardist, but the guy they had hired started getting squirrely, so they called me and asked if I would come to the studio to meet them. It was probably 1 a.m.,, and I had done a show that night at The Whiskey with Sparks, and was partying with friends at The Tropicana Motel, where I was staying. I went with a girlfriend, which Scott thought was obnoxious, because she was gorgeous and wearing hot pants. Michael and I jammed for a minute on piano and synth, and we talked a little bit. He said they would let me know. The other guy kept asking for more money, so they called me at the last minute and asked if I could fly to Santa Cruz in a couple of days and rehearse a few times, and then go to Europe. I was looking to make a change and said, 'yes.' After the tour, we ended up in the studio to finish *Scene Beyond Dreams*, and I think I played on 'Tremble,' and the title track. I think it's important to point out that the band really came together when we became a four-piece band. Our bass player quit just before we did *Reconciled*, and we had a big gig in San Francisco at the I-Beam; Michael suggested he play bass. About halfway through the show, we all looked at each other and smiled. As soon as we got in the dressing room after the show, Michael said, 'This is it, isn't it?', and we all agreed. It was just undeniable. It felt so right."

Being the new guy in the band and the youngest member, one would think you had a little different musical perspective and influences. How did this manifest on *Reconciled*, when you helped co-write some of the key tracks on that album? What was it like coming into the band and working with Michael so closely, on what, for many, is the album that really broke through and introduced them to The Call?

"I think Michael was looking to make some changes in his music. He was really into New Order and some of the other British bands, and we had that in common. We both liked The Smith's first album, and that is why Michael sang 'I Still Believe' with that melody and the falsetto parts. He asked me to send him anything that I recorded that he could write to, so I sent him a lot of stuff. I was thrilled when he started using some of the songs. We did that the entire time I was with the band. I was really lucky to have the opportunity and did not appreciate that until he died and I went back and looked at the body of work that we co-wrote. I think I kind of took it all for granted in the moment and didn't realize just how powerful and exceptional his songs were."

Each album has its own flavor, if you will. What was your favorite album and why?

"My favorite album was probably *Into the Woods*. It didn't get any love from the label because they decided to drop us, but it was such a strong record. I think it has some of Michael's greatest lyrics, and our arrangements got better. 'It Could Have Been Me' is an incredible song, and 'The Woods' has the best lyrics of all the songs Michael and I co-wrote, at least for me."

Can you give me a [basic] timeline or history if you will of your time in the band?

"Joined for *Scene Beyond Dreams* (1984) and exited after *Red Moon* (1990). We reunited in 1997 for *To Heaven and Back*."

I've heard from Scott and Dicky talk of humorous nicknames and how they came to be. Can you elaborate on what you remember about everyone's nicknames and how they got them?

"I always thought 'Dicky' was his real name. It was probably a year before I found out it was Tom. Scott had a mischievous twin they called 'Zack.' Zack came out after a couple of shots of Jack Daniels. Michael never had a nickname as far as I can recall. I started out as Jim Bidet (B Day) because I spoke French, but I soon became Granny because of the way I cleaned up after everybody on the Winnebago. I couldn't stand a messy cabin."

What do you remember about The Call's / Michael's writing process?

"Mostly, that he wrote down every line he thought could work as a lyric in a notebook, and he would go there to look for bits of lyrics or lyric ideas all the time when he was working on a song. He wrote in the hotel room, on the Winnie, backstage - anywhere an idea came to him. We worked out song arrangements and parts at sound-check, a lot. We wrote 'The Woods' at a sound-check in Omaha, when I absentmindedly played the opening riff, while trying to set a delay effect and was not even looking at the keys. Michael stopped me and said, 'what was that?' I played it again and started making the chord changes under the riff. We worked it out and played it that night. I have no idea what he sang."

Do you recall any session in the studio that particularly stands out? Or perhaps a particular story about recording a specific album? Did The Call have a process in the studio or was it more live and organic?

"It depended on the environment and the engineer. *Let the Day Begin* was very live. We recorded with monitors at full volume and had a lot of bleed on all the tracks. No headphones. It was wonderful."

"There was an interesting moment at The Captain and Tennille's studio, in Encino, when we were recording the vocals on 'I Don't Wanna.' The engineer was fussing about with the snare sound while Michael was doing the first take, and after the take, Michael said, "what did you think of that, Jim?", and I said, 'that might be the one.' Michael agreed and asked the engineer to play it back. The engineer was not sure he had recorded it and had to check. Fortunately, he did, and it is the vocal on the record. One take. Michael might have fixed one or two things, but I'm not sure. I think it is one single take from start to finish and it almost didn't get recorded."

"Another time we almost overlooked the best take was the drum track for 'I Still Believe.' Michael had become obsessed with BPMs (beats per minute) and fluctuations, where we would speed up or slow down during the song. Michael clocked the take and was disappointed that we sped up 4 BPMs for the chorus and slowed back down for the verses. Before we decided to move on and try again, I said, 'That track has some kind of wicked magic going for it. Are we sure it's that big a deal?' I think Scott suggested we check for BPM fluctuations on a hit song, so the engineer played a Beatles song and then a Stones song. They both fluctuated 10 BPMs or more. Michael threw the BPM device in the trash and said, 'Let's move on to the next song.' Later, when we were working on the overdubs, we all commented on how wonderful Scott's groove and dynamics are on that track. The idea that we almost threw it away because it wasn't machine-like enough, gave us all a good laugh."

"Michael did most of the vocal for 'Oklahoma' late one night at The Power Station in New York City, where we were recording *Reconciled*. Michael had had a couple of shots of Jack and said he wanted to try to sing it. I remember the engineer thought it was a waste of time because we were tired, and it was late, and Michael was buzzed. Dicky said, 'Let's go, he wants to sing.' I think Dicky had a feeling Michael was on a roll. Michael took the bottle in with him and had the song done in, probably, two takes. Much of the lyric is adlibbed. Been was channeling his hometown roots that night. 'We were hugging in our hearts that night.'"

You took a break at one point in the 90's. Why did you take a break? What did you do while you were away?

"I had married and was about to have my first child; I didn't want to miss all of that because of being on the road. [And] I had fallen into a lucrative business, writing music for commercials, so I had an opportunity to make the change. I had also lost some of my joy for the band, as I didn't feel like I was contributing anything authentic to the music anymore. I had allowed Michael to steer me into playing what he wanted to hear and not what I heard in my head. I had a love for progressive and punk music that had become totally suppressed over the years. I remember feeling one night on stage that I was faking it, and it shocked me. I knew right then that I had to move on."

Post year 2000, after The Call, what have you been working on? I know you have written commercial songs and themes etc. Can you elaborate on that?

"I lucked out and had a good run writing music for movies, movie trailers, commercials, network design (ABC 4 Note), corporate logos (Warner Home Video), etc. It gave me enough free time to produce other artists (Andy Kim, Mairead), and I had a wonderful studio in Hollywood for several years. I even got to co-write a song for Ricky Martin with Dave Resnick (Sonia Dada) and Rob Rosa (Menudo). Mostly, it all provided enough money to raise my kids and enjoy a good life in Los Angeles for about 20 years."

How did you feel about the tribute shows and album in 2013 / 2014? On a personal level, what did you feel about getting up there with Robert to pay tribute to Michael?

"That experience was one of the most joyous and emotional projects of my adult life. When Robert asked us to consider it, and we got together and played a few of the songs, I knew immediately that it was going to be intense and rewarding on many levels. It was clear that Robert could pull it off, and that was no easy feat. Michael's singing range was extraordinary, and there were a few songs Robert wouldn't even consider. But, most of the material was adaptable for Robert or worked exactly as it was written. His bass playing really impressed me. Again, Michael's style was not easy to emulate, and Robert had to play and sing at the same time. Then, there were the lyrics to memorize. Michael packed a lot of lines into a song, and I was astonished at Robert's ability to retain and recall all of that information. He suggested that growing up with the songs had put them in his subconscious and stored them as partial memory, which gave him an advantage. However he did it, it was amazing to watch."

Finally... Do you know of any unreleased tracks or lost sessions/songs?

"I think there is a song somewhere that I co-wrote with Michael called 'Welcome to My World,' but I'm not sure if we recorded it or not. It would have been part of the *Red Moon* sessions."

Jim Goodwin and Scott Musick in Norway.
Photo used with permission of Jim Goodwin.

Dan Russell Interview October 16, 2020

Dan worked with The Call and Michael for many years. What began as a friendship and shared book, continued to be a lifelong friendship with the band and especially, Michael. Dan worked with several other artists and started his own label fueled by passion and the need to support the artists and music he loved.

Dan, could you start out by giving me a bit of a bio / background on yourself and how you started out in the music business?

"I've been around so long, I can't remember too much. However, I've worked in many capacities to advocate for artists that I am moved by."

I know at one point you worked with U2. Could you elaborate a little on that and tell me how you got involved with U2, and to what capacity, and time frame, you worked with them?

"I met them at the beginning of their amazing career and we became friends, and of course, I am a real fan of theirs, and adopted a 'let me know if I can help' attitude with them. I've worked with their management company, with other artists. I did road management work and marketing work with U2 for a brief period of time, during the Zoo TV world tour, I coordinated their guest relations."

Dan, could you tell me a little bit about how you met the The Call and got involved with them? Could you give me a time line and details of events leading up to working with them?

"Again, it all started as being a recipient of their music, and seeing them in concert, and feeling compelled to connect with them. In the mid-80's, I would attend their shows in Boston. They always profoundly impacted me. I finally got to meet Michael, when I handed him a book and my phone number was inside the book. It was a book by Brennan Manning, 'The Lion and the Lamb.' Michael read it within a couple of days and called me, and that begin our direct relationship. We read a few books together; there was no official capacity at that point. We just became friends and read the same books for a while."

Once you were working with The Call to what capacity did you work with them and for how long?

"I remember sometime in 1988, getting a phone call from Michael, and he said something about how he had just written a song. They thought it might be real important and wanted me with him as he brought that song forward. I told him he could have about eight weeks of my life. I would be happy to support him. This song was 'Let the Day Begin.' I officially started as his road manager in 1989, for the longest tour I've ever been involved with. I think we crisscrossed the country a dozen times, following the energy of that song and the follow up single, 'You Run.' Michael and I became close and somewhere along the line, I became his manager. I worked with Michael, as his manager, through *Red Moon* and all the subsequent releases, as well as, a solo record and the yet to be released solo record that he turned in to Quest, just as Quest was closing its doors."

You released a couple of The Call's albums on Fingerprint (your label), how did that come about?

"The album, to *Heaven and Back,* happened because The Call was out of a record deal, but still together. I found a studio in San Francisco that would take my credit card and allow the band to all live there while they recorded it. We put out a maxi single for the song 'Love is Everywhere,' along with that album. We also put out *Live Under the Red Moon,* which Jim Scott recorded at a small club south of LA. I never had great marketing or distribution, so I was I was trying to find a partner to get that. I still wish, to this day, more people could've heard that music. Michael's second solo record was with Jim Keltner and Bruce Cockburn, and they hung out at the studio for about a month. Only a few of the songs have seen the light of day. Presently, we are working on getting the rights back to all the records and we know we have *Reconciled* coming back to re-master and re-release. Warner Brothers has been really great about giving the masters back and we look forward to getting *Into the Woods,* as well. We're aiming at all of their masters. We're going to try to find any other tracks to clean with them, but certainly we want to re-master everything and figure a way to get them out."

Are there any stories that come to mind of significance that you can tell?

"I don't know, there are so many stories, so many memories from being on the road with the band, to being on vacation with Michael. Michael was very involved with my family, and had formed a strong bond with my son, and would call him several times each week to see how he was. He was checking on him about all kinds of things, from school, social life, music, faith, and if he was keeping his room clean. They started hanging out when he [my son] was two years old. He would come on family vacations with me and we would have a blast. We also played music together, and even talked about going on the road as a duo with acoustic guitars."

I know you were especially close to Michael; on a personal note, could you tell me about knowing Michael, as a friend and what he was like?

"Michael was a very deep, and sincere, and sweet man. He, like all of us, had struggles and challenges, but he kept at it, kept living, kept giving. If anything, I think, Michael like many of us, had an incorrect, low self-esteem perspective that from time to time got the best of him. He never really knew how important and wonderful he was. I've never been as close to anyone as I have been to him. His passing ten years ago made me quite upset. I had to clean out his apartment, and donate his clothes, and close out his cable, and his mail. I thought that was expecting a lot of me. I, like many, are completely shocked he died at the age of 60. I recall him saying [once] that both of his parents died when they were 60, as well. I can only assume that he is healed [now], and whole, doing wonderful now at the next phase of his soul's existence. He will always be a big part of my life."

Why, 20 years after The Call officially disbanded, do you think they still have such passionate, dedicated fans? Why is their music still so relevant?

"There is an enduring authenticity and passion that few artists have. Michael was a prophet of sorts. He boldly wrote what was on his heart and he did not write for commercial success. He gave 110%. I think, because he toured so extensively, and each of his performances were as intense as they were, connected him deeply to so many people… And, because he was not afraid of saying the truth, I think people, if they could hear it, find it refreshing. I don't know many bands that consistently wrote from the heart and soul as profoundly as The Call did."

How did Michael, and The Call's music, affect and influence you?

"The Call / Michael spoke to me. His music gave me a rare and important fellowship. Their music makes me feel that I'm not alone. Their music strikes me at a much deeper level than most music does. I love the way Michael approached his instrument and of course, his lyrics. Michael is authentic."

Do you have any other stories or thoughts about Michael?

"I will talk about him for the rest of my life, about his sense of humor, his sense of compassion, and his dedication to the music and to his son. He was also really generous with my kids."

****

January 21st, 2021 – I picked up once again with Dan Russell to fill in a few blanks from our first chat and to cover the topic of Mark Heard and Michael.

Can you elaborate on the connection between Michael and Mark Heard?

"Yeah, you're talkin' to him. Mark was my best friend and we had a studio together, and Michael, of course, was a real good friend. Sadly Mark passed away when he was 40 years old. Michael had played on Mark's 1992 *Satellite Sky* album. So, when I did the Tribute album in 1994, Michael decided to kick in a track right away. I don't recall if I asked him or he just said, 'I'm doin' it.' We had a triangle. Michael was the Comedian. You couldn't hang around with Michael without him going into a 2, 3, or 4-joke series. One time in San Diego, I was down there with a buddy and we were at LAX. Michael was going to be stuck there until four in the morning (he was there with BRMC). So, he asked if he could ride back with us. So I said, 'If you tell one consecutive joke after another all the way to L.A., and never repeat yourself then you can get in the car.' So, he did that for like two hours. Michael was in the back seat, just one after another. So, we gave him a 'free' ride back with us [laughter]. He had a notebook he carried with him a lot, with all of his jokes in it. He lost it, unfortunately. It was a full notebook, maybe a hundred pages front and back, both sides, of jokes. It's a major bummer it got lost because it would have been a great source of material. So, I was the prankster with The Call team. One time, we came over Hoover Dam from wherever we were. We had a tour bus and a big 20 foot trailer behind it. So, a couple of the guys wanted to stop and take a pee. So, we pulled the bus over in the breakdown lane. So, all four of the guys got out to take a pee side by side. So, I told the bus driver, 'Here's 10 bucks, pull the bus forward about 50 feet.' [laughter] …and we had a bunch of traffic. All of the guys were standing there, holding their hose, side-stepping, trying to keep behind the bus and trailer. So, we did a lot of funny things back then."

"Michael used to spend holidays with us. Carol had moved out and the divorce was imminent. It all kind of blew his mind; so, he decided to move east with me, and my family. I had my studio and about six people working there. He would come in and sit at my desk and just look down at the floor. So, everyone noticed, 'Look at how sad he is.' So, I had a 2-year old boy named Jesse. I went and got Jesse from my house and brought him back to my office. I came up to Michael with Jesse in my arms and asked, 'Hey can you hold him for a little bit?' I had a ton of work to do. Michael wasn't really the 'jump-up-and-hold-the-kid' kind of guy, or that's what you'd think, but he did, and he held Jesse, and that started the relationship with Jesse. Those guys would go out for three, or four, or five, hours at a time and they became super friends. From then on, in Jesse's life, Michael was his mentor. They would talk once a day, or at least every other day, about girls, math, science, school, faith, mom and dad... So, Michael would call me to find out the scoop with Jesse (when he was like a 13 year old) and I'd tell him, then he'd call Jesse. When Michael passed away... Well, he'd used to call me like three times a day. He'd always start his phone call with, 'Remember me?' So, he called from Brussels, using the promoter's phone, and we talked about 30 minutes. We were planning, about a week from that day, he had announced his intention to retire from working with Black Rebel. So, about a week from that day, I was picking him up at the airport when he got back from Europe, and he, I, and Jesse were going to go to Martha's Vineyard. We had rented a house. We were going to discuss music, guitars, and sounds. We had made an offer on the house next door to me, and we were going to move my studio into that house, and Michael was going to live there. Michael was going to focus on kids like Jesse and work with them like a mentor. Jesse was his first project. We were cuing up for that. Thirty minutes later I was driving in my car and Grant called me (the road manager), he told me to pull over. I thought that was weird, but I did. Then, he told me, 'Michael just died.' Then, we lost the offer we had made on the house about a month later. So, that was a pretty rough ending. For me, I used anger as my crutch for a time. No one was there to go into his apartment in L.A., so I did it, but I did it with anger, because I couldn't grieve. You know, because if we would go on vacation, then 'Uncle Michael' was there. He was 'Uncle Michael' to my daughter and my son."

"So, back to Mark Heard. I had worked with Mark for a long time. I worked independently with Bruce Cockburn, Michael Been, and Mark Heard, and they're all brilliant, but they didn't know each other. So, I would send demos to Bruce and Michael. I kind of lived with Michael on the road all the time; so, if we were in Georgia, I would try to get Mark to come out. In some ways, Michael was kind of shy. If he had a big ego, he might have been much more successful. He didn't have that 'commercial' ego. Michael's lyrics were kind of heavy. A lot of the more successful people they keep it light. Michael was just such a powerful baritone singer."

"Speaking of that... Have you heard the story about The Call backing up Bono, doing demos for Willie Nelson? [No I haven't.] You know I've known, and worked with, Bono since he was 19. He was a very passionate, and a charismatic front-man and a Christian. Back then, he would carry his big, leather, King James Bible around with him. So, anyway, Bono was in L.A. in 1990, and we went to see the 'Bulgarian Women's Choir' (I think). I had brought Michael and Mark. So, we talked to Bono and he said, 'I have a bunch of songs that don't make sense for U2 and I want to pitch them to Willie Nelson.' I said, 'Cool, so what's keeping you from it?', and Bono said, 'I don't want to ask my guys to play it and I don't have a band to demo these songs.' That is kind of the story on, how did Bono get on the *Red Moon* album? So, I said, 'I have a band and we're doing a record.' We were at Oceanway, and I told Bono, 'If you come do backing vocals on one of their songs, they will back you up on your demo.' So, he got a studio at Oceanway. I just don't know what happened to that cassette I had of those songs. It was basically The Call, backing up Bono on those demos. I don't even know if it ever got pitched or not. So, they spent four or five hours with Bono doing that. So, then, Jim Scott was in the next studio working. So, we got done and Bono was getting ready to leave and I said, 'Wait you got to walk down the hallway and sing.' So, we set a mic up in the console room for Bono. Michael then sang the part he wanted Bono to sing; so, then Bono could do it. To me, it was too far down in the mix. I should have had Bono do something where it was a big stand out part. Then, of course, I get a phone call the next day from New York, from U2's management, saying, 'Hey what are you doing with Bono in the studio with The Call?' I (jokingly) said, 'Yeah we are going to put a sticker on the album, "With Special guest Bono of U2!," or maybe we'll just make it a single.' They were like, 'Oh, no don't do that.' [laughter] So, that kind of brought the guys together."

"Anyways, [Back to Mark Heard] so, Michael would call me up and tell me a joke. I'd call Mark and tell him that same joke. Then Mark would call Michael and tell him the same joke. Then Michael would say, 'Hey I just told that exact joke to Dan, thirty minutes ago.' I am grateful to have had Michael for 25 years, as one of my best friends. We used to sit around the piano together, he'd be on one end of the bench, and I'd be on the other. Michael would go for like, two hours playing one song after the other. He would play Hymns or songs by The Band, and we'd sing harmony together, and end up in tears, same with Mark. If both of those guys were still alive I believe they would have made an even greater impact. So, Michael wanted to retire and work with teenagers and pass along his legacy. We have three or four guitars that Michael helped my son Jesse pick out. In my studio, I have Michael's Ampeg bass amp that I bought off of him. I also bought a Fender twin off of him. I absolutely wanted to keep this stuff in (The Call) family. My kid, Jesse, still uses them. He has stuff from Mark Heard, and Michael, that he still uses. Right now, Jesse is working on a Martin Scorsese production, and he is using some of that gear. I just like the idea of firing up the Ampeg and using it on a record. Nobody else knows it, but it belonged to Michael Been."

"So, Michael played on *Satellite Sky* for Mark. I only had two bass players that I would use, and I've done over a hundred different albums. I would use Fergus Marsh, the bass and stick player, and Michael Been. Nobody can top those two guys. It was Michael's bass playing and his voice. His signature sound. Back when he was playing guitar with The Call as his principle instrument, he would explode. He would close his eyes and sing a verse or two. He would get so much passion in there, he would physically just jump! Sometimes back then, they would play at places that had sit down tables and service, you know, serving food or something. Well, Michael jumped off the stage and landed on a table with his feet and the table tipped over, and there was four people there with plates full of food. He kept the guitar around his neck, and shook off all the food, and jumped back up on stage. So, sometimes he would just explode. So many nights, to borrow an expression, he would, 'leave everything on the stage.' So, then he would go back stage, and Dicky, Jim, and Scott would be talking to the opposite sex (who would tell them – Oh! You're so good...), and Michael would go in the back, just drenched in sweat, and he would just weep for several minutes. He would just explode with emotion. He would get it all out, and dry himself off, put on a new shirt, and then we'd go out. I'd be the one to see him in that condition. Every time he did a 'Call' show, he would do it like it was the last show he would ever do in his life. It was always so exciting. I think we did, like, 305 shows in a row, before I went home one [tour]. That took about 18 months. Then, when he got off stage and went to a club, we'd have a blast, but when he was into the music, he was so, so, passionate. I think it was Jim who made a couple of sock puppets on the bus. One was Michael, and the other was Michael's guitar tech. He would do a whole routine. I'm sure it was Jim or Scott, probably Jim. I think there is a video tape somewhere."

"I think I've told you before about how I met Michael. I would wait outside the clubs at 2 a.m., and they'd be coming out of the club and they'd see me like I was a groupie or something. I was actually working with U2, and other bands at the time, but they didn't know that. I didn't really flash that around. So, I would see their show and be so moved, I knew this band was so important. When *Modern Romans* came out, it blew my mind. So, I would wait outside the club and they'd walk by me and try to avoid me, like I was some nerdy groupie. Finally, in '83, I got a book. Often, Michael would walk by me, and kind of put his hands together, and nod, and say, 'Hi!' So, this one time, I just held the book out, and he responded, and took the book out of my hand. My number was on the inside of the book. I said, 'If you like it give me a holler.' That began our relationship when we started exchanging books back and forth. He called me three days later from D.C., playing the 930 club, and he had already read it. He said, 'the book was fantastic,' and had brought voice to some things he had been thinking about. So, that's how our relationship really began."

"So, then a funny a story about the Tears for Fears tour - Boston, $10 a ticket, about 10,000 people could fit in there. We were in the third row with some friends. Michael was playing the Telecaster and put his foot up on the monitor to position himself while he was playing. He was pulling on the guitar strings, like he was going to tear the guts out of the guitar. This monitor wedge was large and had like two 12's or 15's in it. All of the sudden, I saw smoke coming up over the top of the monitor and Michael kind of just looks down at the smoke. People just assumed it was an effect, then suddenly flames came out of the monitor. Michael just kept playing and then, two techs came out and grabbed this four foot monitor and took it real quick. They tried to put it out with towels, but it was like someone had put gasoline on it. It was almost like a cool effect for a blistering lead guitar part. Almost like Jimi Hendrix putting lighter fluid on his guitar. Michael just made the most of it, like it was supposed to happen. Michael took credit, like it came from his spirit, and that his guitar playing blew up that monitor. He told me later, 'I'm glad you were in the third row because I'm so hot you coulda' got burned!'"

"Michael was both cursed and gifted. He was cursed, because he was such a great talent, and just didn't commercially quite make it, like the failure to get proper support from record labels. That kind of lack of success plagued him. He was like, 'Why do I have these songs and feel like this if it is only to sell 3 or 400,000 records?' Like when 'Let the Day Begin' came out as this massive hit in two formats and MCA decided to consolidate their warehouses and change things just as their song was sitting at number one, they ran out of vinyl. I had to go into MCA and say, 'this record sold 2 million copies, we want the royalties.'"

[So] "I was the guy who delivered *Red Moon* to MCA. My task was to deliver the master copy of the record. I had to deliver it and then, they had to accept it. If they didn't accept it, then as far as they were concerned, you didn't do the record, and you were liable for all of the advance they gave you. So, the guy at the label said, 'I don't like it, go back and do another record. There better had be a 'Let the Day Begin' part two or something.' So, I had to tell them, 'this is the record.' This is how Michael and the guys felt. They put their heart and soul in it. This is the next album. He yelled at me some, and then said, 'So, I suppose you want tour support now? Go talk to my secretary and she will take you to figure out the tour support.' I went to the secretary and told her I needed to present a tour budget. So, she and I figured up how much [everything] would cost. We added it all up and I figured we would need like $88,000, or so. Then I had to take it back in and present it. I hadn't even intended to get money that day. Then, the secretary took me down to the office and in an hour's time, I had a check for $88,000. After that, The Call was dropped from MCA so we didn't have to recoup it. So, I went back to Michael and he asked if they liked the record. Did they accept it? I said, "Well they really wanted something that sounded like 'Let the Day Begin,' but here's a check for $88,000. Then, we did the tour and we didn't need any tour budget, short fall money. The band lived within their means, and made much better money than we had assumed. So, when they dropped the record, we didn't have to pay back the $88,000. It just kind of went away. I went and took a verbal beating for The Call, and ended up with $88,000. So, Michael and I thought it was a good day's work."

"He was a very unique, special guy. I was lucky to be his 'brother.' I would be on tour with U2 and be on the phone with Michael all the time. That's where my heart was, with Michael and The Call. I could go on about Michael, and The Call, for the rest of my life."

Producer of Red Moon - Jim Scott Interview - Oct. 23rd, 2020

What about The Call and their sound really stood out to you when making *Red Moon*?

"The year The Call released their *Red Moon* record, when you listen to that the sound. It is coming off of, sort of, the 80's power pop sound [era] and all of the bands, they were in competition with in the 80's. That record, the *Red Moon* record, to me, sounds like it is from right now. It's very Americana, very 60's, very Beatles-like in some ways. The bass playing is unbelievable, the drums are beautiful, natural, and full. Levon Helm-style drums in the room. You know, nobody does that; nobody has the courage. You know, everybody is afraid of having a bad drum sound. Scott didn't have a bad drum sound. He had a beautiful drum sound. [Recording drums that way] It's hard to stand behind it, myself included. Recording engineers, mixers, everybody has got to have 'that' drum sound. We were, like, screw it, lets just have a good song. And, of course, Jim 'Granny' kept his keyboard sounds traditional, but you know, the synthesizers had a beautiful sound. They sounded great, you know, and then, Dicky's guitar... I mean, every left-handed guitarist I've ever worked with has been amazing. He could lay it down. I mean, what a team. It was beautiful!"

What do you remember about the sessions when they were recording *Red Moon*?

"Well there were a couple of stories. There are a couple of things that are maybe unanswered questions, as far as I am concerned. There are a couple of things on that record that I remember, specifically. They always make me smile, when I think about it. They also sort of amaze me when I think about it. The period when we made The Call record, it was recorded on analog tape. It was 2" wide analog tape and the tape recorder had 24 different channels, so you could record 24 different things. Then, you were out of real estate and you couldn't record anything else, unless you had a couple of tricks up your sleeve; you know, go back and erase something, or record two things at once, on one track. I mean, unless you wanted to spring for a synchronizer and sync up two tape recorders, you had to be creative. So, it was a 24-track world. Generally, their band setup was the same on about every song. So, the drums were on a couple of tracks, and the bass was on a couple. Dicky had a couple of channels, and Granny (Jim) had a couple of channels, and Michael had a vocal track, as we recorded the initial, live take. After that, we would get creative and do a few over-dubs. Then, we'd put in the background vocals or a tambourine and maybe lay down a guitar solo. But, from my memory, from song to song, the setup was arranged very much the same on tape and the tracks. It was pretty standard, so you would know track number fifteen was always going to be the vocals, for example. Well, Michael always did a vocal as we did the [initial] recording, a live vocal, or a guide vocal. The intention was that he would always redo the vocals. That was just the plan. And I will never forget this… It has never happened to me on any other record I've ever done. "

(Jim Scott has worked with hundreds of other bands like Tom Petty, the Red Hot Chili Peppers, Dixie Chicks, Sting, The Rolling Stones… The list is amazing!)

"So, we went to do the overdub on the first song. He went to sing the vocal on the first song. In those days, when you were organized… Each reel of tape had 16 minutes, 37 seconds of tape on it. So, that's how much time you would have on one reel of tape. Then, after you got organized, you would put three of your songs on one reel. So, then it was your master reel, or your main reel. After we recorded everything, all of the songs, we would take all of the master takes and put three songs on a reel and then three more songs on a reel, and so on. So, at the end of the day, your entire album is on three or four reels of tape. Nice and neat songs, one through ten, on four reels so you don't have to hunt around to find stuff. So, we start and Michael sings a vocal on the first track and then Michael says, 'Jim, just let the tape roll! I want to sing the next song too!' He said, 'Don't stop just let it roll right into the next song.' I told him wait a second we need to stop so I can look at the tracks and make sure where everything is. He said, 'No, don't stop, just let it roll.' There is about a minute of leader between the songs, you know the next song. I am like, 'wait, what is the next song, anyway?' Just in time, I determined that track 16 was available for the vocal. So, we punched into track 16 and he did the vocal. Then again, he said, 'Okay now what's the next song?' So, we didn't stop the tape recorder. Basically, we didn't stop and he sang the whole album in one take! We did one song after another, in one take. We didn't go back and painfully comp vocals. You know, a lot of artists will do five takes and comp the vocals, picking the best take on each verse. You pick the highlights and have no mistakes. But Michael on *Red Moon*, my memory is, every vocal was a one take vocal, all done at the same time, all done within about an hour. We just rolled the tape, he recorded it, and we went on to the next one. I haven't really told that story too many times. I've just never seen anything like it. I truly believe that we did not go back and touch up much. He didn't re-sing, or start over. We spent more time on background vocals trying to get those really beautiful. We had everybody singing around the same mic. We didn't have enough tracks for everybody to have their own track. We had to Beatles-style it and had everyone around the same mic. It was quite a sight. I really remember it. I mean, generally, everybody wants to do another take and another take... 2, 3, 4... you know... 100 takes, I mean whatever they want to do, until they feel like they got it. Michael, he was a real leader. Michael was a very, very, strong leader. He was very possessive of the band, and very possessed by the band. He was very passionate. More than once, I would spend all day at the console and I couldn't get up to go to the bathroom, because he'd say, 'No, No. Wait. Sit down another minute.' Then there was Dicky. He really played great, you know. Back in those days, they were signed to a major record company [MCA], and we were working at a good recording studio. They had hired T-Bone Burnett. There was budget for this record. Part of the budget was we could rent equipment if we needed to, if we needed something special. Dicky, like a lot of guys, rented some amplifiers. He decided to experiment with some different amps. He really wanted to get a good guitar sound on every song and he wanted to try different things. It was pretty common to rent special amps, drums, keyboards... whatever you wanted or needed to make your record. So, we got all of these rental amps and they were all stacked up. All of these Fenders and Marshalls, pretty much whatever you could want. I'm there with Dicky and everybody is waiting around. We'd plug in one amp and he'd play and be like, 'No! That's not it.' We'd try another and he'd play and be like, 'No not that either.' He'd say, 'That's not the sound, no, that's not the sound either.' So we changed the mics and we changed the cabinets, and we kept trying and trying. Finally after a while Michael was just like, 'Dicky! As soon as, you play something good, it will sound good!', and Dicky was like, 'Oh, okay. Maybe you have a point.' I was like, 'Oh, maybe the pressure is off. Maybe this isn't my fault after all.' So, I set up some microphones and of course, Dicky played great. It sounded really good. You know, nobody was mad or anything, but you could tell they were getting frustrated. Michael could be a little frustrating too, but he was also really funny. He had a beautiful smile, and a beautiful laugh. That was a great moment that I remember well. I've had a good laugh about that more than once."

"What was a real heartbreak was we worked so hard on that record. A beautiful record, and we put it out and then the record label dropped them, and it didn't get promoted like it should. "

"One other thing about that record, when you're done and you mix it and you get everything to sound just right; then you record the mix down to stereo, from that tape you ultimately cut the vinyl and make the CD or whatever. In the final process of the mix, you have to get it mastered. The mastering process is pretty simple. You basically have one more smart guy, with a good ear hopefully, and he listens to it and he rebalances it one more time. He'll tweak it and give it a little more bottom, or more top. He balances the levels between the songs, so one is not louder than the other. Generally, people who are good at it, are really good at it. It's one more chance to make it better. So, I remember we mixed the record, and then Michael listened to it and said, 'we got to remix the record. I don't like the mix.' So, we got to remix the whole thing. I was heartbroken and was like 'Really?' and Michael said, 'I just know we can do better. I know we can do it better, and faster, so let's take a few days and do it again.' Back then, it was common for it take about a day to mix a song-so, one song, one day. The second time we mixed it, I am pretty sure we did it in just three or four days. So, then we put it on a two track. We were happy the mix is done and we send it to the mastering guy. He gets done and sends it back to us and we are all excited. We knew it was going to sound great. Michael puts it on and says, 'Ugh...I don't like it. We're not done yet. Something is wrong.' He said, 'I can't figure it out. I just don't know what it is.' I told him, 'I don't know, it sounds great to me.' He takes it back to the Mastering Engineer, Brian Gardner; he is the top dog in town. He is still one of the best in the world. So, Michael goes back to Brian Gardner and says, 'Come on let's just do it one more time. We can make this just a little bit better.' So, they just barely sped it up by, like, ½ of a percent. They didn't change anything else. They sped it up just a fraction. It gave it a brightness, and a freshness, to the tempo, and that was it, we had *Red Moon*. Now, if you try to play along with *Red Moon*, the album is sharp just a tiny bit. It's an old trick. I mean, if you try to play along with *Back In Black;* it's sharp, they had to of sped that up. There is a lot of records that do that. Honestly, I would have never have thought of that for Red Moon, but Michael did. It was about the feel."

"Then when Bono came in to sing… Most of the time, when a person does an overdub, especially a background vocal, they go stand in front of a microphone in the vocal booth, or out in the studio with a pair of headphones. The play back is in the headphones, and they sing along, and the mic only picks up the sound of the voice. Well Bono didn't want to do that. He wanted to sing in the control room with the big speakers going. He wanted them blasting, so he could 'Feel it!' The problem is, with the speakers blasting in the room, the microphone is going to record it. Then, you have the potential for a feedback loop, and then, the music the mic records competes with the vocal you want to play loud in the music, and you have the levels set in the song. Now, here's a vocal that has more music bleeding thru, throwing off the mix. So, here's Bono singing with this music coming through, and we were like okay whatever you want. We only had him for an hour, so we let him record in the control room with the speakers blasting. So, we had to do it his way. I mean, it's no kind of judgment or anything, it's just how he liked to do it, so, it's what we did. You got to be flexible and get it while you can."

So was everyone there when Bono did the vocals? Or was it just him?

"I think everyone was there. I mean the control room was kind of small, so maybe the guys were out in the studio and only a few of us were in there - my guy, me, Bono, maybe T. Bone, I don't recall. T-Bone wasn't there much. He was kind of in and out. Maybe he was there for a couple of days, then he wasn't, then he'd come back and check in, or he'd show up when you needed him. There are a lot of producers that have their own style, but I think he would have been there when we had Bono there. T-Bone is an interesting guy and has quite a story."

Something the band is working towards, hopefully, is revisiting unreleased tracks and cleaning up some of them and reworking others. We have a few and would like to record some new songs.

"That would be great! Please tell the guys to get in touch with me... Jim, Scott and Dicky. I would love to hear from them. My studio is amazing. I am lucky to have such a nice place to work. I would love to help the guys record a record, or mix a record, or help with anything. I love them, they are beautiful guys. I am very, very proud of the record we did, and it broke my heart when they got dropped and it didn't get the support it deserved. [*Red Moon*] It's a special record and a very creative record, too."

"Oh and one more thing, I have a little secret about the live album [*Live Under the Red Moon*]. I recorded the live album. We had a recording truck. I think we recorded down at the Golden Bear, in Huntington Beach. We recorded it multi-track, but part of the process back in those days, you would also run a stereo mix, so it was easy to run back and check it out. We also ran a cassette tape of it, that way we could listen to it on the way home, so you could see how you did. So, I took the cassette home. I had the cassette. I don't remember exactly, but I think it was Granny [Jim] who called me and said, 'Hey we are trying to find the live *Red Moon* recording. We are trying to find it.' Nobody could find the tapes. The tapes were mysteriously missing. They were gone, but I had the cassette. It was of the live, on-the-spot mix, there was no chance to fix anything. So, they took my cassette and mastered it. They actually made the album off of my cassette."

About two months later I spoke to Tom Ferrier (Dicky Dirt) on December 16th, and December 18th. Here's what Tom had to say.

"When I start thinking about it, I've got quite a lot of stories to tell." – Tom Ferrier, December 16th, 2020

"So, you asked me just how the band got started? It all started off in the late 70's, with Scott and Michael in their band called Airtight. That, of course was with a guy I played many times with, Dale Ockerman. He was a keyboard player. That band was probably '77 and '78. Then, I came in around 1979. They had lost their guitar player. Around Santa Cruz, there was this great little music scene in the late 70's and early 80's. It kind of happened because the whole Haight-Ashbury thing in San Francisco had burnt out, and all of the artist wanted to get out of town. So, they kind of drifted down into the Santa Cruz mountain area, and you had these bands like Moby Grape and stuff, and those guys were up in the mountains. It was a time in California, and especially Northern California, when there were lots of drugs, lots of people not working, and lots of artists. It just somehow lead to this beautiful, little, music scene. The drug culture wasn't so much the 'band guys.' Because you had an audience that wanted to stay up all night long, they were very energetic, and they were always there. So, there was this really lively kind of scene. There were about ten really good bands that interacted with each other a lot. So, there were just a handful of guitar players, a handful of drummers, and a handful of keyboard players. Very few keyboard players, a few bass players, and very few really good singers. So, Michael really stood out when he came to town. He was the best singer in town, by far. So, one night I got a call from Dale Ockerman, and their guitar player had just quit. So, they asked me to come down and join in. So, I did. I didn't really know any of their songs, but I had heard them before and I was a pretty quick study. Michael and I just kind of had this connection.

So, the next day I got a call from him [Michael] and he asked if I wanted to join the band. So, he asked if I wanted to come down and rehearse with them, and it kind of took off from there. So, then I was in the mix with the 'Okies' and we had a unique sound. That only lasted for about a year and then Dale wanted to leave, and so, there were just the three of us [Michael, Scott and Dicky]."

"Then we went to this studio in the Santa Cruz valley, called Mars, and we recorded, I think, eight songs just as a 3-piece. We sent it off to L.A., because in the 70's, you would make a tape and send it off to L.A., and hope somebody would actually listen to it. Trying to get into labels and trying to get a record deal, so far, Michael and Scott hadn't had any luck. This tape we made, the Mars tape, was really just stripped down songs. Just guitar, bass, drums and [Michael] singing. Not a lot of other fancy stuff, which is really the way you should do a demo. Don't send a finished, completely produced song, because, the record company will just want to re-do it anyway."

"So, then we got this kid who was in a local band, Greg Freeman. He was totally unassuming and about ten years younger than us. He came from a different school of [music] playing, but he just kind of fit right in. So, there was this real ease of playing together, Michael and I always kind of had that from day one. It was just kind of the thing we did together. You can tell it if you listen to all of those records. Especially on those first three records, where he played a lot of guitar. Sometimes we sounded, like maybe it was only one guitar. That was one of the things about the chemistry of The

Call band, we didn't sit down and labor over how to play these things, or how to do these things, or how to come up with parts. It was really quite unspoken. In fact, we would tell a lot of jokes, then throw on our instruments and just come up with stuff. It was really quite effortless. That kind of became this unspoken formula we had. Greg was in the band the first three records and it was great, but he hated touring and Michael wanted to get back on bass, so, that's how we finally got Jim. Jim came in during the third album, during *Scene Beyond Dreams*. Once again, the reason he came in was because of a formula we had. It was because he came in and we played with each other in a very unique way. In a church you would call it 'Call and Response.' Where you throw out something and get something back, same thing in a rock band. Somebody plays a lick, and you answer that lick. You know, or compliment it in some way. Jim was that way. If you go back and listen to those records you'll hear that. I will play a little guitar part, and he'll answer with a little keyboard part. There is a lot of that, that goes on. Then Michael of course, when he got back on the bass, he just sewed it all together with his amazing, fretless bass playing. Michael, he just plays, not like anybody else you know. He'd play lead guitar bass, which is really cool. It was totally unique. Where I come from as a musician, early on, I really understood my strengths and weaknesses. I was a good rock guitar player and had a good sense of melody, but because I was so dyslexic, I wasn't so good with words. I was always looking for someone to collaborate with. I was always looking for somebody who could sing and was good with words. I was lucky enough, early on, to hook up with Michael and Scott.

Michael, he was a great poet, and he could put his poetry into rock 'n roll. He just hit at that wonderful time as the 80's happened. We weren't a new wave band or anything, but what was featured at that time was personal song writing. Michael he was a song writer. He was full of them. He just had a lot to say, and a lot to talk about, and write about. It was really neat, because we had that great honesty, we both knew each other's strengths and weaknesses, that kind of complimented each other in our playing. Michael had such strong little wrists that he was great at intricate little picky things, whereas, I had a sense of kind of psychedelic rock, which he really loved. Those things just kind of meshed together well to create that sound. Anybody that came and played with us kind of heard it immediately."

"You asked me about Garth Hudson. Garth heard that immediately. We sent him that tape and he listened to it and got back with us almost immediately. He said, 'This is good stuff. I can play this stuff. I want to come down and play with you guys.' We tried to come up with a sound that was our own, something everybody tries to do, I guess. A lot of people just try to copy what's going on. We kind of went against the grain, a little bit. We just wanted to get our own little niche. You know, make our own little sound. Garth Hudson, he was the perfect guy to add to those first three albums. When I first met Michael and Scott, and I joined up with the band, I went up to their house and started hanging around. We would listen to all of the records that we all liked. They were huge The Band devotees. They just loved those guys. In fact, the album *Red Moon* is kind of a tribute to them [The Band], that kind of sound, and the songs about family, and stuff. So, it was a tribute of sorts back to them, they were total devotees. So, early on, this guy was from Capitol Records, a rep from Capitol, he was trying to get us to go over to Capitol, and he took us out to dinner and stuff. He asked us, 'If you wanted anyone else to play in your band with you, who would it be?' and we were... 'well, we kind of like who we are.' But, he kind of pressed us on that and Michael said, 'Okay, Garth Hudson. That would be a dream.' The Capitol Records rep said, 'Well guys, I just happen to know him.' That's how that connection was made."

"So, the funny thing about Garth was, he was hysterical to go out on the road with. He was like a little old Santa Claus. He would be late to the bus every morning. You'd have to knock on his hotel door to get him up. You could never understand what he was saying. So, he would just play it for you. What was ridiculous about the things he would do? It was so much fun to listen to him play things and just sit back, and alright, let's just listen to this, now. There would be seventy-two notes that would go by and he would say, 'You know the fifty-ninth note? Could you go back and punch in there?' He was a trip. So, when we were doing stuff on the bus, on tour, he would tell us stories. Of course, we were all telling stories, but he also had narcolepsy. So, we'd be driving along and he'd be telling a story. We'd all be kicked back, staring out the window. He was talking and then all of the sudden, he would just stop. We'd kind of turn around and look at him. His head would be back and he would be snoring [loud snoring sound]. We'd look at each other and be like, 'Should we wake him up?' Eventually, (usually) Scott, would go, 'GARTH!!!', and wake him up. He'd come to and be like, 'OH! Where was I?' He made for a really fun time. The first album we ever did, we did at the Manor, just outside of Oxford, about three hours outside of London. It was the greatest thing. It was an actual manor. The guy - you know Virgin Records - Richard Branson, in the 70's, England went into this terrible depression and recession, and he [Richard] went in and bought a bunch of these mansions and turned them into different things. This particular one, he turned into a recording studio. For about $2,000 a day, we all got to stay there, we got fed, we all had our own big fancy bedrooms, butlers and maids, and we had a studio on the premises. That's where we did the first album. So, we brought Garth and his wife, Maud, over. It was really a trippy experience, because... I know you had asked me about Steve Huddleston. Steve was a friend of theirs from Oklahoma. He played a little keyboard, a brilliant guy and was also an engineer. He also, eventually, worked for an airline. He flew over to the Manor when we were there. So, one of the things they had on the grounds was a lake. They had a river, and they also had a go-cart track. They had these really cool little go-carts. The track was not just a circular track, it kind of had little things like a tunnel and things. Whoever did it, spent a lot of time doing it. So, Steve Huddleston came and these little things would only go about 15 to 20 miles per hour. So, when Steve came to the Manor, the first thing he did was took off all of the governors. So, then we could get them up to about 40 miles per hour. Of course, then we wrecked those things and tore them up.

It's like the story about Scott Musick, wrecking and tearing up the car. He was really into wrecking things. [Laughter] He would never wreck himself, but he would wreck everything around him. He was trying to teach one of the kids who worked at the Manor, I think he worked in the kitchen or something. So, we had this car and a huge long driveway. So, anyway the Rockford Files were on T.V. at that time, late 70's, early 80's. Scott wanted to show this kid how to do the 'Rockford Turn.' Rockford did it, which was... he would get going about 35 miles per hour backwards and just whip it around. So, he dropped the whole chassis out from under the thing. He scared this poor kid to death."

"Then there were stories about Scott driving home at three o'clock in the morning. Driving from Santa Cruz, back up to Boulder Creek, on this little tiny road they called Highway 9. It was a twisty-turny, little road. You could only drive about 20 miles per hour. I won't tell you the stories. They are his stories to tell, but I played with some guys that lived up there. One friend of mine that played in The Dicky Dirt Band, which was a blues band I had in the early 70's, a friend of mine went off of that at about 50 miles per hour in a BMW. He just sheared off the top of Redwood trees, flying over this gulley and landed in a big tree. Because he was so drunk, he was able to climb out of the tree, grab his guitar and walk home. So, anyway have Scott tell you his stories about driving on highway 9 at three a.m. he's got some good ones."

"So, yeah getting back on track, you had asked me about Denny Cordell. It was kind of an interesting thing that happened. Right as we made our first demo, the 'Mars' tape.

It was kind of floating around L.A. and a friends of theirs, Phil Seymour [went to high school with Scott] from Oklahoma, he had a band with Dwight Twilley. He [Phil] came out to L.A. and wanted to make a demo. He heard about us, I think maybe through talking to Scott. Denny, who had been with Shelter records, heard about us through Phil. Phil told him, 'I know these guys in Santa Cruz that have a band now and I would really like to use them.' I remember Phil came up to Santa Cruz and we rehearsed and then went to the Crow's Nest and played a set or two. Then, Phil went back to L.A. and talked to Denny. Then, Denny heard us play at the Crow's Nest and he realized we were a complete band, not just a backing band for Phil [Seymour]. So, then we went and did this demo for Phil and at the same time, we did a few songs for Denny and very soon after that Denny said, 'I have you guys a record deal with Mercury Records.' So, in a way he became our first manager, or agent. Sadly, I don't think much became of Phil's demo tape that we did. There were some cool songs, but Denny was very taken by us, and by Michael, especially. So, that's kind of how we all made that connection. That's how that all happened with Denny Cordell. Denny was kind of a funny guy."

"Some of that stuff we recorded back then, I have on cassette tape. I intend to get with someone and put it all on CD or something, but I have a ton of cassette tapes of old stuff that wasn't released. So, we all have this stuff in our closet on old cassette tapes."

"Talking about these tapes really makes me want to get all of us together again."

On the topic of getting together and recording new stuff, when I talked to Jim Scott he mentioned that he was willing to help you guys out and even offered his studio if you were interested in recording new material.

"Jim Scott is such a great guy. We had a really great time working with him [on *Red Moon*] and I really enjoyed it. To do any kind of new recording, we have to do it the right way. All three of us (me, Scott, and Jim) have to be involved at a minimum. I'm sure we could do it very quickly. We want to be happy with the result and have control of it. We were never really happy with the sound we got on the [Live Tribute] album. We didn't have control and the guy made the sound weaker. Scott told me he didn't care for [the mix] and said, 'If Michael were here, he would never stand for this.' So, anything new that we do, we must have input, and control, as to how it sounds. So, to have Jim Scott, again, would be fabulous. He did *Red Moon* and *Live Under the Red Moon*. He was fantastic. What eventually became the *Live Under the Red Moon* album was, well after the show that we recorded, I went out to the truck to listen to it and we ran off a couple of cassette tapes. Ten years later, when we decided to release it as the *Live Under the Red Moon* album, we had to pull these tapes out and [master them] make them sound like that. So, I know we have the technology, and a lot of songs that we can go back and do that with, as long as it has us involved. It has to be us, we can do something with it."

(Changing gears...)

"So, one time back in the early days, Scott and I went to a party with this girl, who I think was also a Tulsa girl. Her name was Marcy Levy. She co-wrote 'Lay Down Sally,' with Eric Clapton. So, if you co-wrote a song on a Clapton album, even with just half a writing credit, that was pretty good. I remember she had just gotten a check for like, a quarter of a million dollars. So, she'd just bought a house in the Hollywood Hills. We were down there making demos and stuff. It was neat, because, here was this girl who was just playing in bar bands, but it goes back to the whole Tulsa thing and Denny Cordell [and Leon Russell] setting up Shelter Records [and Church Studio] in Tulsa. Anyway, so, that was Marcy Levy. I don't know what happened to her, I think she made a solo album after that."

(Marcy Levy was also professionally known as Marcella Detroit. She moved to Tulsa to pursue her music career working with Leon Russell and Shelter Records. She worked with Bob Seger in the early 70's, eventually she went on tour with Eric Clapton, sang backing vocals for Clapton, and worked with him for four years.)

"So, how I got the name 'Dicky Dirt.'"

"We all had nicknames in the band. Michael we called 'Max' [also Maximus]. The reason we called him 'Max' was because he had, early on he got this giant bass rig, it was called the MAX 2000, and we called it the 'Max 2000 Fry King!', because if he turned the volume knob up anywhere past a one and a half, it just crushed everybody in the band. So, that was how he got the name 'Max.' Then we called Jim Goodwin, 'Jim

Bidet,' after the French toilet. [Jim was also nicknamed Granny, because he cleaned up after everyone like a grandma.] Jim Goodwin, the first time we went to Europe with him, um... He was an exchange student when he was a Senior in high school. He went to Paris for a year. So, 'we,' being from Oklahoma, and California, and being in France for the first time, and being introduced to the bidet, we thought it was hysterical. You know, a toilet that shot water back up at you. So, Jim was the guy who told us all about the bidet. So, we nicknamed him 'Jim Bidet,' and it stuck. We also called his record company 'Tile Face Records' and I don't think that needs any explanation. Scott Musick, he had a million different names, because, Scott would go into different characters. He would come up with these weird characters, and at one time we called him Zack Musick, for awhile. Zack, came from Jack Nicholson, because, he could make that face in photos and of course everyone would say, 'Stop making that face.' You know, that look, like he just stole something from you. Well, that was his 'Zack' face. Now the name 'Dicky Dirt,' you have to back it up to the early 70's. I had this friend named Michael Knight, he was my drummer. We had a band, this was probably '71 or '72. We all lived in this house together. It was a band house and we would have parties. We would have a gig, and then after the gig we would invite everyone back to our house. So, this was long before a skit they did in '75 or '76 on Saturday Night Live. Maybe you remember the 'Lord and Lady Douche Bag' skit. Anybody from that era should know what that was. It was a thing where there was someone introducing people as they came into the ballroom. Lord and Lady Douche Bag was the punch line in that skit. So, anyway, it was funny naming, and this was about three years before that skit. I remember when I saw that on Saturday Night Live, it was hysterical. So, my friend Michael Knight, my drummer, was sitting across the room in the house, and I walked in with whoever my girlfriend was at the time. So, we open the door and he was sitting there, in a big loud voice, introducing people as they walked in. Right off the top of his head he said, 'And now entering the ballroom is Dicky Dirt and Greta Garbage.' He said it in a musical way, and that name never left. About a year later, I named my band 'The Dicky Dirt Blues Band,' and then I brought in a horn section and it became 'Dicky Dirt and His Fabulous Perversions.' I had that name through a couple of other bands until finally I joined Michael and those guys in Airtight. That name, it just wouldn't go away. It was always there. So, when we started The Call, or Motion Pictures, we started doing all of these interviews. So, the interviewers would refer to me as 'Dicky', and they would ask my name, and then in print it would come out as 'Dicky Dart', or 'Dirty Dick', so, I said, 'Okay, we've got to nip this.' So, I said, 'Okay, let's just make this my 'inside' nickname that you guys call me and people won't know what you are talking about.' So, I decided to keep it like that and I would be Tom Ferrier now, for interviews and stuff. So, then we go to England for the first time, and in London they had a whole bunch of clothing stores and they were called 'Dicky Dirt's,' because it meant shirt, and there was a campaign in London that said, 'Dicky Dirt wants to clean up the city.' So, they were sponsoring a clean-up. They put all sorts of garbage cans out around London, with little signs on them saying, 'Dicky Dirt says clean up the city.', and of course they put me in a garbage can and took pictures of me. So, I knew that the name would never leave and it has always been there. Although, it's just my friends that call me that. I even had people that would call me 'Richard Dirt.' They would ask me if my real name was Richard. So, that's how I became 'Dicky Dirt.'"

"So, I wanted to talk about some specific things that happened on some of the albums. They are fun stories, I think. One of the things that happened was on the *Let the Day Begin* album. There was a song on there that Michael and Harry Dean Stanton wrote the lyrics to. ["For Love"] So, when we were doing that record, Michael wanted to have Harry Dean come and play harmonica on it. We were up near Ventura, in this studio called Ameraycan Studios. So, he met Harry Dean doing The Last Temptation of Christ, and they liked to hang around, and they wrote that song together. Well, Michael wrote the song and Harry threw in some lyrics. So, one night we recorded the song and wanted Harry to come up and play on it. Now Harry was probably about 70 years old or something back when we were doing this record, and Harry Dean Stanton is a real character. [In fact, Harry Dean was 62 at the time.] He was an artist, story teller, actor, renaissance man, and Jack Nicholson's best buddy. So, we asked him to play with us on the song. So, we are sitting there at ten or eleven o'clock at night, and we waited. Remember, this is before cell phones. So, you know, you make a call and say I'm coming, and then go get in your car. So, then we don't know where he is. So, around three o'clock in the morning, he staggers in, and he had taken L.S.D., because he wanted to be really out there for the session. So, he had gotten lost, but he came in and you will hear him in the background on that song, a faint harmonica, and that's Harry Dean Stanton."

"Then the lead song on that, 'Let the Day Begin,' well, the whole slide guitar part on that was an interesting story. I had never played slide guitar. We recorded the song and it was the last song we recorded for the *Let the Day Begin* album. We went down to L.A. and we were in a studio that Little Feat owned, or worked in a lot. So, we recorded the basic track for 'Let the Day Begin,' and then I was supposed to play a solo on it. So, I was kind of kickin' around with this, and that, and couldn't come up with very much. So, everybody decided to go to dinner. So, they all went to dinner and I stayed there with the engineer. I was just kind of playing all of these different kinds of solos, and they just didn't sound right. So, I said, 'Okay, let's slow down here and let me have a drink. I've got to think about this.' I know it's a cliché, I had seen it done in an old Rolling Stones clip or something, but I took the Jack Daniel's bottle and I put it on the guitar and kind of made a slide sound. The playback was going and the engineer said, 'Hey that sounds really neat. How about playing slide guitar on it?' I said, 'I don't know. I've never played slide before.' So, I had a couple of more drinks and tuned my guitar to an open tuning, then I could just play in an open key. So, I got this slide and just kind of goofed around on this thing. I was just goofing with it. Then Michael and them came back from dinner, stuck their heads in there and Michael said, 'That's it! That really sounds cool! Do that.' I was just kind of full of myself and I did it. So, then we all got drunk, had a good time and went home. Then, in the morning, we came back and took a listen to it. I thought it was kind of funky and Michael really liked it and over time I really dug it. What's funny is, I figured I would never really have to do that again. I'm not really a slide player. I don't want to go out and embarrass myself and the band. Slide is something you can study for a thousand years to try to become a great slide player and that is something I never did. Then, of course the album comes out and the song goes to number one. Of course, then we were going on Arsenio Hall or the Pat Sajak Show. So, we are going on television, and I'm thinking, I'm going on television and millions of people are going to watch me. So, I am sitting back and thinking, 'why did I pick the slide for?' [Laughter] I don't really know how to play this. So, with my talent, and God helping me, I went out and pulled it off, pretty much. Michael was the one to always encourage me. He would say, 'I really love that.' If you listen to that, Michael and I kind of did that thing once again, where we kind of backed up the groove, and started doing this interaction with each other, and it was just kind of that natural thing. We would just very naturally play with each other. So, that was the magic of The Call band, going to a live performance and hearing how we interacted with each other as players, and pushed each other forward, and complimented each other. We just had an uncanny connection with each other. The thing to understand is it wasn't contrived. We didn't sit down and plan to do it. We didn't really write out things. It became so easy to make records that Michael would walk in with a couple of chords, and part of a melody, and we would sit down and write a song, in like ten minutes. Then, we would spin the tape and play it a second time and it was like magic. You know, we might go in a studio another day and you could spend all day trying to top that and we couldn't. So, we had a great natural ability to really interact and really make wonderful music. I feel like we never had a bad performance. That moment on stage, that's everything to us. You know, that was it. That's what it was all about. Off stage, we were just a bunch of cut ups. We were comedians. We didn't take ourselves very seriously, at all. We didn't try to be too intellectual or too heavy-handed. The music, that was the thing, that's where the passion came from. We were all that passionate about that time on stage. We was always wanting to deliver that performance. I was always looking for someone like Michael Been, someone really serious about what he was doing, and really serious about the music, and have it really be connected, and mean something. That's what I loved about him, and that's what he loved about me too, that passion of the moment, that delivering of the message. I was always amazed at the fact that between songs, he might say something funny, but then I would watch Michael and he would turn for a moment, kind of towards the drums, and he would close his eyes for a second and he would put himself into that next song. He would get ready to deliver it that way. So, for me, we never had a bad performance. We were always spirited, and we were always passionate. We always knocked people out. We didn't do a lot of drugs or anything. We always wanted to be there, and be present for any performance. Our formula was maybe a couple of puffs and a shot of Jack Daniel's."

When talking to Jim Kerr of Simple Minds he mentioned that the guys in the band liked to get together and party with you guys since he didn't drink.

"That's right. [Laughter] Their dressing room wasn't as much fun as ours. If they wanted to have fun they would come over to our place. That happened a lot. You know when Jim [Kerr] was married to Chrissie Hynde, if she wasn't touring with The Pretenders and we were on tour, she would pop in. We would play for forty-five minutes or so, and they would play for 2 ½ hours. So, she [Chrissie] would pop into our dressing room. She could drink anybody under the table and she had the greatest stories. So, when she came by, eventually their road manager or someone would come by, and tell Chrissie everybody was already on the bus, and it's time to go. With those guys [Simple Minds], we had a wonderful time and they were wonderful musicians. There was this funny little thing that they used to do. Wel,l before we went on our second tour together we were all in New York making albums at the same time. Peter Gabriel was making an album, Simple Minds was making an album, and we were making an album. So, Michael went over and sang on a couple of their songs, and Jim Kerr came and sang on ours. So, they would always do this thing where Michael would come up on their encore and sing backing vocals on 'Alive and Kicking,' I think. At the time, they were wearing these kind of funky Shakespeare outfits, big drapey shirts, baggy pants, and these kind of little ballet shoes. So, every night in the dressing room they would have one of their wardrobe people run over and put one in our dressing room, it was for Michael. They would send him a little outfit, and of course Michael never wore it. It was kind of a funny, running joke. You know, years later they recorded 'Let the Day Begin,' and they were kind of influenced by us a bit. So, a couple of years later, we were touring in Europe, and watching a rock 'n roll show on television and Simple Minds were on there, and they were dressed exactly like us. Boots, tight Levi's, black t-shirts and leather jackets, it was funny. With those guys, we had a really good time, Michael especially, with Jim Kerr. Michael and I loved Charlie the guitar player, he was kind of the loosest in the group and, he loved to come out and hang. He loved to go to clubs. We also did an MTV special around that time, like 'Live from the Ritz' and Charlie came up and played the encore with us. I think it was at the end of that tour maybe in '86."

"I just remembered a funny thing. This was before Jim [Goodwin] was in the band. So, Michael, me, Scott, and Greg Freeman, during the *Modern Romans* album, we went to this place outside of Malibu and headed up into the mountains about 5 miles. This place called Indigo Studios. So, we didn't have the money to fly back and forth to Santa Cruz and stuff, so, they had a barracks kind of thing there. So, we stayed there for about a month, went home, and then came back for about another month doing that record. So, there was this loft thing, an open loft. There were a couple of beds on the bottom, and a couple up top, and you went up on a little ladder. It was like we were in camp. So, we were making this record, and Garth [Hudson] came out and played for a little bit. So, we are all in there in the middle of the night. We were all sleeping and all of the sudden, they say, they heard me making these noises, and I sat up, and I said, loudly, 'You never told me it would be like this in this guitar world.' Then, I fell back down into my pillow. Everyone started laughing and they started saying, 'Did you hear that? Did he really just say that?' Then, in the morning, they told me the story. Now whether they all made it up or not, I don't know, but, it was one of highlight memories making the *Modern Romans* album. I've been reminded many times about 'Dicky Dirt and his Guitar World.' So, ask Scott about that one, I think he was the one who bunked right next to me."

Part 2: Tom Ferrier / Dicky Dirt Interview Dec 18, 2020

"Something popped into my head about Simple Minds. Some of these English [or European] bands we played with, they had these traditions that they would do with the opening bands that did the whole tour with them. Not pick-up shows doing different venues, and places here and there, just straight through the same opening act and the headliner for the tour. So, anyway, these English guys, [European Groups] they like to do these funny little things at the end of the tour. So, Peter Gabriel, [Laughter] when we finished his tour, we were in Paris or something like that. So, the last gig we played with him, we had kind of heard rumors that they would do stuff like this, but we didn't really think much about it. We weren't really sure what it was all about. Every once in a while, one of the crew might kind of say something, but Peter never said anything. So, when we played our encore, I think our encore was 'Walls Came Down,' we came out and started singing it, and all of the sudden, from the side of the stage, this was an indoor event they had these 5 or 6ft tall trees in pots throughout the auditorium. Well, we weren't paying much attention, because we were behind a curtain. So, the curtain opens, and we come out and are doing the encore, and all of the crew guys, and band guys, brought out all of these 6ft trees, and lined them up right across the front of the stage. So, we were then singing our song behind a hedge, [Laughter] and they were all standing off to the side, just laughing their asses off. So, what we did, and we were told later that nobody had ever done this before to Peter Gabriel - you know, he was kind of like a god in Europe - we, and actually a couple of the wardrobe people, and some of the guitar techs, they came to us and said, 'You guys have got to go do something back. Peter really loves you, so it would be really funny if you did something.' So, we went into the makeup room, and this was the 'Shock the Monkey' tour. So, they painted us up in monkey makeup, and we put on some of Peter's outfits, but they were the ones that were kind of beat up and torn. So, they were kind of ragged. So, we were ragged monkeys. He had this huge stage that had this giant backdrop to it, and the players were kind of in tiers. The keyboard was on another level above, and the other instruments were lower. The drums were kind of in this sunken thing. Anyway, we were in these outfits, and the way you got on the stage was to go up a ladder, up the back, and kind of from the top. So, when he was doing 'Shock the Monkey,' we all of the sudden came over the top, dressed like crazy monkeys, acting like monkeys. [We] walked up to everybody in the band, and took their instruments away, and started playing the song. Peter was playing the keyboard so we left him. He was kind of essential to it, since he was singing and all. Scott got on the drums, and Michael took the bass. I couldn't take the guitar because he was right handed, so, I was just jumping around like a monkey. I'm sure somebody filmed it somewhere. It was a very hysterical moment."

"Simple Minds, when we finished their tour, we didn't do anything back to them, but their gesture was kind of a cool thing. What they did was, we were in some kind of a theater, and they had a big curtain behind us. A big giant curtain, and we were playing our set, and when we came to our encore, we played 'The Walls Came Down.' When it got to the last lyric, and there's that break, and we started in with the 'Ya, Ya, Ya, Ya's,' right then, behind us, the curtain opens, and we didn't know any of this was going on. The entire band, roadies and everybody, had stacked up every amp and speaker that they had. When we kicked into that, they kicked in and made this hellacious loud sound, and played the encore with us, singing and musically. I could feel the wind blowing on me from the speakers and all of that stuff. That was Charlie and Jim's [Kerr] idea."

In my conversation with Jim Kerr, he told me that they love the song "The Walls Came Down" so much that they recorded it, and are planning to release it on their new album.

"Those guys are very cool, and we had a great time hanging out with each other. I know they were kind of influenced by us. You know, we were about 10 years older than all of those guys. We had come through a different journey to get there. We had started in the late 60's and early 70's, back then you didn't just jump out on a big stage and start making records, you played bars. We played bars for ten years, so, we had chops. Those guys were always very interested in what we had to say. I remember many nights sitting around with Jim [Kerr] after hours, talking about the groove, 'How to make it groove.' I remember Michael and I used to, when they were playing, lots of times we thought, or I always thought that, because I'm a guitar player, that Charlie wasn't loud enough out front. He kind of got swallowed up by the hellaciously loud keyboards they had. So, we would go under the platforms, under the stage, and go on Charlie's side of the stage, underneath him, and listen to all of the cool stuff he was playing.

Then later on we would tell Charlie "Come on, you got to turn it up. More! More Charlie!" They were all very sweet guys. Very sweet guys."

"Okay, so here's something cool that has to do with making records."

"During the *Into the Woods* album, we did that in '87, [Released July 7th, 1987] in the valley, in L.A., over the hill from Hollywood. We were in this studio. Michael had found this producer he wanted to use. This guy named Don Smith. He kind of co-produced the *Into the Woods* album and engineered it. He had just done one of Tom Petty's records. So, where he wanted us to go was out in the suburbs, a studio called Rumbo, [Rumbo Recorders] and it was built by 'Captain and Tennille,' and in the middle of one of the sound stages it has this little turret thing, like what you would find on a sailboat. That was the Captain's chamber. That was where she sang. It was a glass thing that had one of those wheels, like you would have on a ship, in it. So, the Heartbreakers kind of lived all around there. They were good friends with Don [Smith]. So, sometimes they would just pop in the studio, and see what we were doing. One night, I was working on 'I Don't Wanna,' and I usually did my stuff late at night. I like coming in at night and doing overdubs and stuff like that. I was working on that, and not getting anywhere, really. All of the sudden the door opens and it is Mike Campbell, one of the Heartbreakers, Tom Petty's guitar player. He comes in and asks what we were doing. So, we play him the song and we get to talking about it, a bit. I had been messing around with some of the machines trying to get a really sustained sound. I wanted to hit a note and it would just last for days, but I wasn't getting that from this stuff. I'm still messing around and Mike kind of drifts off, and comes back a few minutes later with this thing. He said he had just gotten it, and it was the latest deal, the latest gadget; he said it would do exactly what I was talking about. We plugged it in and it did. So, the solo on 'I Don't Wanna,' that was the first take with that thing. Then, I went back and tried to do it again, but we used the first take. The solo on it turned out how it did because of Mike Campbell. I like to give him credit for that. Those 'Heartbreaker' guys were really sweet. The other guy that used to come by all the time was Benmont Tench, the piano player. He had a house just a couple of miles away from the studio. A few times, he invited us back to his house to have a drink. His house had a sunken living room. Right in the middle of the living room, he had a grand piano with stools all around it. It had a table cloth on it, with a bar setup on it. He would sit at the piano where the keys were and we'd sit around on the stools and do musician stuff. One of the games we'd play was to 'stump' Benmont. We'd try to come up with a song he couldn't play. We never could. I remember, because he had albums stacked in milk crates from the floor to the ceiling. It covered all of the walls in his living room, true story."

"Another story, it's kind of a me and Been [Michael] story. Me and Been were very competitive with each other. We had a funny relationship; It was cool. We worked really well together. He would always pull me along for these interviews. We would really flow with each other, and we were good at setting each other up for punch lines, and telling stories, and things like that. Early on, when we were making a bunch of demos, one of the demos we did was with Andy Johns. He was Glyn Johns brother, the guy that did the Beatles and Stones albums. He was the guy who did the *Exile on Main Street* album. We were doing demos with him at the Record Plant. It was 1980 and everybody was way too high. We did some stuff that later led to us going to England and that's where we did our first record. One night, we were sitting in a hotel room, me and Michael. We were sitting there and that was when [John] Belushi was on a number one T.V. show, had a number one movie, 'The Blues Brothers,' and a number one album out in the country. He was huge, and they were playing at the Universal Amphitheater. We saw it on television. Michael, he said something like, 'You know, I know Belushi. We could probably go to that, if we wanted to.'

I said, 'Yeah really, okay.' Then, we kind of forgot that for awhile. Then, we saw it on t.v., again. We were in Hollywood, in a hotel. So, Michael says again, 'You know, I really know Belushi.' So, I said, 'Okay, big shot if you do then, let's do it.' So, he got on the phone, and I watched him make two or three phone calls. He started out with the box office. Two or three phone calls later and he was on the phone with Belushi. I still didn't know what to think because he did stuff like that. Michael was a jokester. So, then he gets off the phone and says, 'Okay, now we're going.' So, Michael says, 'Let's get a cab.' I'm still thinking this is crazy, and he's got to be pulling my chain. Sure enough, we go to the amphitheater, and go through all of the checkpoints. We go out back of the amphitheater, where he had a trailer with this little fence around the front of the trailer, and all of the rock stars, movie stars, and beautiful women were there in this area. Like a hundred people were in this area. He [Belushi] comes out of the door on the trailer, and he looks up and sees Michael. So, he has his security guard clear out the people. Then Belushi says, 'Hey guys, come on in.' Sure enough they were old friends. They were hugging each other, telling all of these funny stories. Then John's wife came out, and his mother came out, and they all started reminiscing about this event that had happened. They were both in high school, in Chicago, together. I think both were seniors in high school. They were both in speech and drama type classes, and they would go compete in these events, drama and comedy and such. So, they would go and give performances. When they did it, and it came to the finals in the city of Chicago those two guys went head-to-head in the comedy division. They both had these skits, and they both ended up acting them out in front of me. They were both just cracking themselves up. Michael's routine was better. One of the rules they had was you couldn't be destructive or break things. You couldn't go that far with your physical comedy. Because Michael's was better, Belushi ended up throwing himself through a wall or something. Michael ended up winning the contest. So, Michael called my bluff and it was pretty cool. We got to go stand on the side of the stage and watch a 250-pound Belushi do cartwheels across the stage and perform. The next day or so, we got invited down to the studio and they were mixing the live performance. While we were there, we got to meet Ringo Starr. That was pretty cool. Michael had a kind of colorful past, because those two guys were kind of rivals back in Chicago. Michael grew up in Oklahoma, but in high school his dad, who I think worked for Wilson Sporting Gear, got transferred to Chicago. So, Michael ended up in Chicago, and that's when he met Belushi. So, that connection was made. We were actually talking to him about wanting to do something, because he was kind of the biggest name in show business at the time, and 6 months or a year later, he died." **[A year and a half later based on when the movie and album came out.]**

"The first time we went to England, we went to Olympic Studio. Denny Cordell ended up taking us there. He had asked us where we wanted to go and we said, 'We don't know. How about Olympic Studio?' We said that because it was where The Stones, Zeppelin, and all of these other people had recorded. Not that we were looking for a 60's sound, but we just knew that is where these people had recorded. So, we get to Olympic Studios and it hadn't been updated in years. The gear wasn't that good and it had become kind of a blown scene. The one thing we got out of that, was that across the street was an Indian restaurant; None of us had ever had Indian food before, real Indian food, authentic Indian food. Well, that's where Michael fell in love with Indian food. We went to that studio, and it didn't really work. So, we didn't really know what to do. We were hanging out one day, in this little apartment we were in, and Denny [Cordell] kind of bailed on us. So, we were kind of stuck there. So, we organized a little tour. We toured with a band called the Jags. We went to Liverpool and all of these little places. What was funny is eventually, we ended up doing the thing by ourselves. When we went to the punk bars, it was really cool. They really liked us. When we went to other places, I remember one in particular, it turned out to be kind of cool in a unique way. It was at a prep school or something. It felt like we were in a Monty Python skit. We walked out on stage and it was just all guys in suits and skinny ties. We started playing our stuff. What reminded me was I saw a picture of this, not too long ago. So, we do two or three of our songs and we just get blank stares. Michael is starting to get a little upset, because we are just not going over. So, I say, 'Hey, let's do a Chuck Berry song.' We played a lot of stuff like that when we were jamming; we loved all of that stuff. Early on in Airtight we really liked to play a lot of that stuff. So, I kicked into the opening lick for 'Oh Carol!' and it was like in a movie. They all jumped up and took off their ties and started going nuts. So, luckily we had that stuff in our back pockets. You know, we were four guys from a little beach town, from Santa Cruz. We were four Americans. That first time in England was great bonding times for the four of us, we really got to know each other, especially after being left there by Denny Cordell. We ended up going and ransacking his house. We found a bunch of different passports, in different names, with his picture on them. So, we thought he was an international spy or something... We later found out he had a wife in Argentina, or something, with a horse ranch. So, he was quite a character, that Denny Cordell."

"Also, during that first trip to England with Denny Cordell, now you'll have to get details from Scott Musick, but Scott Musick, if you didn't hold him down, he would crawl out of the car and get on the roof. He did this a few times. Well he did it once in London. I really don't know what prompted it, but we were probably drunk. Well, Denny had a SAAB with a luggage rack on top, and Scott got up there. Well, there were two crew guys, or something, in the back seat, on either side, holding on to Scott's legs, and he was on the roof of the car, surfing through London. You know, we were just four guys from Santa Cruz, but we were 'on our way.' We thought we were invincible. We were living our dream. We were young and on our way to being 'Rock Stars!' Well, you know, in our minds. We were fearless. That was kind of the beginning of many, many, years of Scott Musick being very entertaining, and doing all kinds of crazy stuff. Scott was the most fun guy to ever be on the road with. He was always doing stuff to make us laugh. Besides that, he was just a great drummer!"

"What was it like being in The Call? Well, it was the greatest experience ever. We played fantastic with each other and we had fabulous songs. We never had a bad night. We never brought any drama into anything we did. We always loved each other. That's hard to do for 25 years. Not many bands can do it. Usually, people will eventually have drug or emotional problems, or just hate each other, or 'hey, you fucked my girlfriend,' or, 'I want to kill you.' You know, maybe just go in different musical directions. You can't plan for those things. It just happens. At any point, if any one of us had just speared off somewhere different [me, Michael, or Scott], you know it just wouldn't have lasted, but we had that thing. We had that chemistry. We didn't have to talk about it, or work on it. It was just kind of there. We just really loved what we did. Those two hours on stage every night really was everything to us."

"I got a good one for you. Garth Hudson, the first time we met Garth Hudson, he came down to the studio we were in, making demos. We made demos for about a year, before we finally got a real record deal and went to England to record our first album. Like I mentioned, the guy from Capitol Records sent Garth Hudson a tape of us, and he got right back to us. Well, we are at the studio, waiting for Garth to come down. We're thinking a semi-truck is going to pull up with some crew guys, or his entourage, and he shows up in this little white van. He knocks at the back door and asks, 'Can anybody help me load this stuff in?' So, they loaded it in and helped him set it all up. It was pretty funny. So, he told us how much he liked the stuff, and started asking us how we wanted him to do this and that. So, we walk back into the booth, and Garth has all of his stuff set up. He has this kind of classic keyboard set up of three tiers, you know, his Hammond organ and his setup that you've seen him play on stage before. So he has it set up, his three keyboard tiers, and this is when we were first exposed to just exactly how much of a fantastic musician he really was, and the entertainer he was. So, he starts in with one hand playing this kind of clarinet, Dixie-land melody, kind of thing. Then he goes down to the other keyboard, and starts going back and forth, and kind of has this rhythm going on. Then, he looks at us and smiles. He reaches down and pops open this box he has, while he is still playing this other thing. It's still going on, and then on the other side, he's doing something else. He pulls out this long balloon thing and blows it up, while he is still playing. He puts the balloon under his arm and starts playing the bottom keyboard on the bass notes, and starts playing this tuba bass lick, and with the other hand that is free now, he starts playing another melody. So, he is like his own Dixie-land band. We were all just standing there in awe, cracking up. We all knew what a fabulous old coot he was. He was just a fabulous musician. That was our first introduction to him. Then we just went and jammed, which was great. We were all from that school of improvisation, just jamming, we loved to do that. Garth was just great at it. We had a lot of fun playing with him. At one point when we were playing live gigs, he wanted to get one of the tech guys to set up some pedals so he could have me plugged into him [his setup]. So, he could morph me and what he was playing together. You know, the kind of creative stuff you would expect from Garth Hudson. One time, he made a sample of a goose at the Manor. He recorded all of these sounds from the goose, and sampled them on his keyboard. He put some effects on it, and these really weird sounds, and at the root of it was the goose. That's who he was, that and narcoleptic. [laughter] So, we just lucked out, to get to play with a guy like that, you know, get to hang with him. He was wonderful."

On the first album, what inspired the direction you guys decided to go? What inspired the songs you ultimately recorded for the first album?

"A lot of it was inspired by the first time we went to England, to Olympic studios, and we did that little tour. So, we got exposed to a lot, and a lot of that type of music that wasn't happening in California. So, it was that kind of punk movement. We all were really into the cooler punk stuff, like The Clash, and we went to the clubs a lot around there. So, a lot of those songs were influenced by, and written after, our first time of going to England.

Based on the first album, many people assumed The Call was an English band, both from the sound, and the fact that they recorded in England.

"Some of the songs have specific lines in them like 'Fulham Blues.' Fulham was a suburb of London. That song was kind of about us being left there by Denny. We were kind of just stranded for awhile. We were in London, and had a little money, so, we were having a good time. So, there is this line in that song about the 'Fulham bag men.' For some reason, during that time we got really drunk, and we put garbage bags on. I don't recall why, maybe we were making uniforms or something. We probably had hats, too. We were in somebody else's house. Once again, we were kind of ransacking it. [laughter] We would go out on the streets at, like, midnight or 2 o'clock in the morning. We were out there just goofing around."

"We were waiting at the Fulham station

For the last train east

A one-way ticket

The foreigners searching for the living

They got your sidewalk citizens

Mookin' all around

The tunnels were dark

We drove underground

Things look different

Things feel strange

You're out of luck

You could be in danger down here

You ain't at home (don't stare)

You could be in danger down here

When we rose to the surface

We were all stunned

The shock of what's real

Like the sound of a gun

You can't miss it

All the carney lights flashing

On the midway stroll

The blind getting fleeced

By the lovers of gold

Oh, it gets lonely

Man, it gets cold

You're out of luck

You could be in danger down here

You ain't at home (don't stare)

You could be in danger down here

(there'll be no staring down here)

We were growing so reckless

We were hurtin' for fun

There's no turning back

To where you'd begun

It's behind us

I remember well walking for hours

Through the scenes of old

An old soldier singing out

Bearing his soul empty handed

We stood there freezin'

On the empty streets

There'd be no rescue tonight

It seems we've been stranded

I said stranded

You're out of luck

Brother you're in danger down here

You ain't at home (don't stare)

(there'll be no staring down here)

You're out of luck

You could be in trouble boy

You ain't at home (no)

You could be in danger

Danger

But you will be taken care of"

[The Call – The Call, Fulham Blues 1982 Mercury Polygram Records] Written by: Michael Been

[Printed with permission from The Call]

"So, then there was a soccer stadium down at the end of the block, and we tried to hit golf balls into the soccer stadium. Nobody came out and yelled at us, maybe they were afraid of us and thought we were psycho or something. So, there was this period of us just kind of being left in England, and the whole episode was this wonderful kind of bonding thing for us, for the band. The four of us together in a house in a 'Strange Land,' and we really came to love each other. So, I will never forget that. That's when Michael was kind of carefree. It was all fun, and our dreams were coming true, whereas, later on, as our career went along there was more stress, and more money, and more struggles, and the whole 'dealing with the business.' He had to work harder to find those times when it was carefree and fun.

Michael took on so much himself. Besides being a control freak, he wanted to be a part of everything. The record business is a horrible business. They try to screw you at every turn. So, he took on so much of that. So, like I said I was kind of comic relief for him. We were complete opposites, but we had this kind of musical soul thing with each other. So, I would always say, like thirty seconds before we walked out on stage, the people are going crazy and the lights are coming down and we know it's about to happen... I'd whisper into his ear, 'Let's just have the time of our lives. They Love you.' You know, to break that tense thing that he would have going. But, that's what I loved about him, he was a consummate performer. Every song he sang, he meant. He never just mailed it in. There was never a night where he said, 'Oh I don't really feel like it tonight.' That is what we did. That is what we were serious about, giving that great performance. Not only was it for the audience, but, it was really for us. That was 'oxygen' for us, you know, the live gigs. You know, when he went to play with his son, [Robert (B.R.M.C.)] we were amazed at how, you know, he just kind of stepped away from that. We also understood, because he wanted his son to have that chance. He did those first four or five albums and he taught them how to do it. It was their ideas, but it was [Michael] molding that. Giving those guys the confidence they needed to be the pop stars they are.

The real drag was right around the time he died, we were finally starting to have a conversation about getting [back] together. We were going to do it at Scott's, because, Scott had that house up at the lake. He also had his friend, Danny Timms, who had access to a studio at the time, so we were just going to go to his house on the lake. Sit down and write some songs, and do whatever we wanted, and just hang out. We hadn't really done that in awhile. Michael had kind of become a little estranged to us. I mean, we talked occasionally on the phone and if he came to town, I would go to the gig. But pretty much we were married and connected at the hip for 25 years and we were talking about it. We went to Dan Russell and told him to put a bug in his ear, and get him to take a break. I'm sure B.R.M.C. would like him to go away for a little while, [laughter] have him come up and hang with his old buddies. You know, when he died, it was terrible. It would have been nice if we could have had a chance to reconnect. We were all so close you know, kind of married to each other. We spent way more time with each other for 25 years than we did with wives, or girlfriends, or anybody else. When we heard that Michael had died, all of that kind of melted away. All the angst, and what if's, or 'I wish it could have been this way.' All of the, 'Why don't we get together?', and it just kind of washed away. Then over time, we were kind of able to realize the great stuff we did. So, since then we've try not to focus on what we didn't do, but the great stuff we did do. Not what we weren't able to do. We kind of stopped as a band at the peak of our existence. You know 'Let the Day Begin' was kind of it. We had a number one song with 'Let the Day Begin,' and we could fill any place we wanted. Then 'Red Moon' came along and the whole fiasco with MCA. You know 'Let the Day Begin' hit number one. MTV was playing it every five minutes, and at that time they were switching over from records, and tapes to CDs. They were closing down record plants and opening CD plants. So, they thought maybe we'd sell a half million records or something over a few months or so. So, they didn't press that many, and all of the sudden, it is a number one song and video. It was totally in demand, and they ran out of records. So, they couldn't get it together fast enough, and we weren't really a priority to them, you know. There wasn't any internet at that time, so, we just kind of fell off the charts. Instead of coming to us and apologizing, they got kind of pissy and wouldn't take our phone calls. So, then we made 'Red Moon' and they dropped us. So, there were all kinds of things that kind of tried to stop us, but in the end we were able to make, like, nine studio albums and thirteen or fourteen records in all, with live and compilations. We survived somehow and they couldn't get rid of us."

The Call early 80's in England. Scott, on Dicky's shoulders, with Greg Freeman and Michael.

Photo courtesy Greg Freeman Collection

Scott Musick Interview January 10, 2021

What is the story behind how you and Michael first met?

"Michael and I met because I had just been in a band with Danny Timms. **[Danny a lifelong friend has also played with Kris Kristofferson, and the Highwaymen, among other well known artists]** I came back to Oklahoma from California, with the intention of attending North Texas University the next semester. I had been offered a scholarship and decided that would be my best move. Danny was playing a national tour and arranged a stop in Tulsa on his flight home. He came to tell me he had met, and was playing with, a good singer/bass player. Danny believed that the three of us could form a good band and get a record deal. With little-to-no arm twisting, I went back to California, and started playing with Michael and Danny. After jamming on whatever rock 'n roll and blues for a few weeks, we started learning The Band songs, which was very challenging. We spent most of the next two years doing that in Danny's garage."

What would you say clicked with you and Michael, leading you to work together for over 25 years?

"All of The Call members over the years played well, and effortlessly, together right off the bat. We never dissected each other's playing, looking for the perfect part. Our styles came together naturally. We usually recorded rehearsals, especially when learning new songs. Been would start a new song and we would just fall in and play along. Several times, he would have specific parts for our instruments. Parts he had thought of while writing the song. We would then play the song again with the pre-arranged parts. We never had anything against this, because we wanted the songs to come across the best they could. We weren't there to jam. It always happened the same way. The next day we would show up to rehearse and Michael would say, 'I listened to the tape last night. Forget the parts I had. Just play the parts you came up with when you first heard it.' So, to answer the question 'What made us click?' I don't know. We just did."

So, now let's fill in a few missing pieces of the puzzle. What was the connection with Motion Pictures, Phil Seymour and Denny Cordell?

"So, Phil Seymour and Denny Cordell? I met Phil Seymour while in high school, in Tulsa. He came to the Paul McGhee studios for drum lessons. I was Paul's assistant teacher. Phil became my student and we became good friends. In the mid 70's, Phil and Dwight [Twilley] came to stay at my house in southern California while they shopped their demo. I warned them that it may take awhile, weeks, maybe months before they received any real takers for their music, because thousands of people were in town taking the same approach with the same goals. They headed out the next morning and returned that afternoon, saying they had a record deal with Shelter records."

Tell me about England and recording the first album at The Manor?

"England and the Manor."

The Call album [album #1] was recorded at two studios, Townhouse studios in Shepards Bush was first. The Stones were currently in another studio there. Our recording room was huge. Led Zeppelin had recorded *Led Zeppelin II* there. Our producer / engineer was Hugh Padgham. He had been the second engineer (in training) on the Led Zep recordings. He had some great facts and stories."

"Hugh, of course, knew the room and desk (board) extremely well, and recorded great tones on all instruments. The Frog & Firkin Pub was close by. Hugh recommended we try Dog Bolter – the pub was noted for serving this beer, brewed in their basement. It was said to be a psychedelic brew. Sure, we tried it. It was true, we bought a gallon jug to go. We put it in the fridge in the corner of our giant recording room. So, I had some Dog Bolter – Delicious. When I stood up from my drum seat to cross the room for more, I felt that I was much shorter, closer to the floor than when I was sitting down. It was fantastic beer. I had to cut back on that. The Townhouse recording went well and then we moved to The Manor studios outside of Oxford, England. [It was] a beautiful old mansion where the carriage house had been converted into a recording studio. Garth Hudson joined us at this stage of the game."

"We were so honored that Garth Hudson would play on our record, blown away actually. Then, even more so, when he continued to work with us on all tours and recordings for over three years, amazing player, amazing man. One rainy night while practicing my 'Rockford turns' up and down the road leading to the manor, I slid into the driveway and bumped into the studio building. Garth was working on some overdubs at the time. At breakfast the next day, I tried to apologize for the interruption. He said, 'Yeah, at first I thought it was on track 16, then we realized something hit the building.' He said, 'No problem. It's the first sign of life I have seen in this band.' I *LOVE* that guy."

1980 to 1990 Favorite Album.

"To pick my favorite track or album, I would have to sit down and review them all. My quick answer would be *Reconciled*. I like all of the songs and performances. Great content, spiritually, and politically. Cool guest appearances too."

"*Red Moon* is a favorite as well, with a more organic sound of the instruments, as the 80's slipped away. I especially love Jim Goodwin's sax and keyboards."

What led to you and Michael playing with The Band?

"[Once again going back] way back in a past millennium, maybe 1972, our mutual friend Danny Timms, [who] brought Michael and me together. We [all] became 'Band' fanatics. As a trio, we started learning and playing The Band songs in Danny's garage. We did this daily for probably two years, every day and night. Having Garth Hudson play with The Call was far beyond a dream come true. We had never even imagined it. After Garth had worked with us for over three years, he left to go back to playing with The Band. They had decided to play shows without Robbie Robertson, since he basically quit The Band after *The Last Waltz*. In November 1985, Garth called me at home and explained that The Band had dates booked around California, and Levon had to go to Spain. He had worked on a film there and something went wrong with the sound track, this being long before the days of Pro-Tools and email recording. Levon had to go to Spain to re-record his lines. He asked if I would play drums on their gigs. Of course I would, as terrifying as it sounded. I asked, 'who would play guitar on these shows?' I reminded him that Michael knew every measure of every 'Band' song, and would not only want to do it, but could sing any missing vocal part due to Levon's absence. We met up with Garth, Rick, and Richard at LAX and headed for Ojai, California, to play that night, no prep, or rehearsal of any kind."

Thus exemplifying the commitment, the connection and professionalism that formed in the early days of The Call and working with Garth.

Levon and Garth of The Band – Photo courtesy Paul Goeltz

Chapter Six:

Paying Tribute

On August 19th, 2010, at the age of 60, Michael Been passed away back stage at the Pukkelpop Music Festival in Belgium. Michael had been running sound for his son Robert's band, Black Rebel Motorcycle Club (B.R.M.C.).

Michael played John the Baptist for Martin Scorsese. He was friends with Jim Kerr, Bono, Peter Gabriel, Robbie Robertson, Garth Hudson, Bruce Cockburn, Barry McGuire, and so many others.

He was a lyrical genius, a masterful bass player, and had an angelic, yet commanding voice. He was the primary song writer, founding member (with Scott and Tom), and the heart and soul leader of The Call.

The day Michael passed, I was in Scott's office in Tulsa, Oklahoma, oddly enough, talking about the possibility of The Call doing a reunion show in Tulsa at Cain's Ballroom. I was standing by Scott's desk when he got a phone call, and was told the news of Michael's passing. In that moment, a chapter closed and it seemed likely they would never play together again.

Over time, the concept for the tribute show and album formed and came to be in April of 2013. Michael's son, Robert, father's bass guitar in hand, stepped up to the microphone two nights in a row to pay tribute, first at Slim's, and then at Troubadour. The evening was emotional, but still had the energy and power you would expect from The Call.

In 2014, the band releases a tribute album commemorating the event. It was released on LP (vinyl), CD, and DVD. The DVD also featured vintage The Call music videos.

In 2017, The Call again reunites with guest vocalists to give a powerful performance in New Orleans, LA.

[Jim Kerr] Remembering Michael...

"A little over two decades ago I had the pleasure and honour to spend a fair amount of time with Michael Been while touring America. Simple Minds may have been the head-liners, however there was no doubt that is was us who looked up to our opening act – The Call - fronted by none other Michael Been. We may have just topped the Billboard charts but we all knew it was Michael who was the "real deal" especially in comparison to ourselves, who at that time had buckets of chutzpah well enough to disguise for the most part the fact that by enlarge we were still well wet behind the ears."

"Michael in turn had already lived "an artist's life," having traveled far and wide both in body and mind from the dusty back roads of Oklahoma. A preacher and a teacher no doubt, he was always much more than your usual "ten a penny" careerist '80's rock star. That said as driven as he was with his beliefs, the very ones that infused his music; Michael far from sanctimonious, was always a hoot to be around."

"To my mind, he had a similar soul that one perceives in true American greats such as Robbie Robertson and even Dylan himself. But even more wonderfully he also had the wickedly spirited comedy of John Belushi draped all around him. For that reason I easily recall the difficulty in picking myself up off the floor numerously after he had acted out one of his genuinely hilarious anecdotes. As I say, it was a pleasure and an honour to have hung around with Michael Been, and for that reason it is with sadness and with feelings of extreme fondness that I recall this warm and friendly man only hours after his sudden death."

"That The Call were denied the kind of commercial success that their music merited, is an obvious understatement. Too American for the Europeans perhaps, and too English sounding for the American mainstream, Michael's face was more suited to Biblical epics than the once ubiquitous MTV. (Beards and bellies were not associated with authenticity back then in MTV land. And Michael to be frank was way too authentic to take seriously the falsities needed to play the success game.) For that reason I was not surprised to see him turn up in Martin Scorcese's The Last Temptation of Christ."

"Michael Been may have departed but I am convinced that his songs will live on and continue to be discovered by the on coming generations. I look around the current musical landscape in search of those coming through who may be cut from the same cloth as Been was."

"Today that search is fruitless, but I would never give up hope. Hope was what the music of The Call was all about. This may explain why many thought our bands made for a great bill, and with so much in common."

Jim Kerr (Simple Minds)
August, 2010

****

"I was extremely upset to hear about Michael's untimely death. I have so many great memories. He was a great songwriter, never properly acknowledged, and such a passionate singer."

"Although Michael's darkness was very evident in his music, he was always open, warm hearted and a pleasure to be with. I will miss him."

Peter Gabriel – 2010

****

"I really enjoyed working with Michael and having him on my album." – Bruce Cockburn Oct 18th, 2020

Michael's music and death clearly still affects us all.

When talking to Jim Goodwin I asked him to reflect on the experience of paying tribute to Michael at the shows in 2013.

"On stage, it was a very surreal experience. In the fog and lights, Robert looked a lot like Michael, especially when he was playing the iconic scroll-top Ampeg bass. Scott, Tom, and I sounded exactly like we had 25 years earlier. We had the same equipment with all the sounds stored in the memory banks. There were moments in the show when I wasn't sure what year it was as the sound, visuals, and emotions were so similar to the original performances. It was very much an out-of-body experience, or like a sense of time travel. The emotion was the most notable. I had a much deeper appreciation of the material since Michael's memorial, and there was the memory of Michael that infused the entire effort, and, of course, the emotional feedback from the crowd. They were mourning Michael and empathizing with a son who had recently lost his father, and three band-mates who had lost their leader, friend, and spiritual mentor. Our shows always had a church-like quality to them, but this was another level. You could literally feel the love pouring from the crowd onto the stage and washing over us like a wave of healing light."

"One of the unintended benefits for me, personally, was having my adult children there. They had never seen me play on stage and knew very little about The Call. After the show, they were very moved by the material and the performance and felt that they had a much better understanding of who I was and where I came from. I made sure to thank Robert for making that happen. It was just a wonderful unintended consequence of his willingness to make the effort and spend the money to make those shows happen."

Photo of Michael Been courtesy of Jim Goodwin.
Used by permission – Jim Goodwin collection

The Call played a rehearsal show at Slims April 18th 2013 - the day before the Troubadour tribute concert, both shows featured Robert Been of B.R.M.C., Michael's son.

Pass for both tribute shows at Slim's and Troubadour.

Dicky Dirt (Tom Ferrier) rehearsing at Slim's for the Troubadour tribute show that became the live tribute album. April 18th, 2013.

Full band rehearsal at Slim's with Dicky Dirt, Scott Musick, Jim Goodwin, and Robert Been.

SLIM'S
THE CALL (FEATURING ROBERT LEVON BEEN OF B.R.M.C.)
Thu. April 18, 2013
DOOR: 7:00 PM I SHOW: 8:00 PM
SLIM'S - 333 11TH ST., SAN FRANCISCO, CA 94103
6+
$30.00 + $4.00 FEE
GEN. ADM. SEATING LIMITED
Ticket #: 7K079SWH
NO REFUNDS OR EXCHANGES

Ticket for Slim's featuring Robert Been April 18th, 2013.

The album & DVD came out approximately a year later.

Troubadour marquee April 19th, 2013 tribute show.

Another way many have paid tribute to Michael and The Call through the years was to cover one of their songs. Most often "I Still Believe (Great design)" or "Let the Day Begin." Some you might call "Sister Bands" and others simply admirers.

Russ Taff – "I Still Believe (Great Design)"

Simple Minds – "Let the Day Begin"

Simple Minds – "The Walls Came Down"

Time Cappello – "I Still Believe" – Lost Boys

B.R.M.C. (Robert Been) – "Let the Day Begin"

Todd Rundgren – "The Walls Came Down"

Alana Levandoski – "Uncovered"

Protomen – "I Still Believe (Great Design)"

Union of Sinners and Saints – "I Still Believe"

Kevin Max – "Let the Day Begin"

Talbot McGuire – "Let the Day Begin"

The Heightsmen of Boston College (1994) – "Let the Day Begin"

The "Waco" limited TV series David Koresh plays "I Still Believe" out the window of his compound.

The David Koresh / Waco portrayal is somewhat controversial. When I asked Scott to comment on it, he simply said, "I don't know what to think about that."

After looking into the question of did David Koresh really do it? That is unclear. The series was written from the actual accounts of two different witnesses. It seems he did play a song out the window to the federal agents. Was it really The Call, or were they just making "good TV?" We do not know.

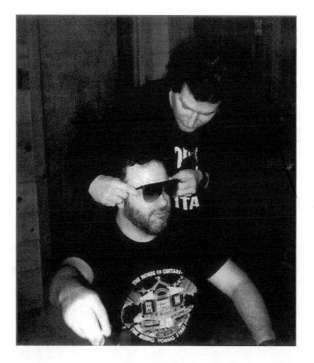

Michael Been and Dicky Dirt. Photo courtesy of and used with permission Jim Goodwin collection.

April 22nd, 2017, The Call reunited for what may be the last time. What may be "The Last Call" for The Call happened at a club called Siberia in New Orleans, LA. Jim Goodwin felt the call to stand up and have his voice heard. Due to the current political environment in our country, Jim felt he could no longer just sit silently. Jim felt it was time to take a stand. It was time for The Call once again, maybe for one last time, to March On!

March On!, Jim's new organization to join forces with other progressive movements to stand up and make a difference, had its first rally and concert with The Call headlining. This was with several other local bands and bands from across the country. One band was Alarm 58, fronted by Mikel Lomsky. Alarm 58 joined forces with Jim (in Oregon), and his cause, to put on the show. Scott (and myself), came down from Tulsa, Oklahoma. Dicky came in from Santa Cruz, CA. After a few days of rehearsals, things gelled like they had never stopped. The Call brought in friends Michael Divita, Ray Ganucheau, and J.D. Buhl as guest vocalists. Ray also played bass.

The club was small and the crowd about 100 people, but the air was electric and the bands were on fire. Several local acts played short sets. Finally, Alarm 58 took the stage and really got the crowd warmed up.

After Alarm 58, Jim takes the stage and explains March On!, and why we were there. Telling the crowd how we can all make our voices heard, make a difference, get out and vote, and help change things for the better. Time to "heed the call," you might say.

Then, for the first time in almost exactly four years after the tribute show at the Troubadour, The Call takes the stage... and they were on fire.

Club Siberia Show – April 22nd, 2017

I asked Jim Goodwin, "In 2017 The Call reunited in New Orleans for your March On! project. Can you tell me more about March On!, and why you felt called to have a rally/event and reunite The Call at that time? I know you are a man of conviction and passion. Please feel free to elaborate on what called you to take a stand and try to make a difference in troubling times."

"It all came out of the Women's March. I was so moved by that, and it was so clear that [the President] was on a path to divide the people and further corrupt our already corrupt system. I realized how relevant so many songs by The Call were to the situation, and it seemed like an opportunity to extend the energy of the Women's March. I put the idea out there on social media and got a few key responses from people that could help make it happen. One was Carlo Nuccio who lives in New Orleans, and is a musician, producer, and activist. He said, 'New Orleans is where all marches should begin,' and he was able to help us with a venue and support bands to fill out the show. Another key player was David Resnick, who supported the project with his enthusiasm, and money. And, the third player was the band Alarm 58, who I was producing in Bend, Oregon. They had a serious activist side, and their singer, Michael Divita, did an amazing job of singing Michael Been's songs with great effect. They put on a good show as the opening act, arranged for the transportation of all of our equipment, and fronted the money to cover the rest of the expenses. It would not have happened without them and a lot of the credit goes to their leader, Mikel Lomsky, whose enthusiasm was key to making it all come together. We had hoped to do a series of shows around the country, but it didn't work out. In the end, the New Orleans show was the only one we did outside of Bend. One of the most emotional aspects of the March On! show was my friend J.D., who flew himself to New Orleans to sing "Modern Romans" and "Turn a Blind Eye." I had played with J.D. in Berkely, CA, in the late 1970's in the punk scene, with his band The Jars. He was teaching school in Northern California, and contacted me immediately about being involved. What I didn't know was that J.D. was suffering from advanced cancer. A trip to New Orleans was on his bucket list and despite the pain, he got himself there, rehearsed, and performed with us. He passed away about a month after the show. He barely had the energy to rehearse and was resting at a hotel right up until show time, but when he got on stage that night, he was like a 20-year-old kid. He nailed both songs as the consummate professional that he was, walked off the stage, and headed straight back to his hotel room to rest. I never saw him again as he flew back the next morning. It added another layer of emotion to the show."

Scott Musick, and Ray Ganucheau during rehearsal.

Road case – pre-show rehearsals – April 21st, 2017

Dicky Dirt at rehearsals in New Orleans, LA - 2017

Jim Goodwin's keyboard rig for the New Orleans show.

Even though Michael (Been) wasn't there, you could feel his powerful presence and spirit through his words and music. Playing *"War Weary World," "What Are You Made Of," "Everywhere I Go," "I Still Believe,"* and so many more. Michael Divita gave a great performance, nailed the vocals, and really helped hammer home the spirit of the evening, inspiring people to stand up, and take action, and to March On!

Jim Goodwin during rehearsals for the March On! show
April 21st, 2017 New Orleans, LA.

Scott, Ray, and Jim during New Orleans rehearsals.

Dicky Dirt on stage Club Siberia – New Orleans, LA.

Chapter Eight:

"I Still Believe"

New Orleans was hoped to be the beginning of several more shows. The plan was developed to do a show in Tulsa, OK, at Cain's Ballroom, almost exactly thirty years after the last time The Call played Cain's. Everyone was excited and the show went well in New Orleans. Many video conferences later, Cain's Ballroom was reserved for April 20th, 2018, almost exactly a year after the Club Siberia show. The plan was to have a local Tulsa act open, then Alarm 58, and finally The Call. Sadly, due to scheduling conflicts we were unable to get everyone there. However, we had a show to do. Our friends Bria and Joey Guns, opened the show. Scott Musick, Tom Ferrier, and Matt Martin went on next, with Michael Divita again doing some songs by The Call and finally, Alarm 58 closed the show. Since Jim Goodwin was unable to attend the show, it was no longer a *"March On!"* rally, but instead became a benefit fund raiser for the Leon Russell monument fund. All funds went to help build a monument to Leon in Tulsa at Memorial Park Cemetery. What many people were not aware of is The Call's aforementioned connection and early ties to Leon Russell via Denny Cordell, Dwight Twilley, Phil Seymour, and Shelter Records.

Scott, Dicky, and Matt Martin playing Cain's Ballroom for the
Leon Russell monument benefit show above.

Tom Ferrier, Michael Divita, Scott Musick, and Matt Martin
rehearsing "The Walls Came Down" for Cain's Ballroom show.

Scott and Dicky playing Cain's Ballroom April 20th, 2018.
Used with permission from Mikel Lomsky and Alarm 58.

The famous Cain's Ballroom – Tulsa, OK.

Played by The Call January 30, 1988, and again 30 years later
by Scott Musick and Tom Ferrier April 20, 2018.

****

"I met Tom Ferrier (Dicky Dirt) in the late 70's. He was in a popular Santa Cruz band, The Artichoke Bros. He sat in and played with Michael and I on a gig or two and I loved his loose rock 'n roll style. That's what we needed. We were Airtight at the time. The first The Call band was Michael, Dicky on guitar, Greg Freeman on bass, while I played drums and sang harmonies. We went through a few personnel changes over the years, but the core was always Michael, Dicky, and me. The lifers. Jim Goodwin was the perfect addition. He put up with us as long as he could." – Scott Musick

ALARM 58 · April 20, 2018 · Cain's Ballroom

With Special Guests:
Scott Musick
&
Tom Ferrier
of THE CALL

Free Show - No Cover!
100% of Donations Collected Benefit:
The Leon Russell Monument Fund

Doors open at 6:30 p.m. - Show starts at 7 p.m.

VIP Tickets Available!
Early Entry. Meet & Greet.
+ Photo Ops w/the bands!
100% of VIP Ticket Proceeds
Benefit the
Leon Russell Monument Fund
For more Information:
KCHpromotions@mail.com

Cain's Ballroom
423 N Main St, Tulsa, OK

VIP Tickets Available
For a $100 Donation
to the Leon Russell Monument Fund

cainsballroom.com/event/1652237

Also Featuring: Bria & Joey Guns

2018 K.C.H. Promotions

Poster designed by Knoel C. Honn

Scott and Dicky having fun busking in downtown Tulsa, OK - 2018. If the people walking by only realized who was playing that day (calling themselves Busker-Du) by the Woody Guthrie Center.

Dicky Dirt before the Leon Russell monument benefit show.
Busking in downtown Tulsa, OK - 2018!
Photos copyright Knoel Honn 2018.

Scott and Dicky playing a local gig fall 2018 – Tulsa, OK.

Scott and Dicky photos taken by Knoel Honn 2018.

Chapter Nine:

March On!

After the benefit concert at Cain's in Tulsa, planning continued to do other shows. The hope was to do a limited tour in support of the March On! movement. Unfortunately, the funding was not there and plans for the March On! tour had to be scrapped.

MARCH ON!
CELEBRATING WORLDWIDE CHANGE

Even though the March On! concept was no longer being pursued, interest was still there to do more shows with The Call. The idea was conceived to bring in all available, original members, consisting of Scott Musick, Tom Ferrier, Greg Freeman, Steve Huddleston, and Jim Goodwin, with guest vocalists. Plans were being pursued to possibly go on a limited 80's bands tour, and to do some 80's cruises. Unfortunately, again due to scheduling issues and the Covid-19 pandemic, these plans have been put on hold indefinitely. When the worldwide health crisis is finally over, hopes are to finally attempt to do a limited run of shows, so The Call can March On! one last time. Only time will tell if they do March On!, or if New Orleans, LA was their "Last Call."

With the 40th anniversary of The Call upon us, plans are moving forward on several projects. Though the band formed in 1979, and really cut their teeth in 1980, it was 1981 when they officially became The Call (according to Greg Freeman's date book). So, The Call's "Official" 40th anniversary is 1981 to 2021. Celebrating this event is the release of this book, a planned album of unreleased tracks, potentially some new tracks, a documentary film about the band, a 35th anniversary re-release of *Reconciled* (and other albums), and yes, the possibility of a limited run of live shows in the near future.

So, perhaps The Call will "March On!" one more time, as we celebrate 40 years of music!

www.TheCall40.com

Celebrating 40 years of Music.

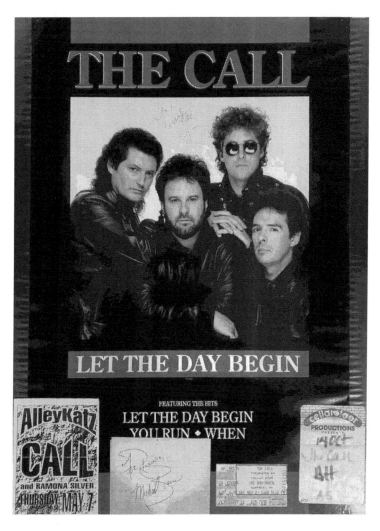

Photo courtesy of Ronnie Long. *Let the Day Begin* poster and images used with permission of The Call.

Chapter Ten:

Notified – The Official Call Newsletter

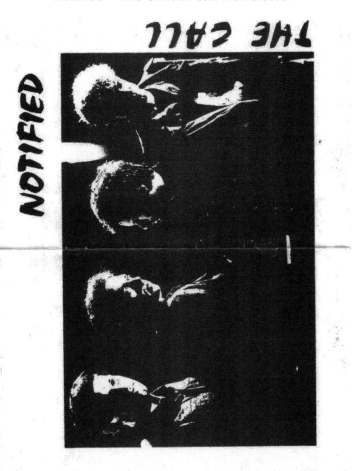

The First Issue of "Notified" comes out in 1987 as a folded 5.5" x 8.5" Newsletter with news, interviews, lyrics and photos.

NOTIFIED

Hello and welcome to the first issue of NOTIFIED.

The response to The Call Info Service has been great. We've received many wonderful letters-there are lots of Call fans out there! In one letter, the writer describing a Call concert and meeting Michael afterwards said, "It was a pleasure to meet Michael Been. I don't know if he'll be able to understand that I don't normally (i.e., never) go seeking out performers after concerts, but I wanted to try to thank him and the band for what their music has given me. The performance moved me so deeply that I wanted to tell him in person, but all that came out was 'I love your music.' I hope he knew what I meant."

Thanks to all of you for your letters and support.

After The Call's current tours of Europe and the Southwest United States end in October, the band will take a break until January. During this time, Michael will be in Morocco filming an upcoming Martin Scorsese movie. More about this in the next issue of NOTIFIED-- which will also include an interview with drummer Scott Musick, future tour information, and more.

                                        Maria

NOTIFIED is published by
The Call Information Service
P.O. Box 606
Salem, IL 62881

Compiled and edited by Maria Braden

One year subscription (4 issues)
$5.00- U.S. and Canada
(check or money order)
$10.00 - Europe and rest of world
(international money order)

Photo Credits: Robert Specter, Matt Mahurin, Eric Meyer, Tony McLain, Gary Heaton, Pat Johnson.

Special thanks to Jean Nesterak, Gary Braden, and Gary Heaton.

issue one
1987

An Interview with Michael Been

WHAT DO YOU THINK ATTRACTS PEOPLE TO THE MUSIC OF THE CALL?

We get an amazing cross section of people. I'm sure different people get in on different levels. As many people may like The Call for its rhythm as its lyrical stance. There are certain fans that are extremely passionate about it, and have had traumatic situations in their lives where the music really helped them.

I personally like music that speaks to me about my life- not my fantasies- not my ego. When a band writes a song and I can say "that's how I feel- that's what I think- that's my experience," it creates a kind of community. Loneliness, or better still, aloneness, is a basic emotion we all share to varying degrees, and the music that appeals to me is the type that eases that aloneness.

THE CALL HAS A NUMBER OF WELL- KNOWN FANS; BOB DYLAN, U2, AND OTHERS; ALSO GARTH HUDSON AND ROBBIE ROBERTSON PLAYED ON YOUR ALBUMS, AS WELL AS JIM KERR AND PETER GABRIEL. THIS IS PRETTY IMPRESSIVE STUFF-

It's nice that they appreciate our music and it's nice to get to know these people on a personal level. We toured with Simple Minds in 1983 and again in '86, and we've all become good friends. When we were first asked to tour with Peter Gabriel, we didn't know too much about him except that he'd been in Genesis. During that tour, though, we all got to know each other very well. Peter is one of the most interesting, unassuming people I've ever met.

The most exciting thing to us was THE BAND- Garth and Robbie and Levon and those people- because THE BAND, to us, was the greatest band that ever was. They were an incredible influence on us. I went to see The BAND when I was about 18, and I recall the exact moment that changed my life. Richard Manuel was singing a gut-wrentching version of "Rockin' Chair", and I remember looking through the crowd and seeing people with tears in their eyes. I'd never seen that before. I knew immediately what I wanted to do.

2

Incidentally, about two years ago, Scott and I played in
California with Richard Manuel, Rick Danko and Garth Hudson on
THE BAND's reunion tour. Levon Helm was doing a movie at the
time so Scott filled in on drums. Robbie Robertson was busy
with a previous commitment and I played guitar. Scott and I
really enjoyed playing all those songs we've loved for so long
and playing with THE BAND was an incredible experience.

IT SEEMS THAT MICHAEL BEEN HAS A LOT TO SAY IN HIS SONGS.
ARE YOUR LYRICS POLITICALLY ORIENTED?

Our music is interpreted and classified a lot as political or
social and I suppose it is in some ways. But rather than being
concerned with major political issues, our music is more into
personal politics. If it's talking about war, it's more a
symbolic reference to wars that are going on inside individual
people than on a grand scale confrontation. I think that our
most political songs, like "Walls" and "Blood Red", are very
personal because they're trying to provoke a passionate
response in the listener- a very personal reaction to a
universal situation.

DO YOU FEEL THE BAND HAS A COMMON BOND WITH OTHER POLITICAL
BANDS?

Some bands have a violent revolutionary attitude. We would be
much more inclined toward a non-violent approach. But I think
that what they're doing is important because there is too much
apathy in this country. As an artist, you have a
responsibility to do something.

YOU SAID YOU WROTE "BLOOD RED
(AMERICA)" AS A RESPONSE TO THE
CURRENT ADMINISTRATION'S APPROACH
TO SOLVING THE WORLD'S ILLS-

I think anything's possible with
that kind of thinking- we are
capable of the worst thing that's
ever happened in the history of
the world. But I think the thing
we've got going for us is that
historically the pendulum always
swings back- and there's always a
reaction to that kind of
insanity. I'm very patriotic,
but I'm patriotic to the human
being rather than the flag they
stand under.

YOUR LYRICS SOMETIMES SEEM TO HAVE BIBLICAL REFERENCES-

Well, I try to write about my own life experiences, and I'm a
Christian myself, so I write from that point of view. Although
it wouldn't be the type of Christianity commonly practiced
these days. I believe it's a vain presumption to think that
all people in the world should believe what I believe or that
it would necessarily be right for them. I only know that it's
right for me. I'm not interested in selling religion;
Christianity or otherwise.

3

THE CALL HAS MADE FIVE ALBUMS. IN RETROSPECT, ARE YOU SATISFIED WITH YOUR WORK?

I really like all of our albums, and each one for different reasons. In 1980 we went to England to make some demos and play some gigs and at that time there were emerging some great bands- Joy Division, The Clash, The Pretenders, Gang of Four; and we saw them all. The British punk bands weren't so concerned with technique and orthodox standards, they just played like their lives depended on it. The music was fresh and we were part of it. In fact, everyone thought we were an English band. We went back to England later on to record our first album. We were exploring music during that time; trying to determine our own direction. The Call was a compassionate album, but it probably came out as anger.

Modern Romans is our most political album. There was a great deal happening politically- Granada, Lebanon, our government saying the Russians are evil and the Russian government probably saying the same about us. That kind of thinking inspired me to write the last lines of "Walls Came Down." The album reflected the times.

Scene Beyond Dreams, I call our 'metaphysical' album. It was an abstract parallel of the transitions we were going through. Those were the heaviest of times for us. Some personal tragedies and strained relationships caused a great deal of introspection. Lyrically it was a more poetic approach. We were also in the middle of reforming the band with Jim Goodwin. Musically, the change in instrumentation brought out a different sound.

We did Reconciled in the summer of '85. The band hadn't had the luxury of playing very much together prior to making that album. We had gone through two years of not having a recording contract. We fell into a business hell and the band became lawyers over legal bickering with our former record label and management company. We didn't have anything definite other than the band itself. Then we got the Elektra deal and we started rehearsing, and things started clicking and feeling wonderful again. We believed in the band, and I think that all the adversity that we went through strengthened us.

Into the Woods is my favorite album, without a doubt. There's so much of all of us in the album. I really love it. When we finished the album I didn't want to listen to any of it for awhile, after having heard each song about 200 times in the studio. So I separated myself from it. When I did listen again, it was really wonderful. I was enjoying the album and not concerning myself with studio technicalities.

DO YOU SUPPOSE ANY OF YOU WOULD RATHER BE DOING SOMETHING ELSE?

The Call is 'home' for all of us. We absolutely love this band. We have that level of commitment- a mutual respect for each other. The band is very special to us; that's why we do it. We've played in a lot of different bands over the years, and it's a miracle when you can get four or five people together, and their minds are all in the same place, and want to play the same kind of music and get along well. This is just the best thing we've ever had.

4

RECONCILED
tour

1986 was a busy year for The Call. After the release of *Reconciled*, the band began preparing for a tour that kept them on the road for seven months.

In April The Call set off on a very compatible bill, supporting Simple Minds on their three month tour of the United States and Canada. Since this was The Call's first tour in two years, it was for many, an opportunity to see the band live for the first time.

The Call would open with "The Morning" and continue with many of the cuts from *Reconciled*. The band closed its set with their 1983 hit "Walls Came Down", and the audiences often took the song literally. The Call has described themselves as primarily a live band - - "when you step out on that stage in front of hundreds or thousands, the natural thing to do is play really hard for those people."

After the Simple Minds tour, the band could be seen headlining smaller clubs around the country. These shows afforded more playing time for the band, and it was here that music from their previous albums could be heard. "Tremble", "All About You" and "Turn a Blind Eye" were among the earlier cuts played. One noteworthy performance during this time was the May 29th show at The Ritz in New York City, which was taped and later aired on MTV.

September and October brought the Spin Magazine College Tour, with The Call headlining the East Coast concert dates. This tour was also the subject of an MTV special, with interview segments as well as performance clips.

After several months of touring, the band was ready to take a rest before beginning work on their next album. But actually, some of the work had already begun as several of the new songs, "I Don't Wanna," "It Could Have Been Me" and "Day Or Night" had already been written and performed at some of the last concerts on the 1986 tour.

While the quality of both the lyrics and music made *Reconciled* a highly listenable album, only a live performance provided a true reflection of The Call's powerful intensity.

5

Tremble

First born, grace begins
More bones, more skin
Veins surround me like a nest
Tie me in, first caress
Home

    A womb to grow human in
    A world to grow human
    Tremble

First breath, light surrounds
More sight, more sound
Immortal art, hands in wood
Freedom's form born to be rejected

    Hopefully we labor on
    Endlessly we labor on
    Tremble

Last words, life begins
More bones, more skin
Grave clothes are cast away
Love returns faithfully
Home

We mock the world
'Cause we cannot see
We mock the world heartlessly
Cold

    The last one to enter
    Dearer than the first
    The last one to enter
    Tremble
    Hopefully we labor on
    Endlessly we labor on
    Tremble
    A world to grow human in
    A womb to grow human
    Tremble

from Scene Beyond Dreams
written by Michael Been
published by Neeb Music/Skyhill Music

WITH OR WITHOUT REASON

"the song seems to be about the inability of the intellect or reasoning mind to understand certain basic truths about life" - Michael Been

How you gonna tell your story
Are you gonna tell it true
Either with or without reason
Love has paid the price for you

How you gonna cure this feeling
How you gonna right this wrong
Either with or without reason
The weaker do protect the strong

Listen in your hour of comfort
Just listen in your hour of pain
Either in or out of season
The hunters still pursue the game

Oh, there's somebody waiting
Oh, there's somebody near
Oh, there's somebody waiting
Oh, there's somebody here

Now lately I've begun to wonder
Just who is talking when you speak
Either with or without reason
The stronger still pursue the weak

The wisest of the fools can tell you
Anything you want to hear
Wither with or without reason
These are truths you hold so dear

Oh, there's somebody waiting...

I dedicate this inner chamber
I dedicate this harvest toil
Either with or without reason
The language of the heart takes hold

Now don't you see that love offends us
When it rises up against this waste
Either with or without reason
Evidence of sin and grace

Oh, there's somebody waiting...

from *Reconciled*
written by Michael Been
published by Neeb Music/Tarka Music

VIDEO

Inspired by Martin Scorsese's "Raging Bull", Michael Been wanted a stark, black and white setting for The Call's first video. The officials at Polygram Records were against the idea, alluding to the fact that most videos are color and flashing lights.

"But they finally gave in," says Michael. "There was no money behind it, because they thought it was such a risk. But it did stand out."

"The Walls Came Down" video was filmed in an old firehouse in the Bay area. The band was accompanied on keyboards by Garth Hudson of THE BAND, and Steve Huddleston. The powerful music and lyrics of the song, coupled with the contrast of black on white, did indeed separate it from the sea of look-alike videos that were so prevalent on music video stations.

After "The Walls Came Down" picked up some heavy air play, it became apparent that videos could be more than just colors and flashing lights.

The group's second video, "Scene Beyond Dreams," was directed by Mike Feeney of Video Caroline. It was shot in a flooded, rundown seaplane hanger. Shot in black and white, this performance clip achieved only limited play on MTV. "Polygram didn't know what to do with us," says Michael.

After signing with Elektra, Michael was given a shot at directing the group's first color video. Produced by Juanita Diana of Video Caroline, "Everywhere I Go" was filmed in a San Francisco studio, two Bay area clubs and a quonset hut in Santa Cruz.

Besides the performance footage, there are also off-stage shots of the band. Michael says he wanted to present the band members as distinct characters who "don't take ourselves too seriously. When I like a band, I get into knowing the different people as individuals. This creates more of a bond between the band and its audience.

8

"If you have us perform a song where we put ourselves into it and enjoy it, there's something very real and credible. But if you sit us down and pose us for a picture or make us act, we're very wooden."

Keeping the video simple meant avoiding reliance on "a lot of tricks," and keeping the effects "within the confines of good taste." Although most of the video is in color, it's not a standard color negative. Extensive color treatments were used, such as increasing the blacks "so much that the room itself is eliminated."

"Good videos can be done simply and artistically, without the phony trappings and the personality cult that arise from a childish fantasy that someone then decides to idolize," says Michael.

"I Don't Wanna" is the first video from The Call's fifth album, *Into The Woods*. It is directed by Doug Freel and Jean Pellerin. It was shot at the old Oak Manufacturing Complex in downtown Los Angeles, using Super 8 black and white film.

In the planning stage at this time is a second video from *Into The Woods*. "In The River" is slated to be directed by Matt Mahurin, who also did the front cover for the album. Matt Mahurin's credits include U2's recent "With or Without You" clip, as well as the photography and design of their *Wide Awake in America* album.

9

BLOOD RED (America)

Did we ask for trouble
When we asked for breath
A silent witness put to the test
In a frozen moment
An offering made
Foreign rumors live to this day

Do you feel protected
Inside white walls
A world neglected heads for a fall
A fate suspended
Each day is a gift
A world offended- God, what is this

He says, "We'll walk in the front door
And proudly raise our heads"
I say man you must be joking
Our hands are covered blood red

You've got a way that's easy
The territory's marked
Hurl us backwards- back to the start
A cool deception
A gifted tongue
Nations falling down, down, down

He says, "We'll walk in the front door
And proudly raise our heads"
I say man you must be foolin'
Our hands are covered blood red

I see you standing
Beneath the tree
Your hands uplifted, on bended knee
In a fateful hour
You hear another voice
I must remember what was my choice

He says, "I am the one
The one for you."
A look in your eyes can tell me
    what to do
I feel ecstatic
I feel transformed
More than conquered down to the bone

He says, "We'll walk right through
    heaven's door
And proudly raise our heads"
I say man you must be dreaming
Our hands are covered blood red

from *Reconciled*
written by Michael Been
published by Neeb/Tarka Music

I STILL BELIEVE (Great Design)

I been in a cave
For forty days
Only a spark
To light my way
I wanna give out
I wanna give in
This is our crime
This is our sin

But I still believe
I still believe
Through the pain
And the grief
Through the lies
Through the storms
Through the cries
And through the wars
Oh, I still believe

Flat on my back
Out at sea
Hopin' these waves
Don't cover me
I'm turned and tossed
Upon the waves
When the darkness comes
I feel the grave

But I still believe
I still believe
Through the cold
And the heat
Through the rain
And through the tears
Through the crowds
And through the cheers
Oh, I still believe

I'll march this road
I'll climb this hill
Down on my knees if I have to
I'll take my place
Up on this stage
I'll wait 'til the end of time
        for you like everybody else

I'm out on my own
Walkin' the streets
Look at the faces
That I meet
I feel like I
Like I want to go home
What do I feel
What do I know

But I still believe
I still believe
Through the shame
And through the grief
Through the heartache
Through the years
Through the waiting
Through the years

For people like us
In places like this
We need all the hope
That we can get
Oh I still believe

from *Reconciled*
written by Michael Been and Jim Goodwin
published by Neeb/Tarka Music/Tileface Music
used by permission/all rights reserved

DISCOGRAPHY

THE CALL
(1982-Mercury/Polygram)

produced by Hugh Padgham
recorded at Basing Street Studios,
        London, England
        and The Manor, Shipton on
        Cherwell, England

Tom Ferrier - guitar, vocals
Greg Freeman - bass, vocals
Scott Musick - drums, vocals
Michael Been - guitar, vocals
        keyboards

with
Garth Hudson - synthesizers, piano,
        saxophone - courtesy of
        Warner Bros. Records

War Weary World
There's a Heart Here
Doubt
This is Life
Fulham Blues
Who's That Man

Upperbirth
Bandits
Flesh and Steel
Unbearable
Waiting for the End

all songs written by Michael Been

MODERN ROMANS
(1983-Mercury/Polygram)

produced by
        Michael Been and The Call
recorded at
        Indigo Studio, Los Angeles,
        (1982)

Scott Musick - drums, percussion,
        vocals
Tom Ferrier - guitar, vocals
Michael Been - guitar, synthesizer,
        lead vocals
Greg Freeman - bass

with Garth Hudson - synthesizer,
        saxophone - courtesy of
        Warner Bros. Records
and Steve Huddleston - synthesizer,
        cornet

The Walls Came Down
Turn a Blind Eye
Time of Your Life
Modern Romans
Back From the Front

Destination
Violent Times
Face to Face
All About You

12

all songs written by Michael Been

SCENE BEYOND DREAMS
(1984-Mercury/Polygram)

produced by
  Michael Been and The Call
recorded at
  El Dorado Studio, Los Angeles

Tom Ferrier - guitar, vocals
Michael Been - guitar, bass,
      synthesizer, lead vocals
Joe Read - bass, vocals
Jim Goodwin - keyboards
Scott Musick - drums, percussion,
      vocals

with
Garth Hudson - keyboards ("The Burden")
Steve Huddleston - keyboards
Rick Kelly - keyboards ("Scene Beyond Dreams")

Scene Beyond Dreams	Heavy Hand
The Burden	Promise and Threat
Tremble	One Life Leads to Another
Delivered	Apocalypse
	Notified

all songs written by Michael Been except
"Apocalypse", written by Peter Lewis

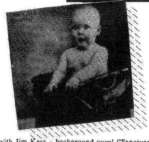

RECONCILED
(1986-Elektra/Asylum)

produced by
  Michael Been and The Call
recorded at
  The Power Station, NYC

Scott Musick - drums, vocals
Tom Ferrier - guitar, vocals
Jim Goodwin - keyboards, vocals
Michael Been - bass, guitar
      lead vocals

with Jim Kerr - background vocal ("Sanctuary" and "Everywhere I Go")
      courtesy of Virgin Records
Peter Gabriel - background vocal ("Everywhere I Go")
      courtesy of Geffen Records
Robbie Robertson - guitar ("The Morning")
      courtesy of Geffen Records

Everywhere I Go	Oklahoma
I Still Believe (Great Design)	With or Without Reason
Blood Red (America)	Sanctuary
The Morning	Tore the Old Place Down
	Even Now

all songs written by Michael Been except "I Still Believe"
and "Tore the Old Place Down" written by Michael Been and
Jim Goodwin

13

INTO THE WOODS
(1987-Elektra/Asylum)

produced by
  Michael Been and The Call
  and Don Smith

recorded at
  A&M Studios, Los Angeles
  One On One, Los Angeles
  Rumbo & Conway Studios,
  Los Angeles

Tom Ferrier - guitar, vocals
Jim Goodwin - keyboards, vocals
Michael Been - bass, vocals, guitar
Scott Musick - drums, vocals

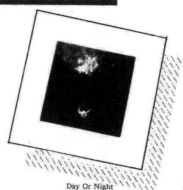

I Don't Wanna
In The River
It Could Have Been Me
The Woods

Day Or Night
Memory
Too Many Tears
Expecting
Walk Walk

all songs written by Michael Been except:
  "In The River" - Scott Musick and Michael Been
  "The Woods" - Jim Goodwin and Michael Been
  "Day Or Night" - Tom Ferrier and Michael Been

The Call's first three albums on Mercury/Polygram Records have been out of print for some time. However, we are pleased to announce that they were re-released August 24th and should be in record stores now.

The first single from the new LP, "I Don't Wanna", was released to AOR (album-oriented rock) stations on June 1, followed by "In The River" on August 26. There's word that Elektra plans to release "Memory" on CHR (contemporary hit radio) stations soon. Whatever is released next, call your local radio stations and request The Call.

The Call heads for Europe September 3 to headline the Elektra Caravan '87. Also on the bill are X and 10,000 Maniacs. The Call has been highly acclaimed in Europe since the release of their first album in 1982.

Upon their return to the States, The Call kicks off a solo tour of the Southwest beginning September 20th in Oklahoma City. Tour dates will include cities in Texas, Arizona and California.

14

THE MORNING

I am standing at the edge of my mind
If I look in, I might fall in- I sense danger
I'm divided, but I've decided it's my nature
But if I look back I might fall back into yesterday

He was weeping as the morning has just broken
He says, "I'm a young man. I got nothing to say.
I got reasons for my feeling so disheartened
I am shocking to myself everyday."

I am standing at the edge of my mind

I wanna run, I wanna shout, I wanna make thunder
Wanna know what kind of spell I've fallen under
Show me, show me
I wanna live, I wanna breath, I wanna love hard
Wanna give my life to you
Lose me in you

He was standing in this dark, dark corner
He says, "I'm a poor man. I got nothing to show."
He said, "Please, please remember me when you
           leave here,
Or I just might follow you home."

I am standing at the edge of my mind

from *Reconciled*
written by Michael Been
published by Neeb Music/Tarka Music
used by permission/all rights reserved

THE WALLS CAME DOWN

Well they blew the horns
And the walls came down
They'd all been warned
And the walls came down
They just stood there laughing
They're not laughing anymore
The walls came down

Sanctuary fades
Congregation splits
Nightly military raids
The congregation splits
It's a song of assassins
Ringin' in your ears
We got terrorist thinking
Playing on fears

Well they blew the horns
And the walls came down
They'd all been warned
But the walls came down
I don't think there are
           any Russians
And there ain't no Yanks
Just corporate criminals
Playin' with tanks

from *Modern Romans*
written by Michael Been
  published by Neeb/Tarka
Music
    used by permission/
      all rights reserved

Back Cover of 1st Notified Newsletter

Notified Newsletter Issue #2

Profile: *SCOTT MUSICK*

Scott Musick's drumming is the relentless pulse of the Call's music. Since their early beginnings in California clubs, Scott's solid fills and cohesive beat have been an integral part of the Call's unique style.

Musical Roots-

Basically self-taught, Scott's musical education began at an early age. "I've been playing since I was a kid. I grew up in a musical environment. My dad was a musician so we always had music in our home. He played drums, trumpet, guitar and sang in combos. My older brother also sang in local bands around Tulsa. I played in the jazz band at school, and it was about that same time I began drumming for a rock band."

"I listened to a lot of jazz as well as rock and roll. The jazz greats, Buddy Rich, Max Roach, Art Blakey -- they all had a tough sound. I was affected early on by the Stones, Beatles, Yardbirds, and the Band. Charlie Watts of the Stones is still one my favorite drummers -- he's straightahead rock and roll. He and Levon Helm of the Band both had well-honed styles for rock and roll drummers. Being from Oklahoma I suppose I was also influenced by country and western music."

Beginnings-

Scott got his first taste of real musical duty in California. "After school I went out to Los Angeles. I played in a couple of bands and from there went to Las Vegas with a club band. That lasted about six months and I went back to Tulsa. I saw this guy I had known in California who suggested I go back and look up this singer named Michael Been who had this really great voice. I did, and Michael and I have been playing music together since then. We played in a lot of bands but after a while we settled in the Santa Cruz area to concentrate on developing our style and writing songs."

Mere coincidence that these two Oklahoma musicians should have such musical compatability? "A few years after we had been playing together, Michael was sitting on the front porch of my granddad's house talking with him about Oklahoma when Michael mentioned that his grandfather had worked in a pharmacy in Tulsa. As it turned out, our grandfathers had been best friends in college and were apprentices at the same pharmacy in Tulsa. It was an incredible discovery."

The Music-

"One of the things that makes our music unique is, of course, Michael's lyrics. Overall, the songs have strong melodies and a good groove. Individually we all contribute by bringing in our own ideas. Jim has been the most modern influence on our music. He plays the synthesizer tastefully and doesn't allow the instrument to dominate a song. Tom's style is very diverse and original -- his guitar moods can range from atmospheric and flowing rhythms to basic blues. Michael has an amazingly solid and complex bass line. As for myself, I've always tried to be very open-minded about music, so even though I'm mainly grounded in rock and roll, I fall back on my entire background and try to take an intuitive approach to our music."

Touring-
Part of the inner dynamic that makes The Call stand out from the crowd in rock music today is the band's intense live performances. "We're a performance band, a live band. We have a lot of power on stage. I guess it's because we really love to play music, and we put everything we've got into it. With a live show, you also get an immediate audience reaction, and we have some great audiences."

Despite their years of collective onstage experience, it's the offstage camaraderie that makes the Call a band. "It's an interesting situation. When you're in a band you spend an incredible amount of time together. You're either soundchecking, backstage waiting to go on, performing or traveling, or in the studio. You have to enjoy the company or you're in trouble."

The Studio-
The Call's background is substantial -- five studio albums and the sixth in the making. "With the upcoming album we basically represented in the studio what we do live. We wanted to record in a method that most closely resembled a live performance as possible, and we like the way it's turning out. We set up in the studio like we would on stage with the monitors in the room. We went into the studio purposely under-prepared to leave room for as much spontaneity as needed. On this last tour we did a few of the new songs at soundchecks, but stopped half way through because they were sounding too good. What I mean by that is you can get into liking a song a certain way, and not see the possibilities of what you can do in the studio."

The Call has done most of the production work on their albums. "My drum sound has been different on each album. There are a lot of techniques you can use to beef up or color your sound and I've used them. But I feel musicians should take responsibility for creating their own sound rather than relying totally on an engineer."

Albums-
The Call has been really quite varied and innovative. "We are all pretty eclectic in our tastes -- we tend to like all kinds of music. With each album we've experimented, so our music has been evolving. We've learned something new on every record and have grown musically."

The Audience-
Can you describe the audience you want to reach? "As diverse as possible. It's true, though, you can never please everybody, and that's not our ambition. I think everyone wants their music to be accessible and our albums are a result of thinking about getting our music to a wider audience, but still doing what we like to do. Our audience is largely people whose first Call album was "Reconciled" and who probably never heard our earlier stuff. But now they're going back and finding those albums to see what they missed."

2

DOUBT

You doubt if there's a heaven
You doubt if there's a hell
You doubt if you'll remember
All the stories they would tell
It's a terrible feeling
Living and dealing with doubt

You've doubted your existence
You doubt if there's a truth
Your plan starts to crumble
But you cannot stand to lose
You're back where you started from
Covering yourself in doubt

You doubted your mother
And you doubted your dad
You doubted your sisters
And any brothers you had
It's a bad situation
Living and loving with doubt

Well, you doubted the beginning
And I'm sure you doubt the end
You doubted your teachers
You doubt all your friends
It's an overwhelming sensation
Confrontation with doubt

I don't know why I started
I don't know if I'll finish
I wonder why I try at all
Sometimes I wonder why I try at all

Doubt can make a strong man
Weaken under stress
And doubt can make a weak man
Totally worthless
God, it's a pity
Doubt

You stage your finale
With meticulous care
Your view is consistent
And then out of nowhere
Your vision is clouded
You face competition with doubt

from THE CALL
written by Michael Been
published by Neeb/Tarka Music
used by permission -
all rights reserved

SCENE BEYOND DREAMS

So where to begin
Let's start with a child
And where will it end
Where the perfect guest
meets his fate
In a scene beyond dreams

I stand where I stand
Convinced by the sight
We hold in our hands
Darkness and light
where they meet
In a scene beyond dreams
And a mother cries
And she cries

So we watch
And we wait
And we watch
And the hero dies

So where do we fit
Earthbound and chained
Can this be it
Visions of prophets
and kings
From a scene beyond dreams

Scattered and armed
Fuel to the fire
Compassion, alarm
Images fade into scenes
beyond dreams

The awaited appears
Branded with lies
Calls to his own
Loved and despised
From a scene beyond dreams
And a mother cries
And she cries

And we watch
And we wait
And we watch
And the hero dies

from SCENE BEYOND DREAMS
written by Michael Been
published by Neeb/Tarka Music
used by permission -
all rights reserved

244

The Last Temptation of Christ

Based on the novel by Nikos Kazantzakis. Director: Martin Scorsese. Screenplay: Martin Scorsese and Jay Cocks. Producer: Barbara De Fina. Director of Photography: Michael Ballhaus. Music: Peter Gabriel. A Universal Pictures Release.

Cast: Willem Dafoe (Jesus), Barbara Hershey (Mary Magdalene), Harry Dean Stanton (Saul/Paul), Harvey Keitel (Judas Iscariot), Victor Argo (Peter), Michael Been (John), John Lurie (James), Andre Gregory (John the Baptist), Verna Bloom (Mary, Mother of Jesus), David Bowie (Pontius Pilate), Juliette Caton (Angel).

The story: Michael gives the following synopsis of *The Last Temptation of Christ.* "The movie is a fictional account of the life of Jesus, not the Biblical story -- although, they certainly interweave. I think the purpose of the movie is to show Christ's struggle with his humanness -- feeling all the joy and pain, and struggling with the same confusion and temptation we all go through. The movie never denies Jesus' divinity, but it focuses on His human side."

The actors: Willem Dafoe played the heavy in several films before starring in *Platoon.* Barbara Hershey, one of the movie industry's most respected actresses, has been in many movies; most recently *Hannah and Her Sisters, Tin Men, Shy People,* and the upcoming *Beaches.* Harry Dean Stanton's credits include *Paris Texas, Pretty in Pink, Repo Man,* and *Slam Dance.*

Filming of the movie took three months. It began in October of 1987 in Morocco and was completed in late December. It's expected to be released to theaters in September, 1988.

Martin Scorsese is best known as the great director of big city street life. His films have long been a vanguard for excellent drama. From *Mean Streets, Taxi Driver,* and *Raging Bull* to *The Color of Money* and *After Hours* the saga continued with the symbolic plot of one man giving up his life for another man. Scorsese calls *The Last Temptation of Christ* "a deeply religious film ...an affirmation of my faith."

Michael Been is one of Scorsese's biggest fans. "I have been a fan of his for years," Michael said of Scorsese. "He was like my favorite director from when I saw *Mean Streets.*"

Likewise a longtime Call fan, Scorsese invited Michael to screentest and ultimately offered him the role of the disciple John in the Biblical epic, *The Last Temptation of Christ.* Michael said of their first meeting, "I met him a few years back when he came to hear us play in New York. I found out he followed the group, knew the songs, and liked the music. He felt there was a similarity in what the band was singing about and the purpose of his movies."

Michael described his time in Morocco as an "amazingly intense, loving experience." He attributes the overall success of the casting and filming to Martin Scorsese's technique as a director. "He's an extremely intense filmmaker. He elicits such convincing performances from his actors simply by choosing people who would naturally fit the role. He's not an acting coach, but rather he sets the mood and level of drama. The ultimate sin to him is overacting -- he likes real drama but not overdone. He's very concerned that movement and facial expression not be exaggerated, since he expects the content of the dialogue to put the scene across."

"And Willem Dafoe I cannot say enough about. He's a brilliant and intuitive actor. All the actors and crew were extraordinary people -- very serious about their work, but at the same time very humorous and real. I made some close friendships during the filming. All the actors were very musical. If we weren't acting we were together making music. Harry Dean Stanton and I became great friends and wrote a song together called "Watch", which is on the new album. All these gifted people confined together for three months -- a very creative atmosphere, so much passion and expression. It was one of the greatest times of my life."

When asked about his role in the movie as an acting experience, Michael replied. "My role is a good first-time supporting part, not too small, not too big." Would he like to do another film? "Let's wait and see how this one turns out. But I did enjoy doing it."

Heavy Hand

I feel the heavy hand of truth upon me
I feel the deadly sin of pride
It separates the highest from the lowly
It separates love from you and I

I hear the taunting voice of sure temptation
I hear the rantings of a child
An inner voice telling me I'm nothing
The voice is mine, subject to the lie

Heavy hand on my heart
Healing words to impart
Heavy hand on my throat
This is no dream
This is no dream

I see the haunting glow of pure surrender
A shapeless light reveals the hidden vow
I can see the countless sons of thunder,
With their knowing eyes circling around me
I feel divisions in this crowd

Heavy hand on my heart
Healing words to impart
Heavy hand on my throat
This is no dream
This is no joke

from *Scene Beyond Dreams*
written by Michael Been
published by Neeb/Skyhill Music ★
used by permission
all rights reserved

5

As their last LP, "Into the Woods", came out to critical acclaim and praise from fans, the Call embarked on a six-week tour with the Psychedelic Furs. The tour kicked off at the Music Hall in Houston, Texas. Between July 18 and September 3, the Call and the Furs played over 35 cities all over the United States.

Even though they were opening for the Furs, at each venue there were enthusiastic Call fans in full force. And judging from the letters we've received at this end, a great many Fur fans crossed over after witnessing the lyrical and rhythmic punch of the Call.

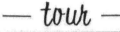

Amid their basic setup and simple but effective lighting, the Call took the stage and set out to take the audience on a short journey through their musical repertoire, although the set was primarily devoted to songs from "Into the Woods" and "Reconciled". The Call often left the stage to a standing ovation.

Touring with major bands, at times, has been a double-edged sword for the Call. While it has widened their audience, the band feels that opening concerts for other acts is not fair to people who come to hear them. "We've gone through a lot of guilt about it," said Tom Ferrier. "And it gets very frustrating -- for them and us -- when we spend six to ten hours traveling and then go play for 35 minutes, when we like to play for 90 minutes."

The Call have been on three tours with major bands. And each time, they were presented to an entirely different audience. The first was with Peter Gabriel in '83-'84, covering the United States and Europe (Gabriel personally introduced them to the audience at the start of each concert). With the Simple Minds tour in '86, the band played for mostly a pop crowd, a lot of 13 and 14-year-old girls. The Psychedelic Furs tour saw an older crowd, 18 to 25-year-olds.

As the tour with the Furs concluded in Santa Cruz, California, the Call left the next day for a 10- city swing through Europe. They were part of Elektra Records Caravan '87 Tour with X and 10,000 Maniacs. The three bands did, indeed, 'caravan' throughout Europe -- all traveling in the same bus. The band described it as "kind of a Magical Mystery Tour".

Arriving back from Europe, it was more dates -- headlining this time -- at small theaters and large clubs in the Southwest states. The sold-out performances everywhere attest the Call's popularity in the Southwest. And it seems the band appeals to no particular age or political group. "When we do our shows, it's a real mixture," said Michael. "We don't have a specific demographic, it's all over the map."

6

After the Southwest shows, the guys went on sabbatical. It was during this time that Michael went to Morocco, to play the disciple John in the Martin Scorsese film, The Last Temptation of Christ. In January, they were on the road again -- backtracking the Southwest tour (Harry Dean Stanton and Garth Hudson joined the Call on stage for a couple of these shows). An extended tour of the United States will begin with the release of the new album.

It's a fact-of-life in the music business, that a group can be very popular in, say, Los Angeles or Dallas, and virtually unknown somewhere on the East Coast. "For us, it depends on how much radio play we're getting in a particular area," Michael said. "Some cities we get so little airplay that the show ends up being an audition. In other cities there's a thousand people all cramped up to the front just waiting for it."

A lot of the Call's impressive reputation stems from word-of-mouth news of energetic and powerful live performances. Their onstage presence is captivating because of the intensity the group projects. Instrumentally, the band works as an ensemble. Solos are rare -- the focus being on personifying the music.

And the quality of their live performances is one of the things that separates the Call from a lot of bands. All too often in today's music, acts are signed before they even perform a single show. By the time the record gets released, they have thrown something together for the stage and hope it works. In contrast, the Call has built a sizable following by playing clubs and opening for other acts. Music critics cite the Call for the depth of their material and the passion with which it's performed:

"The Call opened the evening with an urgent, driving set, highlighted by songs from the band's new album, "Into the Woods", and it's previous one, "Reconciled", and proved why this band deserves more attention than it's been receiving." -David Kronke, Dallas Times Herald

"The Call consciously avoids trendiness and continues making music from the heart. This is a band to watch." -Dave Golladay, Pittsburg Leader

"The Call is definitely a concert band; they perform with style and ease. Frankly, the Psychedelic Furs seemed to take a back seat in quality to the Call." -Sharon M. Browne, Pougkeepsie News

"The Call's music is just good well-crafted rock and roll. By the middle of their set, the sold- out Chrysler Hall was crammed with people dancing in, on and around their seats. The Call were great in concert. The crowd loved them, and so did I." -Lia Braganza, York Town Crier

"This critically acclaimed band counts Peter Gabriel, Robbie Robertson, and Jim Kerr as among it's biggest fans. So what are you waiting for? This is a Call well worth heeding." -Rolling Stone

7

into the woods

"Spiritual adventuring by a California band that dances well clear of high seriousness into a unique groove" says TIME magazine of "Into the Woods", rating it as one of the top ten rock albums of 1987.

Congratulations to Scott, Tom, Michael, and Jim! It's great to see that TIME's choices were not the same super-hype, mega-sales albums that get thrust upon the listener by radio, TV, and music magazines. The fact that a band like the Call, with five exceptional albums sometimes going virtually unnoticed by the rock media, can pop up in TIME's top ten shows someone out there is actually listening to the music.

While the Call's earlier releases -- notably "The Call" and "Modern Romans" -- pointed out the world's obvious problems, "Into the Woods" takes a more introspective look at life's tougher personal questions. "Into the Woods" seems to be a study in contrast between beauty and danger where the imagery of the woods becomes a metaphor for self-examination. "This album reflects a bigger picture," said Michael Been. "Hopefully, it's wiser and more mature. A more psychological attempt at understanding why we humans do the things we do."

"I feel the worse human among us isn't that much worse than the best human among us. Like the person convicted of a crime -- if you follow that person's history -- you'll find that there were circumstances in their life that led them to that crime, and given those same circumstances, any one of us may have turned out the same way."

> It could have been me
> Living in that prison
> Locked in a cage
> Damning the walls
> Damn the division
> Wondering why it had to be me
> Well it could have been you.
> -"It Could Have Been Me"

As always, the lyrics are challenging, and this is especially evident on "Into the Woods". "It Could Have Been Me", in particular, challenges people, and questions why some people are less fortunate than others. "I wrote that song because a very good friend of mine is the chaplain at Vacaville State Penitentiary. Another friend heads up the food project in Berkeley for the street people and homeless."

"We've been poor as musicians, but we've never had to experience real poverty. We've never been racially discriminated against, and never been religiously discriminated against. We've had a pretty cushy life, relatively speaking, compared to people in Calcutta and Guatemala. So you try to live your life with a bit more consciousness than what is demanded of you in America. You try to push beyond that."

8

Michael admits that "It Could Have Been Me" might be more of a challenge than most people want from a rock song. "But you've gotta do it anyway. I was told something by Scott a few years ago. I was writing these songs and I said, 'God, I don't think anybody wants to hear this stuff,' and he said, 'Well, do it anyway.' So, I've been going on his advice ever since."

It's easy to listen to "Into the Woods" several times in a row without feeling you've heard enough. The energy of the Call provides the initial kick, but it's their sense of melody and Michael's provocative lyrics that hold you. However, Michael is not the only one in the Call writing songs for the group. Three of the songs on "Into the Woods" were co-written with the other members. Scott collaborated with Michael on the lyrics for "In the River". Tom and Jim co-wrote the music with Michael on "Day and Night" and "The Woods", respectively.

On each album, the songs have just seemed to dictate the way they are to be played and recorded. "I wrote "I Don't Wanna" one night in a hotel room in Boston at 3 or 4 in the morning," says Michael. "We rehearsed it the next day during soundcheck and played it that night as an encore."

"Into the Woods" clearly transcends, both musically and lyrically, the synth-pop genre of today's music. While most bands seem to be more concerned with their marketability than their integrity as musicians, the Call continues making music with power and vision.

TURN A BLIND EYE

To the desperate young, turn a blind eye
To the old and lonely, turn a blind eye
To our inhumanity
To our death dealing vanity
To the methods of persuasion, turn a blind eye
To the masters of evasion, turn
To the science of control, turn a blind eye
To a world in chains, turn

To the sellers of illusion, turn a blind eye
To masters of confusion, turn a blind eye
To a hollow culture
To the circling vulture
To lovers of power, turn a blind eye
And to our final hour, turn a blind eye
To the resurrection
To a world in chains, turn

I don't want to get involved
It's not my problem
I'll just ignore it
I don't want to feel this

To the starving children, turn a blind eye
To your own redemption, turn
To the horror of extinction
To a world in chains, turn

from *Modern Romans*
written by Michael Been
published by Neeb/Tarka Music

9

New Album..

In February the Call went into American Studios in Los Angeles and recorded some of the music and vocal tracks for their upcoming sixth album. As yet untitled, the album is slated for release in early Summer.

Of the thirteen songs recorded for the new album, ten will be on the release, with the remaining songs possibly being placed on B-sides of the singles. While most of the songs were written by Michael Been, a few are collaborations with Jim Goodwin. Some of the songs that were recorded for the album are:

What a Day	Watch
Closer	You Run
Jealousy	Surrender
Same Old Story	Communication

For Love (with Harry Dean Stanton on harmonica)

Additionally, the compact disc will contain an instrumental titled "Reconciled". Originally recorded during the "Reconciled" sessions, this music was used by Robbie Robertson and Gil Evans for The Color of Money soundtrack.

The new album is being produced by Michael Been and the Call, and engineered by Rob Eaton, who also worked on "Reconciled". There are few, if any, overdubs this time around, capturing the band's live essence.

Many of the cuts on the new album are live takes, as were such previous songs as "Oklahoma" and "Walk Walk". Jim Goodwin recalls that "Oklahoma" was almost made up as they went along. "We had the chord changes down. Then, in the studio, we tried it. Michael just said, 'Roll the tape; I'm going to sing it this time.' I could see him just kind of thinking it out as we were going."

The Call's unique style of music has been unfolding with each album. And although Michael writes most of the material, he's quick to state that the contribution to his songs by the other three fourths of the Call is limitless. "All of them are so creative in kind of a natural way. I always have a tape recorder running or I'll listen intently to what they do. Unconsciously they may be setting up a sound on their instrument or playing some little melody line that if I didn't record it or memorize it, it would just go out into space and that would be the end of it. I know I could take my songs to a different group of musicians and the sound would be something completely different. The sound of the Call is the sound of the way these guys play their instruments."

"Music to me has such an amazing potential to talk about your life and everything about your life. It's kind of exposing in a way, but I came to the conclusion that if we've all got something to hide, and all these dark secrets and the human condition, then conversely we've got nothing to hide. Everyone has a dark side and the wonderful, beautiful side."

"The new album, lyrically, has to do with the inability to communicate our feelings and with running away from our problems, or more specifically, the attempt to run away from ourselves. It's more directed at getting to the root of the human situation rather than explaining things away, either through spiritual images or psychological insights. The point is to get down to concrete facts about the life we all share."

"I believe the way we act out our lives as adults is dependent upon the way we were raised as children. I think the meaning behind such words as evil or sin or psychological terms such as psychosis or neurosis could be better understood if they could be related to actual incidences or occurences that happened when we were children, and continue to happen throughout our lives. Some things happen to us as children that on the surface may appear to be harmless and of no great consequence, but in fact control and dominate."

"To one degree or another every living person was an abused child. Perhaps not physically, but definitely abused mentally, either by parents or the educational system. Things that appear to be harmless or things done with the best intentions have, in fact, done damage to all of us. Parental authority, educational authority; this is what we need to concentrate on, as opposed to political or economic problems. What is done on an intimate, personal level -- the relationship between child and adult -- seems to me to be the place to start. The rest of our problems grow out of this initial childhood experience -- creating an unbroken cycle of the abused child becoming the abusing adult."

"I'm into healing. In almost all healings, it takes a traumatic self-realization. To get healed, you need to get sicker sometimes. I don't think people should remain neurotic, despairing or lonely -- I think you need to go through that, but I don't think it should be the final word. The healing process is painful. As difficult as the process might be, we still must have faith and trust in the process and not try running away from it. Whether, lyrically, I can pull this off remains to be seen."

In cooperation with the Make-A-Wish Foundation -- who grant the favorite wishes of any child who is fighting a battle with a terminal illness -- Tony Bongiovi, record producer and owner of Power Station, arranged a visit to the studio for 14-year-old Jeff Shindle of New Jersey. While at the Power Station Jeff met members of the Call, who were there working on their next album. The Call presented Jeff with an autographed copy of their record "Into the Woods". Everyone involved with this outing were heartwarmed to spend this day with Jeff and experience the wonderful work of Make-A-Wish.

‖The Call leaves May 26th for a tour of Scandinavia.

‖The band is currently checking out a possible producer for a future session.

‖The song "Same Old Story" from the Call's upcoming album may be included on the soundtrack of the Tom Cruise movie "Cocktail" due out in June.

‖A version of "I Still Believe" appeared on The Lost Boys soundtrack. In addition, Russ Taff did a version of the song on his LP "Russ Taff". Scott Musick played on a couple of the tracks on Taff's album.

See you next time,

Maria

Photo credits: Kevin Keller, page 6 and front cover(Jim, Scott, Michael); Kirby Klosson, pages 5,8,9; Tom Knobbe, pages 1,7 and front cover(Tom); Phil Fewsmith, page 9(Tom,Scott); Steve Horbund, page 12; Margaret Maxwell, back cover; Karen Sloben, page 11.

NOTIFIED

issue two

NOTIFIED is published by

The Call Information Service
P.O. Box 606
Salem, IL 62881

Compiled and edited by
Maria Braden

The Call Info Service
P.O. Box 7183
Rockford, IL. 61126

NOTIFIED Issue Three

 ## News in brief

The Call's sixth LP, titled *Watch*, will be released in early March. Michael Been described the new album as lyrically more direct, more practical — not as poetic as *Into the Woods* in terms of imagery. There will be 11 cuts on the CD and 10 on vinyl. The songs are "You Run", "Surrender", "Jealousy", "When", "For Love", "Let the Day Begin", "Same Old Story", "Closer", "Watch", "Communication", and "Hymn". "Communication" will be the 11th song on the CD. The first single release will probably be either "You Run" or "Let The Day Begin". The album is produced by Michael Been and Jim Goodwin, and engineered by Rob Eaton.

For the most part, the Call toured very little this past year. They did one month in America, six weeks in Scandinavia and some shows in California. Upon the release of the new album, the band plans to devote most of the year to touring.

Michael Been and Harry Dean Stanton met on the set of *The Last Temptation of Christ*. There they discovered their musical tastes were very similar, and while sitting around waiting for the cameras to roll in Morocco, the two would play music along with other so inclined members of the cast. They both enjoyed the creative collaboration so much they decided to team up for more of the same back home. Along with Scott Musick and Jim Goodwin, they put together a mostly acoustic show blending blues, folk and basic rock and roll; doing sterling versions of songs like "Knockin' On Heaven's Door", "Long Black Veil", "Borderline", "I'll Be Your Baby Tonight", "Under The Boardwalk", and Moby Grape's "8:05". Initially, the idea was to do just a few shows in California, but since the act was so well received and they all had time off, it was agreed to take the show on the road. I'm not much at reviewing live shows, but the performances I saw were incredible. Vocal harmonies to soothe the emotions even as they expressed them — very relaxed and spontaneous. Or as Joel Selvin of the San Francisco Chronicle aptly put it, "That was the kind of evening it was; a couple of pals hanging out and playing some music. Been and Stanton couldn't have looked more homey and at ease if there had been a campfire at their feet."

Conspicuously absent from this past summer's new releases was the Call's sixth album. You may be wondering, as I would, "Where is it? After all Notified reported the release date to be late summer." There's a saying in the music business that the only thing one learns in the music business is yesterday. That observation speaks volumes. To explain the inconsistencies, first off let me say that at the outset it did look as if the new record would be out by August, at the latest. However, there've been a few changes, the most important of which is a new record label. The Call have left Elektra and are now signed with MCA Records. And without getting lost in all the whys and wherefores, suffice it to say the band is pleased with the change. And it seems the Call's reputation had preceded them at MCA cause the folks there are really pleased as well.

Secondly, I hope all of you possess the virtue of patience. Ideally, this third issue of Notified was to have been published ages ago, but due to the change in labels and an address change for the Info Service (we are now based in Rockford, Illinois), everything was put on hold for awhile.

Though change may come, one thing remains constant: the wonderfully intense music of the Call. The excitement that stirred in me when I first heard the Call's music has only increased over the years. Their music has not fallen on deaf ears, for that same excitement is felt in the letters we receive, echoing a commonly expressed view that the Call deserves to be heard by more people. I think we've all arrived at this feeling simultaneously. Hopefully, the movers and shakers of the music world will come to realize that people can handle intelligent, well-crafted rock and roll on the radio.

In closing, let me thank you for your support of the Call. The band appreciates hearing from all of you. The new album is tentatively scheduled for release in early March. I've heard the new songs and they are really wonderful. But please note; continued play of these songs may result in hopeless longing for more of the same.

Maria

Page 1 of Issue #3 – Notified Newsletter. Due to a format change of the original newsletter from a folded half page to a full page this is the only option to reprint the complete run of newsletters in its entirety.

A Conversation with Tom Ferrier

The Call have always upheld an intuitive approach to music. They've relied on interaction and have avoided technical excess. The personalities and strengths of the band's members are tantamount to the highly individualistic sound of the Call.

Tom Ferrier's superlative guitar work reflects his early influences of rhythm and blues. At the heart of Tom's playing is feeling and expression, and he has kept his playing very close to its original inspiration.

The following is the third in a series of interviews with the Call.

Were you inspired to take up the guitar by other's examples?

I was very influenced by blues guitarists like B.B. King, Freddy King and I loved Ray Charles. I think the fundamental thing that links all music is the blues. The first music I remember listening to when I was very young was the blues. When I was about seven years old I got a walkie-talkie for Christmas and I would pretend to have this radio show and play all my favorite music. After I got my first guitar it became an obsession pretty quickly. I was diligent about practicing by playing along with records, playing them over and over so I could hear every little thing the guitarist was doing. I gigged around in different bands growing up in California. Back then surf music was the rage but I played in blues-based bands. I really liked Clapton, Beck and Page — the white boys interpretation of the blues. When you're learning your craft you copy others, then suddenly there's a time in your growth when you have your own style.

Have you been with the Call since its beginnings?

Actually before because we were Motion Pictures before we were the Call. Scott, Michael and I were in different bands playing bars, doing covers, wanting to do original material. And it was a fluke really that we got together. What happened was Scott and Michael were in a band and their guitarist didn't show up for a gig one night and someone called and asked if I would sit in. We played so naturally together - everything just clicked. We made some demo tapes and when we were ready to send them out we discovered, after a name check, that there already was a band called Motion Pictures, so we had to come up with another name pretty fast. We thought of all the names in the world and decided on the Call. It was just the obvious choice -- it seemed to fit.

The Call are sometimes perceived as a "serious" band - are they?

We're serious about our music and if you want to compete on a high-level you have to be serious. We just do the best we can musically to make ourselves happy and we try to do this as honestly and sincerely as we can.

But I think we got labeled a "serious" band during Modern Romans. We had good success with that album, but the downside was that it pidgeonholed us. The social justice message is just one part of the Call. The songs are about many things.

The Call makes playing music seem so effortless but we know it isn't...

Well, unlike a lot of other bands, we have a respect and natural flow with each other. Creating the songs is effortless in that we each understand what's required of us in terms of playing together and coming up with song ideas. One reason for this is that Michael is always writing songs, so we're never at a loss for new material. And also when you've been playing together as long as we have, you tend to know each other pretty well in the studio. Another reason is that the Call has the best rhythm section there is and if the beats not there, everybody can go home.

Everyone's emotional pictures of a song are different and the Call is a band that people tend to feel an emotional bond with that goes beyond, "yeah, great beat!".

That's true. We have fans who hang on every word of a song and a particular song will touch them deeply. People are affected by what they hear in our music.

It's an inherent thing -- we tend to gravitate toward those people who possess the same qualities we possess. When you hear from your fans or talk to people after shows what feelings are expressed?

We get all sorts of comments really. The pure essence of Michael's lyrics is very spiritual and people get a lot of spiritual images from the songs. But, actually, it runs the full gamut. Some are serious and some just want to take us out for a beer. We take time to talk because we get a lot out of those conversations, as well. Especially when we're on the road -- it keeps you going to hear it's not all in vain.

The Call seems pretty unaffected by all the razzmatazz of the rock music world.

We've been in this business long enough to know that fame is erratic. We have a real need to play and that's what we love and do best, and

Page 2 of Issue #3 – Notified Newsletter

that's enough for us. Of course we'd like to have that hit song but it has to be something we feel comfortable with. We believe in doing songs about the process of living and lot of music today is pretty removed from the real world. We have our own ideas on what makes a song great.

My idea of a great song is when after you've listened to it twenty times it still bowls you over.

I agree. When a song is revealed too easily there's nothing to think about or interpret. We've always been more concerned with making a good record that will stand on its own several years from now.

If the Call were to be observed in their working environment, the studio, would the chemistry be unpredictable?

It probably would but that's what makes us more creative. None of us is insensitive to the other's ideas. We're musically compatible.

I guess the question I was alluding to would be – is there any healthy friction in the band?

Sure, but it doesn't come from ego – it comes from a passion about the music. All great bands have had it. It keeps you from becoming complacent. It's easy for a musician to get in a rut and always play the same. Everyone has blindspots.

What is the biggest obstacle the Call have had to overcome?

The music has always meant enough to us to stick together through all sorts of adversity. We've tried to maintain the highest musical standards and that's tough in this business and it's real tough when the bills are due. It's a strange profession. Just applying yourself to this thing everyday is a struggle. But we have a great time. Some bands get so jaded that they break up because they can't take the road or because of psychological reasons. But we have a lot of fun or we wouldn't be doing it.

The Call's sixth album is due out early next year and you have a new record label. Any comments on either?

We have some great songs on this album, and the sound we got is very live, with few overdubs. The studio we recorded in had a natural resonance like a club. I'm really pleased with the guitars on this one. As for the new label – we've signed with MCA records and we're just being cautiously optimistic. The possibilities are wide open.

Notified

I was dead set against it
Ever going this far
I'm not that ambitious
Going this far

But you heard my thoughts
You heard my saddest
words
I have been caught
I figured I never would,
never would
You have been told
You have been notified
You have been loved
You have been notified

Strength lies in weakness
When the heart volunteers
To drop all defenses
Am I making it clear

You heard my thoughts
You heard my saddest
words
I came apart
I thought I never would,
never would

You have been told
You have been notified
You have been loved
You have been notified

The branch that has
fallen
Wingless birds strike the
ground
Hear the desperate calling
With a deafening round

You heard my thoughts
You heard my saddest
words
I came apart
I figured I never would,
never could
You have been told
You have been notified
You have been loved
You have been notified

from **MODERN ROMANS**
written by Michael Been
published by Neeb/Tarka Music
used by permission –
all rights reserved

Page 3 of Issue #3 – Notified Newsletter

The Call Info Service has received numerous letters concerning the movie, "The Last Temptation of Christ". While most of the letters were inquiries as to how Michael Been felt about the controversy surrounding the movie, it's apparent his appearance in the film caused a rift with some Call fans. It was decided we should address the issue and so the following is Michael's response when asked to comment on the film.

"I liked it. It was very powerful. It brought up a lot of emotions and questions that were important for me. This was Scorsese's and Kazantzakis's attempt to broaden the concept of Christ's humanity through a fictional interpretation. Two thousand years ago the authors of the New Testament had the awesome task of proving to the world that this man Jesus was God. Two thousand years later the task is reversed; to show that this unreachable God was also a man and knows exactly what we go through. A God who gave up His power and took on human weakness."

"There were things in the story that were problematic for me. But there are things in the Scriptures that are problematic for me. Not because they are wrong, but just because I don't understand it. These writings are the works of genius and I don't pretend to understand them fully. I think the controversy, the negative, hateful part, was sad and disturbing. I think it's a shame that people didn't go see the movie because some religious or political leader told them not to. People should think for themselves. It's alright for children to be guided by their elders but for grown people to be under the control of a father figure who tells them what to do and think is not a sign of maturity, spiritual or otherwise. With all respect to the authorities of the Church, I still feel their job should be to teach people to be responsible for their own lives and not keep them in a childlike position."

"There were also many lies told about dialogue and scenes that weren't even in the movie, spread by people who hadn't seen it. There were people who were offended by the movie and felt that by condemning it they were protecting not only Christianity but Christ Himself. What I actually believe is that they were trying to protect not God but their ideas of God. I personally don't prescribe to a fundamentalist or evangelical interpretation of Christianity. Now I don't doubt the faith and sincerity of these people. I'm only saying that the way they go about expressing their faith and ideas is so rigid and judgemental that they turn off a lot of people; whereas if

they emphasized love, compassion, and acceptance as Christ did, people would be knocking down their door. But look, we're all just beginners here. We're all just learning."

NOTIFIED is published by
The Call Information Service
P.O. Box 7183
Rockford, IL 61126
Compiled and edited by
Maris Braden
Photo Credits:
Tim Huskey, Margaret Maxwell

EVEN NOW

Chased, chased
Out into the woods
Footsteps close behind my back
I never knew how close I stood
Shame has brought me to my knees
Love protects the heart
It is just as you please
Fights, fights
Up and down each shore
We may be outnumbered here
The lions start to roar
Cry, cry for all to hear
Cry, the world goes on
Would you lend me your ear for a moment
I still care even now
Chased, chased
By the angry mob
Trying to steal my heart from me
Steal from me my love for God
Watch as stars fall from sky
Wait until the oceans dry up
But even then
I still feel loved
Even so, I feel cared for
Even now
So look in my eyes again
Do you recognize my face
One of despair again
Is it gone without a trace
I feel I'm alive again
Rescued from the void
Here I'm alone with you
Here I'm at home with you
Even now
Look, look
They're running close behind
Those you thought your enemies
Are friends now standing
by your side
Fight for every step you take
Shaped by every lie you've ever heard
Pain, pain
The pain I've been forced to see
Blame, the blame belongs
to no one but me
But oh, I still care   Even so, I still feel
loved   Even so, even here, even now

from **RECONCILED** written by Michael
Been   published by Neeo/Tarka
Music   used by permission – all rights
reserved

Page 4 of Issue #3 – Notified Newsletter

The Call Info Service
P.O. Box 7183
Rockford, IL 61126

NOTIFIED

issue four

Let The Day Begin

Let the Day Begin	Jealousy	Communication *
You Run	Same Ol' Story	Watch
Surrender	For Love	Uncovered
When	Closer	* CD and Cassette only

Lately, I've been having this recurring dream. In this dream I'm being chased by hundreds, even thousands, of disgruntled Call fans demanding to know the release date of the Call's sixth album. This is no dream! This is no joke!

With regard to the discrepancy in the last issue which stated that the album would be released in March, I'll not alibi this by saying, "Well, that's what I was told." Good intentions don't always translate into actions. Release dates depend on a lot of things, not all of them controllable. But enough -- you get the point.

Finally! At last! The new album, now called Let the Day Begin, will be available in stores May 29th. The first single, also titled Let the Day Begin, will most probably be on AOR (album oriented radio) playlists by the time you receive this issue.

My most sincere applause goes out to the Call for this great album. The temptation to go into a lengthy discourse is almost irresistible. But that would be superfluous. The album, in a word, is stunning.

I would like to thank the proper diety for giving us the music of the Call. And thank you for your continued support.

Drop us a line.

Maria

The video for Let the Day Begin was directed by Victor Ginsberg, whose film work includes commercials, documentaries, and videos, one of which was New Order's Blue Monday. Ginsberg, though now a New Yorker, lived in Russia until he was fourteen.

Michael had this to say about Ginsberg and the new video. "I had seen some samples of his work and he was one of a very few directors whose videos don't look like a beer commercial or a Levi's jeans ad. The video is a combination of documentary style footage and part the band and performance. We filmed the band in the Sequoia National Forest. We set up in a grove of gigantic Sequoia trees. It was definitely the most enjoyable experience we've had doing videos."

Page 1 of Issue #4 – Notified Newsletter. Due to a format change of the original newsletter from a folded half page to a full page this is the only option to reprint the complete run of newsletters in its entirety.

Jim Goodwin

This issue of Notified takes a personal look at Jim Goodwin, keyboardist for the Call. The music of the Call reveals Jim's talent for creating moods and nuances. I found Jim to be an insightful and genuinely modest person. And while his musical career is taking off, his feet seem firmly planted on the ground.

Who were your musical influences?

I was very much influenced by the classical rock stuff like Yes, Genesis with Peter Gabriel, Gentle Giant and a lot of jazz like the original Weather Report.

So those are your rock roots?

Well, prior to that, I had taken piano lessons when I was about 9 years old and I hated it. One of my very first lessons I learned the I-IV-V progression and it was weird really that the teacher was even teaching theory at all in this small town in Oregon where I was living. But I was to have learned all these songs in order to win these busts of the classical composers. So I learned the I-IV-V progression, but at that time to me the I-IV-V was "Louie, Louie" and that's all I wanted to play. I would sort of rock on this thing and my mom would come in and say, "Jim, that's not what you're practicing." So I told her that I wasn't into this thing at all and that I hated it. So she let me quit. I played "Louie, Louie" for show and tell in 3rd grade on this little Sears organ with my best friend who sang and played tambourine. That was my first ever gig. So I guess those are my rock roots. Then when I was about 14 I had this uncontrollable urge (to quote Devo) to play music and to take piano lessons. So I hooked up with my cousin in Portland who was taking lessons from this guy who taught theory more than any style of music. He taught you how to play the piano and have good technique and how to write music.

Was it at that point that you decided rock and roll was what you wanted to play?

Actually, my sister introduced me to the whole rock and roll thing by taking me to a Chuck Berry concert when I was about 14 or 15. For some reason I can't remember, we arrived really late for the show and I was the only one without a ticket and my sister didn't want to buy me one since there were only about 30 minutes left of the show. So she and her friends left me outside the Coliseum in Portland and all I heard was this great, loud rock and roll music when someone would open the doors. It really put the bug in me because it was behind these closed doors and it was just this power, this sound and it didn't have any image. I had also inherited my brother's record collection about that same time and he was really into Jimi Hendrix and Cream and I had loved them so much from the time I was very young. More than anything though I loved Peter Gabriel and Genesis. Their very eclectic, progressive rock—how they used flute, oboe and lots of keyboards—all this avant-garde instrumentation. They were my favorite band which is ironic because Michael, Tom and Scott never knew who Peter Gabriel was. They had heard Genesis but it wasn't what they were into. So I was into all this classical rock and it's interesting really because I feel it's the one thing that defines my

contribution to the Call. Even though Michael also has a background in classical music, he and Scott were into rock and roll, blues, rhythm and blues, and even psychedelic music—people like Muddy Waters, Chuck Berry, Dylan, the Band, and Moby Grape. All this straight-ahead rock music and country western as well. And Tom played in blues bands from day one. So while I was listening to this classical rock stuff, at the same time in their lives they had been listening to and playing this really unpretentious, down-home music. I never had any of that blues band rock. I'm the complete antithesis of Tom in that regard. I never played the blues until we did the Harry Dean Stanton shows. People have the notion that you can't really play music unless you have those blues roots. But I think you can—it's just that you end up playing it differently.

All musicians are influenced by what came before because every generation has chronicled its music. That's what inspiration is—the torch being passed.

Yeah, that's true and I feel this wide range of influence works well for the Call. Like Tom, is really pretty traditional with his guitar work although he ends up with these weird sounds because we throw him into these non-traditional situations and he'll add this blues rock thing. Michael and Scott lay down this really honest, but unusual, rhythm section, and I'll add this thing that I grew up with—a more melodic approach.

Page 2 of Issue #4 – Notified Newsletter. Newsletter Interviews reprinted at the end of this chapter.

A lot of today's music relies totally on this technically sophisticated synthetic sound. Are you pretty state-of-the-art?

I try to avoid all that because it's so clichéd and it wouldn't work well with the Call. We go toward more piano and organ sounds. I'm much more interested in the notes that I'm playing than in the sound. I'm not a technical keyboard player. I'm not a programmer. I don't use a computer. I don't sequence my stuff. I don't have state-of-the-art equipment by any means. What I do is play parts and to me melody is more important than the sound. I appreciate the great sounds, but I focus on performance and melody.

It was firstly on 1986's *Reconciled* that the collaborative songwriting approaches of Michael Been and Jim Goodwin were beginning to show themselves.

The most wonderful thing to me about *Reconciled* was writing songs with Michael. It was such a surprise when he asked me if I had any songs to submit. I said, "Well, yes, as a matter of fact, I do." So I gave him a couple of keyboard melodies which eventually became "Tore The Old Place Down", and "I Still Believe". To me it was the beginning of this great opportunity of writing with Michael that has blossomed on *Let The Day Begin*. For me it's the ultimate situation because I'm not a real prolific songwriter and I'm not even really good at writing songs. I'm really good at coming up with a million little chord progressions and melodies. But I never know what to do with them. I just pump them out. I think Michael is the songwriter I've been trying to find all my life because I've always wanted to collaborate with someone but no one has ever understood or appreciated or been able to hear what I've been doing. Michael is such a talented songwriter that all he needs is a spark of an idea and he'll come up with an entire format for a song out of it. And the band is so good at honing it down into a song that usually all it takes is just one line or chord progression. Scott's drumming is so great and Tom's guitar playing is truly brilliant.

Do you write lyrics with Michael?

Not really. With Michael it's only to the extent he'll bounce lines off me and say, "What do you think works better " or "Do you think this is pretentious or vague?" And since we room together on the road, he'll be working on a lyric and he'll say, "What do you think about this?" But mostly I just let him go because he's so good at it. Lyrics are probably the hardest thing to write. I never even have to consider that the lyrics he will put to my music will be anything but great. I'm totally flattered that he can be inspired by my music to come up with the kind of lyrics he writes. I think the lyrics are by far the best on the new album. Michael said at one time he thought the song "When" is the song he's always been trying to write. To me that was the biggest compliment that I could get. I wasn't responsible for it, but in some small way I had contributed to get that song out of him. To be a part of this band is a total honor and a fortunate blessing for me.

People ask me what it's like playing with the Call or writing songs with Michael and I have to say that basically I feel if I had to name the ten best singer/songwriters in the history of rock and roll, Michael would be one of them. It would be like no one you would feel if you had played with Jimi Hendrix or Jim Morrison. It would be the equivalent.

Even though Michael's lyrics leave plenty of room for interpretation, many of the Call's songs are infused with religious connotations. Were you brought up in a religious environment?

My family was Presbyterian but it really wasn't stressed. My grandfather was a lunatic, fundamentalist bible-beating minister. And for a long time my father rejected Christianity because his father represented this Christian faith and to him it was all bull because of the manner in which he was raised. To him it was all just a lie. It was violent and hateful and he totally rejected it. My dad agreed to go with the Presbyterians because my mother insisted we go to church. So we had regular Sunday School and all that. But I was never really into it because of the rigid formality. When I was in high school I had this great philosophy teacher and we read all these philosophies and I sort of believed everything because there was no reason not to believe it and if it works that's great. That's what I liked about the basic ideas of Christianity, which is all my mother ever stressed, that we should forgive each other and be kind to one another.

While deeply concerned with the spiritual journey and with political and societal inequities, it seems the Call are careful not to get on a soapbox—feeling rather that songs should communicate more in an abstract way. But in all the songs it is obvious: the message is love.

It's all about being human and taking care of each other. People need a much more practical approach in living with each other. I think the thing I'm most overwhelmed by in people in general is the fear that everyone lives with. The fear we have of each other and our intense insecurities breed all this violence, aggression and machoism and every kind of hatred and racism. It's always been there and I think it will always be there unless people really start educating themselves to have a higher, elevated spiritual concept of life and living with people. It's part of the natural human condition. We're afraid of each other and so we build these fortresses.

You've been with the Call for six years. What bands were you in before joining the Call?

I toured with Sparks and I recorded and toured with John Cale. It was a strange thing really how I joined the Call. I happened to run into an acquaintance of mine who played bass who told me he was auditioning for the Call and I asked him if they needed a keyboard player and he said he thought they did. I had heard the Call and really liked them. This was 1983 and "Walls Came Down" was having a lot of success. I called their management company and the receptionist said, "Yes, I think they are looking for a keyboard player," and gave me the number of the studio where they were recording *Scene Beyond Dreams*. When I called they said sorry we aren't looking for a keyboardist right now, but Michael told me to come on over anyway. So I did and we became acquainted and Michael took my number. Their keyboardist was just temporary and as it turned out they had some difficulty with him and he left the band. They needed someone immediately as they were about to leave for Europe to tour with Peter Gabriel. So I hooked up at the last minute. I was pretty much in heaven on that tour because here I was playing with this great band and opening for Peter Gabriel who had been my favorite for years. We returned from Europe and finished *Scene Beyond Dreams*. After it was released it became pretty obvious Polygram was burying us, giving us no support whatsoever. So we were left with two years ahead of us without a record label. We played some shows in California during the legal entanglements with Polygram to keep us alive. It was during one of those shows that a twist of fate dictated a change in the band. We had this date booked in San Francisco and our bass player, Joe Read, who had joined the Call when I did, decided to leave the band. We didn't have time to find a replacement so Michael said he would play bass since no one could learn the songs fast enough. Bass was Michael's first instrument and he and

Scott played for years together with Michael playing bass. It was about halfway through the show when we all realized that this was the best show ever. We all played better than we had ever played before. Tom played better because he was the only guitar player. Scott played better because he and Michael had played that way together for so long. And it suddenly made me feel like I understood what I was supposed to be doing. It was a lot clearer what I wanted and needed to do. Everyone's role became much more defined somehow and it felt good. So Michael said he would continue playing bass. And it was interesting because obviously Michael was going to miss playing guitar because he's such a good guitar player, but he had no problem and he seemed to love playing bass and it sounded interesting, and it immediately became apparent that we suddenly had this distinct style because of his bass. He continued to play guitar on the albums as well as bass and now on stage I play keyboard bass when he plays guitar.

I feel *Let The Day Begin* is probably the purest emotional record the Call has recorded. Honest, romantic declarations mixed with sometimes unsettling religious imagery. And while the Call have always been a little left of mainstream, the new single, "Let The Day Begin" is so infectious. It's without a doubt a great radio song.

Yes it is, and we're pleased about that. But it wasn't a flagrantly commercial move to write a radio song—it just happened. I can just hear some critic now saying something like, "the song is great but I expected more from Michael Been." Some critics have labeled him as a dark, brooding songwriter and while that is definitely a part of him it's not the whole picture. The song is upbeat but the words are very intense. This album is so completely live and recording it was a rejuvenating experience for all of us. We wanted that live sound on *Into The Woods* but we just came close. "In The River" and "I Don't Wanna" sound pretty live. We realized for this album we didn't need a fancy producer. We just needed someone to set us up in the studio. We were in a large room with full concert monitors, with side fills and wedges for all of us and we just played loud. We play best loud and powerful. The only thing redone was the vocals. "Surrender" was completely live. Tom's guitar solos are completely live. I listen to *Reconciled* now and it's good, but if we could do it over the way we did this one, it would be ten times more powerful. I think *Reconciled* and *Into The Woods* led up to this album. For what it's worth, you always tend to look back and think 'God, if we could do this and that over', but I don't think we would have gotten to this point to be able to look back from, without having gone through those steps to get here. When someone looks over the group's history, it will be an interesting body of work. A real progression.

What are you looking forward to right now?

I hope we have success with this album just so we can establish ourselves and work to our full capabilities, our full potential without having to go through these two year nightmares and being screwed around by record company executives that don't have any idea what's going on. Unfortunately it's a fact of life in this business, but if you have a certain amount of success you can finally transcend some of that dependency on the record label because they become dependent on you. You're left alone. You've proven that what you're doing is successful and so you don't have to audition and you can get past them and just have them there to put out your record and keep your career going. I feel really productive at this time in my life. So what I'm looking forward to is if this album is as successful as I think it can be, it will help me be that much more productive on every level of my life. I'm at the time of my life where if I'm given any opportunity I'll seize it and try to make something out of it. Whereas back in *Reconciled* time if I'd been given an opportunity via that success I might have squandered the success and money in some kind of unproductive way.

We are all really anxious to get back on the road. It's our career and it's extremely important to us. The thing that has kept us going is how much we believe in this record, but two years is a long time. We all love touring. The people are wonderful, so completely open. And when you reflect back you realize all those moments are so great. Makes you feel good about what you're doing.

For the edification of our readers, plans are now being formulated for a Call tour to commence sometime around the second week of July or thereabouts. As we go to press, no plans have been finalized.

Photo Credits:
Eric Meyer
Karen Stolen
Margaret Maxwell

NOTIFIED is published by
The Call Information Service
P.O. Box 7183
Rockford, IL 61126
compiled and edited by
Maria Braden

Page 4 of Issue #4 – Notified Newsletter

Good bands don't come along every-day, and albums as strong as this even less frequently. Let the Day Begin *is a close-to-fully-realized effort from one of a handful of socially/spiritually aware American bands, all deserving a larger audience. Here's to continued creativity and renewed success for these guys, "with bless-ings from above," of course.* -Greg Easterling

REVIEWS

Let the Day Begin contains the integral spiritual ten-sions that have fueled the great classics. And this record is destined for classic status. -Kathy Kielar, The Express

---

This band pretty much defines power and in-tensity. Part of the reason for the Call's intensity is obviously its lyrics. Michael Been still hasn't found what he's looking for, and his intensely personal struggles with faith, love and hope are illustrated with refreshing directness. Been's one of the few male songwriters to openly tackle the fear-of-intimacy problem ("Closer", "Communication", even "You Run"). -Karen Schlosberg, Bos-ton Herald

The Call's records are mere shadows of what they do in person. The studio scarcely begins to capture the intensity of songwriter and bassist Michael Been's voice. Left-handed Tom Ferrier peppers the songs with a succession of blues licks, power chords and harmonies. Keyboardist Jim Goodwin conjures up drones, electronic smear and eerie atmospheric church organ sounds. Drummer Scott Musick is as slick as an expensive Swiss watch. -Dale Anderson, Buffalo News

The Call weaves its spiritual rock and roll without gimmickry or posturing and though the quartet's music is overwhelmingly serious, it avoids pretentious-ness. -John Wirt, Richmond Times

As I close this review let me give some advice to those of you who plan on being involved in some extracurri-cular activities. Go out and buy *Let the Day Begin*, have a nice dinner, dim the lights, and then play "Jealousy" from this album. This is an incredibly romantic ballad and a work of art on its own. It will surely get you in the mood. -Solomon Rojas, VISTA

Michael Been writes lyrics that explore the hidden side of man--in-security, fear and jealousy--and Been's theatrical voice breathes real meaning into those words. This is music to change your life by. -Linda Joseph, The Speed of Sound

---

The Call has something to say and music to play; Been and the boys deliver their music and message power-fully well on *Let the Day Begin*. -Ray Boren, Desert News, Salt Lake City

---

Page 1 of Issue #5 – Notified Newsletter

Photo of The Call above in Newsletter
By Pat Johnson

On the ____ ROAD

To wile away the hours on a tour bus, musicians usually watch movies, listen to music, write songs, read and sleep.

Tom Ferrier:

What music have you been listening to lately: I got into the Living Colour album for awhile. I like some of their songs, "Open Letter to a Landlord" is a good song, some great choruses. I also like the new Stones record and Dylan's new one. And then late at night I revert back to this record I don't think anybody has it's a strictly blues album by this guy Robben Ford.

A favorite movie: "Kid Creole". That was Elvis at the height of his game.

Name a song you wish you had written: "The Night They Drove Old Dixie Down" by the Band. Everytime I hear that song it makes me kind of well up, almost cry, because it's such a clear picture and emotional message of the Old South and how we destroyed it in one night. The story is as big, and I mean big as in the hugeness and vastness, as any told in a song.

Jim Goodwin:

What music have you been listening to: There's a movie out called "Let's Get Lost" about the life of Chet Baker, this trumpeter and singer from Oklahoma. I've always been fascinated by his work. I was first introduced to him in Paris when I played with the Gleaming Spires. He was in the audience one night and we asked him to come up on stage and play with us and he did. I have two tapes of his music that I've been listening to lately. One is the soundtrack from the movie and the other is a collection of the best of Chet Baker. It's just the greatest, most romantic music in the world. I've also been listening to Tracy Chapman's first record, and a new band from New Orleans called the Subdudes who are quite good; very cajun influenced, with lots of rhythm and blues and vocals.

Books you've read recently: "Love, Medicine and Miracles" by Bernie Siegel. It's all about how your mental attitude is manifested in your body. I've also recently read Kurt Vonnegut's "Welcome to the Monkey House" and some Hemingway and Flannery O'Connor short stories.

Name a song you wish you had written: "I Want To Know What Love Is" by Foreigner I wish I'd written that song because it sounds exactly like something I would write. Not lyrically, but musically, in terms of chord progressions. Anyone who likes the Call's music will hear that it sounds just like something I would write, especially the verses and choruses. When I first heard it I said "I should have written that song", because it was just about to come out of me, but they did it first.

Michael Been:

Song you wish you had written: "Love Will Tear Us Apart" by Joy Division, "Temptation" by New Order, "How Soon Is Now?" by the Smiths, "Ring Them Bells" and "Most of the Time" by Bob Dylan. And anything by the Band.

Books you've read recently: "The Beloved" by Toni Morrison and "The Power of the Poor in History" by Guitterez.

Scott Musick:

Song you wish you had written: "Unfaithful Servant" by the Band. There's a killer song.

Have you read any good books lately: It would have to be Gideons Bible. You can't get away from it when you're travelling.

What music have you been listening to: Dylan's *Oh, Mercy*, which is his best record in years. One of the best songs on the album is "Most of the Time", but they're all so great.

On this tour you are playing mostly large clubs and theaters, a very intimate atmosphere compared to arenas or stadiums. How would you feel about playing stadium shows?

We did play a stadium show on this tour and it sounded great. But the Call will never be a stadium band in the conventional way where you have a wildly exciting visual show. Michael's never going to tell little stories and funny anecdotes between songs. It's always gonna be the kind of situation where people are going to come to listen to the music. We're just that kind of band. And if we can't get over to the mass audience with our music, then we won't.

Page 2 of Issue #5 – Notified Newsletter

Michael Been is one of the most inspired songwriters in music today. Through his songs he has spoken to all of us in some personal way—digging into our deepest emotions. The following interview reveals a bit more of the man behind the songs.

How would you measure success?

Success to me is appreciating what you have. Truly appreciating what you have, rather than the constant temptation and frustration of a goal.

Are the same things that motivated you, say ten years ago, the same today?

No. I think anger was a more prevalent, more powerful motivating factor in my life ten years ago. Today it's hope.

How would you define rock and roll?

At its best it's an art form that inspires, sometimes teaches, sometimes threatens. Its only crime is when it bores. I don't agree with what some people consider the orthodoxy of rock and roll—that it's for kids and addresses adolescent problems. I don't believe that now and I didn't believe that when I first heard it. I always preferred the blues guys like Muddy Waters and B.B. King, who could be fifty years old and still play you right under the table, to this precious youth thing that rock and roll was supposed to be. I go back and listen to records from the last fifty years and there's that human feeling. Music has the potential to be life altering. Most pop music today is totally submissive to the business. There's not one element of subversion in it. It's no longer a healing art. We live in an escapist, cynical culture right now. A lot of people like songs that completely take them out of reality and put them into some sort of fantasy, romance-type world. That doesn't speak to me about my life so I don't write songs like that. I think you really have to look at the power of the arts to at least help awaken people's personal experiences and put them in some kind of perspective. I know music has done that for me. I was powerfully moved by music. It helped me at some of the lowest points of my life and grounded me at some of the highest points. It affirms the reason that I'm alive.

Rock and roll seems to have always been a male-oriented, male-dominated profession. But many women have made major, profound contributions. Who are some women artists that you admire or have influenced you?

In rock and roll it would be Chrissie Hynde, Annie Lennox and Sara Lee. And for other musical styles, Billie Holiday, Patsy Cline, Aretha Franklin, Edith Piaf, Bessie Smith and Mahalia Jackson.

To you what makes a good song?

Melody, lyric and groove in that order.

Have you ever had a particular artist or band in mind when writing a song?

Oh, yeah. "In the River", "Same Ol' Story", and "Memory" were all definitely written with the Band in mind—that kind of atmosphere, a rootsier approach.

How do you feel about the seemingly cozy relationship between rock and roll and the corporate world; corporate sponsorship of tours and commercialization of songs?

I'm not against bands that use sponsorship by corporations. We recently did a college tour with major corporate sponsorship from AT&T. For me to take that stand against sponsorship I'd feel a bit self-righteous, feel like I'm being a naive idealist. As far as taking a song to sell shoes or beer, I think there's a big difference between the two. I'm okay with the shoe thing—shoes aren't harmful. But I'm not okay with the beer thing which is harmful, because I feel alcohol is the most destructive drug in the world right now. But if I was going to take a stand like that's moral, ethical stand—then I would have to follow it to its logical conclusion, which means I would spend my life in prison because I could not pay taxes that go

toward the making of weapons. Many of your major corporations support righteous causes, but they also have investments in South Africa, the Philippines and Central America. You would have to seriously check into each corporation's involvement. You would have to be such a conscientious citizen. I think on many levels it's important as far as things you can do, from supporting the homeless in your area or recycling-not using so much plastic. All those things are wonderful. But like, for example, with Nike you would have to find out if they are supporting South Africa and then if they are, what do you do? I would probably back out. But I certainly don't think if I were to support a righteous cause it would mean I'm a righteous person. That's the trouble with a lot of liberal organizations is when they cross from concern to self-importance. I think you can support a righteous cause and be an absolute scum-bag. You can support an unrighteous cause and be a good person only if you are ignorant of the facts.

Can you name someone historically you would liked to have met?

There are many. I would have loved to have talked with Shakespeare, Dostoevsky, Dylan Thomas, Emily Dickinson, Jesus, Joseph Conrad, Luther, Dietrich Bonhoeffer.

You employ a lot of symbolism in your lyrics. Are you aware of doing this as you're writing?

Sure. Although I don't sit down and say I'm going to write something really symbolic. I tend to write from a subconscious and unconscious place and that's the way the subconscious and unconscious speaks to all of us. The conscious mind, what we are aware of at any given time, is just the tip of the iceberg of our entire being. So if you figure the tip of an iceberg is 10 percent of the total iceberg, the conscious mind is only 10 percent of our total existence. Most of it is going on beneath the surface which speaks to

Page 3 of Issue #5 – Notified Newsletter

us in our dreams, speaks to us in feelings, some of it speaks to us through confusing us with a lot of images that we have to sort out and see if we can apply it to something tangible in our lives. If you have a dream and apply a literal interpretion, I think that can be confusing. People sometimes take a dream as prophecy. Like if you have an accident and get hurt in a dream—that's not so much telling you that you are going to have an accident, as it's telling you that you're living that kind of fear, you're living that kind of anxiety and tension in your life. Nightmares are like that—they're just telling you there's some chaos going on internally that you should deal with and try to figure out what it is. And don't deny yourself professional help if you have a professional problem. Life right now is so chaotic and complex I think people could use some help. But not everybody can afford or has the inclination to go to a psychiatrist or counselor and really work at their problems.

Most of my dreams are fairly pleasant but sometimes I wake up in the middle of the night really shaken, feeling guilty for not being a better person and feeling very contrite for my sins. I do a lot of heavy praying at that time. But this only happens if I awaken between 2 and 4 am.

Those are the hours.

But before or after those hours I don't feel like being so hard on myself and I can go right back to sleep.

And that's mercy—without it we would kill ourselves. We would either kill ourselves or the rest of our lives would be a downward spiral. We would lose hope, that sense of mercy, that sense of redemption.

Do you pray everyday?

That really depends on what you mean by pray. Sometimes I don't pray if I feel like all I'm doing is asking for something. I usually pray for that thing I was telling you before about success. I pray to appreciate what I have. I think that's my biggest fear, not appreciating what I have.

You mean like counting your blessings?

Yeah. That probably sounds silly but it's true. I remember a song by the Smiths "Please, Please, Please, Let Me Get What I Want". To me that's not very wise. But if you turn that around it says please, please, please, let me want what I get.

I remember my mother telling me about a Jesus prayer that her mother had taught her and what it is, you say this little chant like thing, maybe three words, "All for Jesus" or something like that, and after awhile you come saying it or even thinking it. It actually becomes part of your heartbeat, it becomes part of your action. She said that was perfect prayer.

For me perfect prayer is always an action, always constant and not necessarily verbal. It's a prayer for strength, for endurance. "I want to give out, I want to give in. This is our crime, this is our sin". That really is the essence of "I Still Believe".

I had trouble with "I Still Believe" after it was finished. Not with what is in the song, but with how it could be interpreted. *Into the Woods* was an attempt to say that we're not out of the woods yet, the struggle continues. It isn't this theology of glory, where everything is just beautiful here in the garden and all we have to do is stick our heads in the sand and everything will be fine. *Reconciled*, *Into the Woods*, and *Let the Day Begin* have become kind of a trilogy for me. None of the three should be isolated from the other two. And *Into the Woods* and *Reconciled* are two sides of the same coin.

Do you have a familiar place you go to for inspiration—not literally a place, but somewhere in your mind?

No, not at all. I write from wherever I am in my life at the time. If I were to return to the same place for inspiration, I would never grow as a songwriter.

I know you've begun writing songs for the next album...

We do have some new songs, and the lyrics are some of the best I've ever written. They are very practical and useful. At least to me they are practical and useful, and hopefully to the listener.

Are you an observer of the world in your writing?

An observer of myself. Everything else only depends on the soundness of the sight itself. You have to have the foundation within yourself really, either that or you're just pointing out the obvious.

Some songs are timely and some are timeless. An example that comes to mind is Neil Young's "Rockin' In the Free World" with the mention of the thousand points of light or even his older songs like "Ohio"—they are very timely, pointing out a specific and timely incident or problem. Whereas, 98 percent of your songs seem timeless, writing about this inner search that knows no time.

Another example would be from Dylan's new record *Oh Mercy*, "We Live in a Political World" which is an observational song and it's good. "Everything is Broken" is an observational song and it's good, but they don't compare to "Most of the Time" which is a personal examination. For me self-examination is always superior to outside observation.

I'm totally a work-in-progress; we all are. We're all complex people with different personalities. We're part 5 year old, part rebellious adolescent, part disillusioned adult and it takes us a long time to understand all of them. I was not born with the ability to repress the darker side of myself. I don't mean just acting out evil deeds, but the darkness in each of us. I'm not able to not pay attention to it. I pay attention to it and write songs about it. It's not so much that I'm being honest out of some pure motive, it's involuntary. I have to deal with that aspect of life. The bottom line with the songs is, hopefully, a healthy kind of self-examination that is eye-opening and provoking, which challenges us to make a change in our lives. The attempt is really to look at going from unhealthy ways of existing to healthy ways. Not just to see that we are terribly fallible creatures. But at the same time we're far more than that, we're this incredible creation. There's something sacred about our lives.

People often write and ask questions about your songs. One question that has been asked several times is what you meant in the song "Too Many Tears" when you say "I've seen your work everywhere and there's mercy in hell."

I believe that love and mercy will have the final word over law and justice.

Do you feel like you've reached your zenith in your songwriting?

Oh God, I hope not.

— OKLAHOMA —

We were shaking in our beds that night
There were strangers in the streets that night
Preacher cried out hell's been raised
The preacher cried out hell's been raised
Another hot Oklahoma night
Another hot Oklahoma night
The kind of night where you just sit still
The kind of night where you just don't move
We were shaking in our beds that night
We were shaking in our boots that night
Tornado hit and the roof gave way
Tornado hit and all we could do was pray

How was I to know what I was to think
How was I to know what I was to feel
How am I to say what I can't describe
How am I to face what I cannot hide

We were looking in our hearts that day
There was movement in our hearts that day
They were talking but we could not hear
They were talking but we could not hear
Fever broke and the dead raised up
The ground broke open and the dead were raised
The kind of night where you just sit spooked
It's a hard life, it's a hard life
We were looking in our hearts that day
We were hugging in our beds that night
Storm hit and the roof gave way
When a man cries it ain't easy
but he swore duty, body and soul

How was I to know what I was to think
How was I to know what I was to feel
How am I to say what I can't describe
How am I to face what I can not hide

Momma said you know she ain't that strong

We were praying in our hearts that day
God, there was movement in our hearts
They were praying but I could not feel
They were praying but I couldn't feel
Another hot Oklahoma night
Another hot Oklahoma night
Fools part as the day breaks wide
Heaven's doors were opened wide
I quit, so I said give up
He said I can't stop the lights not gone
Once in a blue moon shown against that day
And my heart rips open and all I could do was pray

How was I to know what I was to think
How was I to know what I was to feel
How am I to say what I can't describe
How am I to face what I can not hide

from RECONCILED written by Michael Been used by permission

Listening to the Call is a lesson in the philosophy of thinking. Everything that happens in their recordings is important, the instrumentation, the words, the production and the beat. You can hear the rhythm guitar of the early Byrds, keyboards of The Band, the intensity of the Plimsouls, and verbiage of folk philosophers like Woody Guthrie and Pete Seger. All of this with a lyrical feel toward Biblical intellectualism.

Yet the music of the Call is so much more than the parameters of these things. They drive oh so hard. Scott Musick hits the quarter notes on his snare like he is chopping wood. It feels as if he is going right through the drum. When listening to Let the Day Begin, it is obvious that the band's intensity is based around Scott Musick's drive. The band sort of strides a bit like smart, tough guys pounding the pavement with Musick at the lead. He does not push the band, he struts the band.

There is the occasional fold when the Call lays back a little toward ballad, but they never lose their intensity. The tune "Jealousy" provides us with one of the greatest examples of a drummer using a cross chop at the beginning of the song moving to a hard drive snare then to a reserved shallower snare hit. Three great struts in one tune, all strong, all different and all quarter notes. This band is exceptional. Scott Musick is the pavement pounder these guys walk behind. Get it, you won't be disappointed. -Ken Austin, Pearl News-Nashville

After seeing the Call twice in one month, one has to ask himself, "If this isn't the best rock and roll band in America, who is?" From the first chords of "Surrender" to the final song, the beautiful ballad "Uncovered", this band grabs hold and takes you for a ride you don't want to end. The band played at the Berklee Performance Centre in Boston, a hall that did justice to the music of the Call. The wails seemed to be expanding with every note that was played and every word that was sung. Michael Been sings with such passion and power that you have no choice but to take what this band has to say seriously. The rest of the band compliment each other so well that it is as if they play as one. Been is such an incredible presence on stage it is hard to take your eyes off him part of the reason is the intensity in which he sings. He sings about faith (religious and otherwise) with a directness that is inspiring. Truly the Call show was a very moving experience, one that everyone should go through. Hopefully, as the band continues to grow in popularity more and more people will be taken for a ride, and like myself, never get enough of the best rock and roll band in America. -Rick Malcolmson

---

Page 5 of Issue #5 – Notified Newsletter

Dan Russell has been a very busy guy in music for a long while. He has worked closely with U2 since almost their inception, toured with Robert Palmer, Sam Phillips, was very instrumental in Andy Pratt's career, and recently has been locked in the studio with Mark Heard putting the finishing touches on his latest effort. He and his brother Joel Russell were cofounders of New Sound Productions which also spawned *New Sound Magazine*. And while Dan does not aspire to become a full-time tour manager, he couldn't pass up the chance to go out on the road with the Call for seven months on their *Let the Day Begin* Tour.

Describe a typical day in the life of a tour manager.

Everything from band-aids to major surgery. Actually, just trying to keep the focus and keeping people in focus. Technically speaking, it's making sure all the people who you've hired to do their jobs are doing their jobs and that they are emotionally capable of continuing under a lot of stress. So I spend a substantial amount of time trying to keep lines of communication open and keeping people motivated to do a good job. Making sure there's a degree of comfort and security and stability in an extremely uncomfortable and insecure situation. Basically you try to get things down in such a way that you're just following an agenda that you've already advanced and worked out, so that you're not getting up that morning and saying "what do I do next?". So what you do that day, when you have some time, is advance 3 days down the road and create that agenda. Things like figuring out if the interviews you've been asked to do are bogus or real, and tying up loose ends with an interview so that the artist doesn't sit in his hotel room for an hour waiting for a call to come in. Meeting with record promotion people, working out ID's for radio stations,

and just anything else that needs to be done.

When were you first introduced to the Call's music?

It was back in 1983 when I first heard the Call. I remember following Michael out after a show in Boston, about 2 in the morning—he and a couple of guys from the band were walking down the street. I hollered and said, "Michael". He turned around and looked at me and I said, "Keep going, man, I appreciate what you're doing", and he just kind of nodded. Some time after that I interviewed him for our publication.

Anything can go wrong on the road, and as you can attest, it usually does. Have you ever felt like it's just not worth it?

I've not seen a night when once the music happens that I haven't felt it's all worth it—the individual, unique value of that particular night. Everyday on the road there is a crisis, but it never subtracts from what is happening on the stage at every show.

The Call have a heterogeneous group of fans. But the thread of spirituality that runs through the Call's songs seems to tie everyone together, regardless of belief or background. What is it about the spirituality of the Call's music that is so different from other bands?

The Call offers a balanced perspective of spirituality. They do not come from a traditional church background. Their roots are in the music world. They recognize mercy and grace and they are less likely to judge. They see that they are a product of God's mercy. As we all are.

Jim Goodwin and Dixie Crosby were married on January 5th in California. Dixie is the granddaughter of the late crooner Bing Crosby. Michael Been sang at their wedding, doing an a cappella version of "Uncovered". Carol Been, Michael's wife and a recently ordained minister of the Lutheran Church, officiated at the wedding. Congratulations to everyone!

---

more notes from the underground:

The Call were inducted into the Chicago's Hard Rock Cafe's Hall of Fame this past November. The band donated one of Michael's bass guitars to be displayed in the club. The guitar's case was autographed by the Call and donated to the Christmas for Kids Rock and Roll Auction. Some of the other items also on the auction block was an autographed Keith Richards photo, Stephen Stills' guitar, a vest from Bon Jovi, and a jacket from Billy Joel. All proceeds went to buy gifts for homeless or abused children.

The Call have been invited to perform at an AIDS benefit being organized by Mick Fleetwood to be held at RFK Stadium in Washington D.C. No word yet on a definite date for the show. Originally scheduled for May 12th, the date will now revolve around the upcoming tour of Fleetwood Mac.

On January 8th the Call were the musical guests on The Pat Sajak Show, playing "Let the Day Begin" and "I Still Believe". It turns out Sajak is a fan of the Call's and was in the audience when they performed at The Palace in Hollywood a few nights later.

If you caught the movie "Tango and Cash" with Sly Stallone and Kurt Russell you must already know that "Let the Day Begin" is a featured song in one scene of the film.

The Call will enter the studio in March to begin work on their seventh album. The record could be ready for release by mid-summer. Peter Gabriel, Daniel Lanois, U2's guitarist The Edge, and T Bone Burnett are among those that have been discussed as possible producers for the album.

Michael Been has, at this writing, twelve new songs ready for the studio. How many or

which ones will eventually end up on the record is not known, but here are the titles of nine of the songs:

Like You've Never Been Loved
The Hand That Feeds You
Red Moon
World Without Love
This Is Your Life
What A Day
Family
Floating Back
You Were There

I've heard these songs (one of the perks of having this job) and I can tell you they are gorgeous. Such a torrent of work is genius. And don't be surprised if a chill creeps up your spine when you hear a few of these songs.

The song "Fall On You" by Moby Grape, the quintessential 60's San Francisco band, could be on the new album. The Call played this song at many of the shows on tour. Moby Grape's self-titled first release (which includes "Fall On You") is now available on CD (Edsel Records, import only).

—*Maria*

NOTIFIED is published by
The Call Information Service
P.O. Box 7183
Rockford, IL 61126

compiled and edited by
Maria Braden

Photo Credits:
front cover: Pat Johnson
all others: Chris Knight

Page 6 of Issue #5 – Notified Newsletter

*Hello fellow Call fans! Talk about timing! This issue of Notified is arriving in your mailboxes just days before the Call's seventh album. Red Moon, hits the stores—and the date to circle on your calendars is **September 18th!***

Red Moon is an album that plays directly into the Call's musical roots. Not that the band are waxing nostalgic—not even near it! This is the Call now, with a decade of recordmaking to their credit, playing in the musical vernacular they grew up with and were inspired by.

Red Moon covers many musical bases. How's yer blues?. Any passion for blues/rock was certainly indulged. There are moments of jazz, some fleeting, some ponderable—with equal parts of head and heart. Great harmonies; tasteful, well-arranged horns; and some of the best percussion I've heard by anyone. It's all here under this rubric called rock 'n' roll, and all within the framework of the Call's own distinctive sound.

This time out, Notified devotes all space to a recent interview with Michael Been. Michael spoke candidly with me about the music of yesterday and today. He also lucidly describes the recording of Red Moon. So consider this issue sort of a companion piece to the album. With that said, read on!

Maria

*P.S. U2's Bono sings on this record. Bono shares vocal harmonies with Michael on the album's first single, "What's Happened To You", which will be released to radio on **September 12th**. Please take the time to call your AOR station and request "What's Happened To You". If you need the name and number of the AOR station in your area, call the Hotline at (815)399-5553 and we'll gladly give you that information. Thanks!*

NOTIFIED

Issue Six

Red Moon is a wonderful album and I think it's unique because it seems to be a real studio album.

Well, these days that's a little misleading. The way most records are recorded today is they'll go in and just have two or three musicians lay down a track, and they'll play with a drum machine or click track and keep recording it until at least one and hopefully more instruments have played it well. Let's say the bass player played great, but they didn't think the guitar player or drummer played that great, to perhaps they'll keep the bass track because the bass will be locked into this consistent clock time. And then the drummer—if, in fact, there even was a real drummer, since most records you hear, especially Top 40, are drum machines and not a human drummer at all—will go into the studio by himself and play just to that bass guitar and that click track until he plays it the way they want it played. They'll then bring in the guitar player and he'll play to those two people. Usually nobody is really in the studio together playing at the same time.

That sounds rather boring. But what I meant by studio album is that once the basic song is recorded you take advantage of subtle techniques—add lots of interesting things to the song.

Right. With this album there were more overdubs, more "production". It was exactly the same process as *Let The Day Begin* we went in with a P.A., no headphones, and played the basic tracks live. Although, we didn't play loud this time—*Let The Day Begin* was played very loud at live volume. But the nature of these songs didn't call for that. We wanted a lot of little subtle interplay, so we set up in this tiny area, a corner really, of this big studio. We were all right next to each other. With *Let The Day Begin*, we were going for the way it would sound in a live concert whereas, with this one we were going for the way it would sound if we were playing in your living room for you.

What the Call does in the studio is we play a song until everyone has played well. Sometimes we've played until three of us have gotten it right, then we'll have the fourth guy fix his part. But we've rarely fixed an entire part. There might be a section where someone didn't play it well or thought he could play it better, and he'll fix that section.

This album is so diverse—it has everything from funky blues to jazz. This is the first Call record that the lyrics are almost secondary to me. Not to say the lyrics are inferior—they certainly aren't, they're incredibly moving—but it's such a musical album. With each listen the music just washes over me.

I think we were inspired by the sounds we were using. We used old amps, old drums, keyboards, everything. We intentionally didn't want to use anything made after 1970, except for some synthesizer sounds that we modified to get away from that standard sterile synth sound. There's an inherent quality with the older instruments that we wanted to get back to. We just got so bored with the modern sounds. There's a tonal quality that the old records have that the new ones don't have. The new sounds are considered better in a certain way, but I personally question whether or not they're really better. On this album we used Mellotron and Chamberlin, which were sort of the first synthesizers; but they used tapes.

I'm not a fan of the new technology. I recently saw Steven Spielberg being interviewed, and he was asked whether or not he wanted to use, or looked forward to using, the modern advances in technology in his moviemaking. He said, "I think I have all the tools I need. If I can't make great movies with what's available today, which is basically what they used twenty, thirty and forty years ago, then I shouldn't really be making movies." He went on and said, "Can you make a better baseball bat—without cheating?" I liked that.

I remember Mellotron from the Beatle days. Didn't the Beatles pioneer instruments like Mellotron and Chamberlin? Companies would make new, innovative instruments, and the Beatles would use them in the studio.

Yeah, but it wasn't really companies—it was this guy Chamberlin. They're the most incredible instruments you've ever seen—very primitive. Chamberlin, in the early 60's, recorded symphony musicians—not as a group, but individual instruments, like a violin, a cello, french horn, every instrument of an orchestra. He recorded them onto a tape recorder, using quarter inch tape. And he had great microphones, those old 40's tube microphones that are so ambient. He would have, for example, the cello player pick a note or bow across the string forward and back for 8 seconds or so. He did this with each instrument plus other sounds like a dog barking and all kinds of things, but the main thing are these instruments from the orchestra. He then took this tape and secured the ends together to make a loop, a circle of tape. He then put each tape on some sort of electric pulley system with a weight, so when you hit the key it releases the weight and the weight goes down and pulls the tape over the tape head. So you hit the note and it plays, and when it stops you have to push it down to start the tape again. It's a rather awkward way of playing, and you really have to master the touch of it. Jim played it on this record for the cello and french horn sounds.

But, regardless of the technology of it, the reason the Call used it is because the sounds are so fantastic. They're the old sounds before digital came in—this beautiful, rich sound of an acoustic instrument.

The way that most music is going today, technology-wise, is sonically unacceptable to me. If you hear the sound of an actual cello—say a cellist goes out in a room and runs a bow across a cello, and you have a nice microphone in it—compare that to the digitized sound of the cello setting on a synthesizer, and the synth is so inferior. It's the difference between fresh peas out of your garden, and frozen processed peas. And I think it's a good analogy because we're getting so far away from a natural approach that the music is losing it's humanness. I personally feel it would be best to use an actual cello player or whoever.

but that's not always desirable if you want to keep a band fairly self-contained. But I think you can use an acoustic instrument or Chamberlin-type organ and still create great sounds.

I think many of today's musicians naturally gravitate toward synthesizers and drum machines because computers and their technology have become so ensconced in our everyday lives.

Computers and technology are taking over our lives in all kinds of ways. We've been warned about this for years—that the more technology comes in, the less the human being will be involved. It's happening in our everyday lives, and it's happening in music. It's like the difference between the great old hand-drawn movie cartoons and computer cartoons. How can you compare them? One is wonderful and one is cheesy.

I guess I'm on a crusade to ask musicians to avoid using drum machines and these tasteless synthesizer sounds that are so sizzly and thin. You can get good sounds out of them, but it's very difficult. Many of the things being recorded now are so synthetic it's destroying our hearing. Synthesizers can create overtones and extreme highs that people are getting used to and our senses are getting dulled to natural tones. Musicians and engineers are saying, "I need more high-end, I need more high-end"—it's like a drug—"I need more, I'm not getting off on it anymore." It's like an aural addiction. I think it's best to stay within the acoustic instrument sound range, except for maybe the occasional special effect for dynamics.

I'll tell you a story. They were recording Elvis Costello's album and they had a synthesizer player in the studio, and he had access to like literally a thousand different sounds through Midiing up all kinds of synthesizers. And they were in there, going through all these squeaks and beeps and blips, trying to find a sound, and they're getting frustrated because none of the sounds are right. And what happened is somebody goes out into the studio and hits a note on a piano and they all go, "What was that? That's fantastic!" True story.

But, Michael, some people will tell you it's a matter of taste— that these modern sounds are superior to the old ones.

I don't think so. Those drum sounds of the 40's, 50's, and 60's were so wonderful, so real—they've got a very primitive quality. And a drum set is a primitive thing—there's supposed to be a wildness to it. But instead we have all

those synthetic, triggered sounds—a lot of which is just gated white noise. They take that sound and mix it together with the sound of an actual drum and all kinds of digital reverb sounds. I just find it to be abrasive and unmusical.

I agree. But if you were to ask anyone who frequents a dance club, he or she would tell you that they like dancing to the drum machines.

Drum machines keep perfect time—it's like dancing to a clock, it's unhuman. But that perfect time is also addictive. People don't even know they're addicted to it, it's very subtle. And I don't think it's good for dancing, it's too inhibiting. I suppose you can do the latest choreographed steps to it, but you can't really lose yourself in it and just move to the music. It's very disco to me. It's self-conscious, posing-type dancing. Real drummers, on the other hand, speed up and slow down continuously, following the dynamics of the song.

I was driving home today and on the radio they played "Stand!", by Sly and the Family Stone, and oh, it's just brilliant—it has this trashy ass primitive drum feel. And musicians, especially young musicians, here and in Europe, are terribly inspired by this soul feel—Motown, James Brown, Sly and Family Stone. The drum beat at the end of "Stand!" is the drum beat used by most dance music currently on the radio. It's this high hat playing 16th notes—clanging around, kind of sloppy and flying by the seat of the pants. Now these musicians took this drum pattern that Sly's drummer played because they dug the way it felt. But rather than inspiring a new breed of drummers that wanted to play that way, they use a drum machine that reproduced that drum beat in a most clinical way. Instead of it being sloppy and wild and funky, it became very clean, mechanical and robotic.

People who use these machines should go back and listen to those old records, and hear how twisted and soulless this interpretation of it has become. Young drummers are even trying to play like drum machines. Think about it. It's ridiculous.

And it goes through the whole synthesizer spectrum. You know, you should be able to get almost everything out of different organs by adding outboard sound effects, like choruses, flangers, and harmonizers, or the old original analog keyboards, or even an actual piano. But the minute we go overboard into the digital domain it's like, "we went too far guys, let's go back." I've been tempted by it myself. We've experimented with a lot of those sounds on our albums, but it isn't satisfying to me anymore. Now don't get me wrong, I like many of the bands who use this stuff.

But I know they would be infinitely better if they used real drummers and more natural instruments. I think this equipment being used is ultimately a dead end.

When you use a real instrument the sound and interpretation of that instrument will depend entirely on the style and soul of the player, so the possibilities are as infinite as the differences between each human being. But these machines take away so much of the style of the player—anyone who sits at them is basically going to sound exactly the same.

Now someone like Garth Hudson or Jim Goodwin can use synthesizers and create exciting, original sounds because they're aware of these inherent dangers. They know how to EQ all the undesirable tones out of these instruments. But remember these men are professionals, so don't try this at home (laughs). Seriously, though, in the hands of a lesser keyboardist who maybe didn't even learn to an organ or piano, the results can be disastrous.

Some people, young people in particular, might argue that much of the music of the 60's and 70's sounds exactly the same to them.

Well, I hated most of the 70's sounds. But if a person would go back and listen to the instruments of the 40's, 50's, and 60's, and actually studied them, I don't believe they would think that. I don't think all the old sounds were great on every record, but far more than now.

I really liked some of the early 70's heavy metal bands. I thought AC/DC were great.

Yeah, they were—but I don't think of them as metal. For me it was just a louder, exaggerated version of the blues—bands like Zeppelin, Hendrix, Cream, T-Rex—that was a wild, sometimes drug induced, interpretation.

Talking about drums, I remember in the 60's there was so much cymbal.

The Beatles did that for effect—they liked it. Another reason for it was that musicians and engineers didn't know miking techniques well enough to keep the high hat and cymbals out of the snare drum and tom tom. But even that I like better than what they've come up with today. For example, this loud overdone bass drum sound, where you have all this music playing and then sitting out on its own is this kick drum to show you where to tap your foot. It's stupid.

Did you put any effects on the drums for this album or did you record them differently this time—they sound so great.

Scott used a 1957 Gretsch drum set and an old Ludwig set. The old drum sets were lightweight so that the set would kind of rattle when you hit it. For us it was all very intentional to get back to a real set of drums, no samples. The modern drums are made of really heavy, very thick wood, and the whole reason for that is to get each drum to be such a self-contained sound so that it doesn't ring into another drum. And they are designed for effects to be put on them. But they don't sound worth a shit acoustically because they don't sound like a trap kit, where everything should connect to each other. When you hear them they sound like you've taken each drum and put it in a different part of a gymnasium. So, what we did was we got this old drum set where when you hit one drum the other drums resonate—they're lightweight and they all shake so that you get the sound of a real drum kit.

You added a lot of additional percussion on this album like wood blocks and maracas and lots of horns and vocal harmonies. How will you duplicate some of the songs live?

We really can't totally duplicate it live unless we bring in other players. And for some shows we may bring in a small horn section for a few of the songs.

I think your first and second albums were more like _Red Moon_ as far as studio albums. After that it was more in the synthesizer vein.

Yeah, well, Jim brought a lot of that in and it was good because he's very creative with programming. But he's starting to dig the more natural instruments.

You have a lot of high separation on this album.

That was really from playing quietly. You can get separation by putting instruments or by putting amplifiers in different rooms. But we got it from just playing quietly. If you turn it up loud on your stereo, that's probably louder than we played it.

Aren't there double tracked guitars on this record?

No, not double tracked exactly, but Tom and I overdubbed quite a few guitars.

I counted four guitars plus bass on "A Swim In The Ocean". You come in on guitar to start the song, then Tom on slide, and then the wah-wah, and there's also one more guitar.

There are actually only three guitars on that song. That's not a guitar through a wah-wah—that's Jim playing a clavinet through a wah-wah. Then I overdubbed another guitar playing some licks and fills. Also, that song doesn't have a bass guitar on it. It's just a floor tom, and I think Jim may have added some low piano or clavinet.

On "The Hand That Feeds You", what is that synthetic crash sound at the beginning of the song?

It isn't synthetic. I hit the inside of a grand piano with a drum mallets. I was looking for an ominous kind of sound to set the mood in the introduction. I played percussion and piano on that song. I used the piano as a drum and we put

a lot of reverb on it. It was a grand piano with the lid up and I hit the strings and the music stand with a drum mallet.

You don't usually play bass chords, but in the song "Family" you did.

I have done it before, but on that song I do it a lot.

What song has the backward guitar?

"Floating Back". The solo is Tom. It's actually two different solos playing at the same time. We turned the tape over so that it came out backwards. It was Tom's idea to do that—to fit the song "Floating Back". It was a great idea.

The bass on "What A Day" is so great—you play a lot of high notes. Your bass reminds me of Jack Bruce on that song.

I played a little Ibanez fretted bass—it felt right for that song. On the rest of the album I use my Ampeg fretless bass.

What microphones did you use for this album?

We used old stuff. We recorded at Oceanway Studios, and they've got one of the best selection of microphones in the world.

T-Bone Burnett was involved with this record. How did you meet him?

Scott and I have known T-Bone for about fifteen years. Last March we started talking with him about music and that we wanted to make a different type of record this time; more natural, more organic. He agreed with our approach, mainly about the things we've been talking about in this interview. We talked about him co-producing the album with me, but he was already producing his wife's, Sam Phillips, album and Tonio K's album at the same time. So we booked Oceanway Studios in L.A., where he was working with Sam and Tonio. Oceanway has about five different studios in one building, so he could at least pop in and be involved. He'd come in from time to time and offer his opinion and suggestions. He had some great ideas; for example, the horn line on "Like You've Never Been Loved" was his idea. He's a very talented guy.

Bono sang with you on "What's Happened To You". How did that come about?

Well, Bono came into town for a vacation, but he wanted to record this song he had written. It's a country song and I think he wrote it with Willie Nelson in mind. He tried recording it a few different times and couldn't get it to feel right with the musicians he was playing with. T-Bone heard the song and suggested to Bono that he have Jim and I play on it—it was during the mixing of the album, so Tom and Scott had gone home. So Bono came in and we did the song. It's a really beautiful song and it sounded quite great. After that he wanted to hear some of the things we were doing. He told us he was "a fan from afar". T-Bone wanted him to hear "Floating Back". He liked it and wanted to hear more. We played "What's Happened To You" for him and at the time we didn't have the harmonies, only my lead vocal. So I said how about singing on this one and he said sure. So he and I sang the chorus and the la, la's, and the voices sounded really good together.

Bono doesn't do a lot of harmony singing—his voice is so distinctive. But we wanted the voices to blend like a chorus—to create a dreamy effect. And I knew he would be great on the la, la's because it's kind of an Irish melody. He was a very nice man, and it was good to meet him after all these years.

Did he mention anything about when we can expect a new album from U2?

They're working on songs, but from what I gathered they are not going to put anything out until 1992. I think they want to get into different types of music, and if they make a new album over there wouldn't be a big enough difference from what they've done in the past and what they want to do in the future. I know Edge is listening to a lot of different kinds of guitar playing. He's just recently been influenced by many of the old blues players and country players, and I think they want to take their music in a different direction.

I've loved them since 1980 and I know that they certainly weren't schooled in music.

That's right. And I think that was a great value because if you're not schooled you come up with something really unique and your own, but it's also a limitation after a while. It's great for a time, but then you can't do much other than that. And if you're a serious musician, and I think they are serious musicians, you'll want to expand your possibilities.

I read an article around the time the *Sun City* album was being recorded in which Bono told a story of how one night he was sitting around with Keith Richards and several other musicians playing songs they had been influenced by—songs they had loved in their early days. Bono said that he had felt so removed from that moment because he really had no major influences and no songs to sing from his past. He then decided he would learn all he could about the early music of the blues greats. He also said that he regretted not studying Gaelic, and becoming more proficient in his history through Irish folk songs.

Yeah, we talked about that. To be able to continue and grow musically you've got to become a student of it. a fan, that sits and listens to it. You've got to study it with the diligence that you study anything else.

There are some young artists who are going back to the early sounds and instruments. I really love the Lenny Kravitz record. I saw him live and he was incredible. He had these wonderful blues players with him. He's so 60's in his approach to music in the way you've been describing.

Lenny Kravitz is really getting some wonderful sounds. He's thrown out the modern stuff and I respect that. And I think it's a consciousness. All of a sudden you wake up and go, "Wait a minute. All this modern stuff is weak."

Recording has gotten into the hands of computer people, people who get off on technology. They're not musicians—they don't have good ears. They're going more for efficiency and quantity of choices. Rock 'n' roll to me was always about primitive expression and limitation—limitation is a good way. "Here's the instrument, make something out of it" rather than "Here's a synthesizer with a thousand sounds—pick one you like."

The good things about the digital world, however, are CD's and digital audio tape. Once you record a song using real instruments on analog equipment, the reproduction onto digital is quite good. You lose some of the warmth of vinyl, but it does have great clarity.

You play an old electric Gretsch hollow body guitar on this album and it sounds so good. Rather than having that short, twangy sound of the Telecaster, the Gretsch is still twangy, but it has more style and body. It sounds better than your Telecaster because it has more tonal value.

That's right, and tonal value is what we've been talking about.

You told me a little while back that *Red Moon* is the kind of record the Call would have made years ago, before you had to concern yourselves with what record companies want and what will sell.

An interesting thing about *Red Moon* is that this is the first record that we've made in many years that I did not think one thought about whether it's commercial, whether it will sell. I was talking with our engineer, Jim Scott, and it simultaneously dawned on us that if we don't reproduce this approach, records are not going to be made this way anymore. It will be a forgotten art. We have to do it, because not enough people are doing it. But we're hoping it will create a consciousness. If we can at least get this through to the musicians, if we can get them to hear what we're talking about. I think they'll know it.

I've always found it so interesting to learn something about each song on an album, such as who played what instrument and who sang on what songs. Tell me about the instrumentation and vocals for the songs on *Red Moon*.

Well, on "What's Happened To You" Jim played Mellotron and electric piano. Tom played guitar and solo. I played the piano and bass and Bono and I sang it. And, of course, Scott played the drums.

"Red Moon" is Jim on a grand piano. Scott played the drums with brushes. Jim and I and Scott sang the harmonies. I played a short bass solo. Jim played Chamberlin and Tom is on guitar.

"You Were There" has Tom playing the guitar solo, one of my all-time favorite solos. Jim played all the horn parts on saxophone. It was so great watching him do it—he's a one-man horn section.

On "Floating Beck" Scott played drums and overdubbed maracas. Tom played two tracks of backward guitar and made it work as a solo. I had some chorusing effect on the bass. And Jim and Scott and I sang the vocals. Jim also played an old ARP string ensemble.

On "A Swim In The Ocean" Tom and I played guitars. Tom played slide guitar and I overdubbed another guitar. Jim played piano and overdubbed a clavinet. I changed the sound of my voice on this song. Scott played drums. I really love the feel of that song.

"Like You've Never Been Loved" has Jim on saxophones and electric piano through a Lesley speaker. Scott overdubbed wood blocks. Other than that, it's pretty much straight ahead. T-Bone sang background vocals with us.

"Family" was recorded basically like "Red Moon"—bass, drums, guitar and grand piano. Jim then overdubbed Chamberlin and Mellotron. The pedal steel sound is the Chamberlin. Jim also played a KX-88 synthesizer, but we eliminated all those tones that are equated with that sizzly synth sound. We EQ'd it all out to create a flute-like organ sound, and ran it through a Lesley. It's Jim and Scott and me singing once again.

"This Is Your Life" is the next one. Recording it was fun. We had a lot of our friends in the studio that night and everybody was screaming and yelling and having a good time. It was just the kind of energy we needed—a celebration type song. I overdubbed a twelve-string guitar and Tom played the solo.

On "The Hand That Feeds You" Jim and I played piano. I played bass and percussion by using the piano as a drum. I wanted the song to sound kind of jazzy and dark. Jim played saxophone just beautifully—it reminds me of Chet Baker. Tom played guitar and that's me on the short guitar solo. Jim also played organ. Scott played the tom tom drum pattern.

The basic track for "What A Day" was recorded during the *Let The Day Begin* sessions. Tom really liked the guitar, so we resurrected it for this album. I didn't have any words written, so I was busy writing words as I was singing them. Jim overdubbed a Chamberlin playing trombones.

One last question, Michael. Much of music now is very short term—one trend after another. How have the Call maintained a philosophy of seriousness in their music, an attitude of credibility as a band, in today's musical climate?

We play according to a tradition. It's a tradition where music is not a fad, or a trend, or a style. It isn't theatre, or a beauty contest, or a fashion show. It can be used, or rather abused, to serve those things because music can't defend itself. But musicians can.

Plans are underway, but not yet complete, for a *Red Moon* tour. You'll be 'notified' when dates are finalized.

NOTIFIED is published by
The Call Information Service
P.O. Box 7183
Rockford, IL 61126
compiled and edited by
Maria Braden
photo credit: Dennis Keely

Page 4 of Issue #6 – Notified Newsletter

NOTIFIED

issue seven

Dearest Call fans,

A lot can happen in a relatively short time. My God, we've gone through a war since last issue.

There have also been some major changes for the Call since our last communique. First and foremost, Jim Goodwin has left the Call; amicably, of course (details inside). More big news-the Call have left MCA Records (amicably? details inside).They are now signed with W.E.A. International Records-though don't look for the Call's 8th album to appear until early 1992. Can we wait that long for a new release from the Call? An emphatic "No"! (details...)

The *Red Moon* tour was great. I hope all of you got the chance to see the band. With each new album and tour more and more people are discovering the Call. And they all ask the same question-"Why haven't I heard of this band before now?" A fan from New Jersey wrote, "We are very confused and upset over the fact that a high caliber band such as the Call gets almost no radio exposure at all. We live in the New York Metropolitan Area and you would think there would be at least one radio station that plays a variety of new music instead of the same songs we have been hearing for the last twenty years or more. The songs by the Call are, by far, much superior over most of the garbage invading our airwaves. Why can't we hear them on the radio?"

To answer those questions one can only theorize, but personally I think that about 90% of the fat cat music business is on a mission to moronify the people through what they glibly call music these days. An exaggeration maybe, but, neverthe-less, most music is a snooze. It's ineffective, and that's due in large part to the upper echelon's marginal (sometimes, submarginal) knowledge of what rock and roll is all about. And one needn't even mention the fact that the almighty dollar (and lots of 'em) rules the show; that's a given. "Career moves" have taken precedence over artistic integrity. And music fans, for the most part, have been lulled into submission.

Is rock and roll dead? USA Today a few weeks ago said that rock and roll is "wounded and in hiding". SPIN Magazine has gone further. They've commissioned 13 writers to "embark on voyages in search of the heart and soul of rock and roll." The writers will be going all over the country, some to small towns "unscathed by the media's suffocating grip." Their findings will be in the August issue of SPIN.

There are some great bands around-some wonderful music-you just have search more fervently to find it. And one of the best is the Call. They're still turning out fresh, intelligent, passionate rock and roll. But, gosh, we want to hear it on the radio.

Which reminds me of something that happened last month. I was travelling Alabama in a midnight storm when a monstrous streak of lightening cracked, followed by the loudest clap of thunder I'd ever heard. For just a second everything around me was illuminated, allowing me to actually see where I was going. But as quick as it came my guiding light was gone, and once again I was navigating a pitch black road in a blinding rain.

I'm telling you this story because the eeriest thing happened after that crashing bolt of thunder and lightening. A Montgomery radio station I had been trying to coax in suddenly began transmitting crystal clear, and the song playing was "I Still Believe". At midnight on a rain soaked Alabama highway, thinking about my critically ill mother I was hurrying to be with, feeding my ever-present doubt with questions about why good people like my mother have to suffer so, I really needed to be soothed by that song. Ah, comfort arrives in strange ways.

Take care.

Maria

P.S. We do need to support diversity in the airwaves. Call your radio stations and strongly urge them to play something other than Top 40 and classic rock. And request the Call's music often. Programmers and station owners need to hear from us, the listeners.

Q&A

Where to begin? There've been so many changes for the Call it has taken on almost epic proportions. So, Michael, why don't you just fill us in on what has been going on with the Call.

Well, I don't know about epic, but to begin with Jim has left the group, at least for now. As you know he got married about a year and a half ago and he and Dixie wanted to start a family; in fact, they are now expecting a child. It's really as simple as that. That's his #1 priority. And touring can sometimes get in the way of making and keeping that a #1 priority. He may still play on the albums, but he feels he can't commit himself to the band 100% at this time in his life. Jim comes from a different musical tradition than Scott, Tom, or myself. We grew up admiring the lifestyle of the blues, jazz, and the big band guys who stayed out on the road almost year round and we've wanted to do that from the very beginning. We love playing live and being out in front of an audience. We always have and probably always will as long as we're physically able. But it can be difficult to love touring in the sense that what touring means is getting up and driving 5-8 hours everyday. It means you're separated from your family and friends for months at a time. And some people, after awhile, will decide that this is not what they want. I enjoy family immensely, but I also love playing in front of an audience. Maybe when I'm 50 years old I won't want to go out and play, but right now it's an integral part of my life. And I'd rather play live than play in the studio. When you record you do it in pieces-it's very fragmented. Making records is fulfilling, but not completely satisfying for me, and I know I can speak for Scott and Tom as well.

The Call have a new label and also a new representative who will be working with your long-time manager Gary Heaton.

Yes, we've taken on additional management. The manager's name is Steve Fargnoli. He manages Sinead O'Connor and World Party and also used to manage the Call along with his partners Cavallo and Ruffalo from 1982-84. The Call left Cavallo, Ruffalo and Fargnoli because we had wanted Steve to be our representative, but at the time their management firm was directing Prince's career and Prince demanded that Steve move to Minneapolis and work solely as his personal manager. So that left us without our preferred choice. Since then Steve split with Cavallo and Ruffalo and he was once again interested in managing the Call.

Steve has ties with the English record companies and he thought it would be a good idea if we signed with Warner U.K., which we have done. Warner U.K. is a division of W.E.A. Interna-

tional Records. They will finance the recording and videos and once that's finished they'll then offer the completed recordings to American record companies. This way the American record companies will know what they are getting.

The Call have had a problem in the past with American companies. A label would be enthused about the group and we'd make a record and then they would either not know how to market the record or not like it because it wasn't what they were expecting. Which is somewhat understandable because we do tend to change considerably from record to record. Record companies would prefer you to make the same record over and over again. But this way they will have the actual record in hand and can decide whether they are excited about it or not.

And that's probably a good thing, a wise decision, because the new record that we're working on now is again a big departure from the last couple of records we've made. And this is caused by the diverse background of the players in the group. We know how to play a number of different musical styles and we'd like to pursue it. Whereas most bands you hear from album to album sound the same because that's all they know how to play.

So that was the problem with MCA?

Our problem with MCA occurred 2 months after we signed with the label. The president of MCA at the time, Irving Azoff, personally signed the Call and was extremely enthusiastic. However, 2 months later, because of his own contractual difficulties with the label and his desire to create his own company, Azoff left MCA. The new president, Al Teller from CBS Records, wasn't that enthusiastic of the Call and the promotion of *Let The Day Begin* suffered drastically. The song "Let The Day Begin" went to #1 on rock radio, but because the president wasn't crazy about the group there was limited promotion. As the next 2 years went on the relationship got worse and worse. And *Red Moon* was such a departure from *Let The Day Begin*, rather than adapt to that album, and promote the record for what it was, they let it go with little or no promotion whatsoever.

How is the new record different?

It's a very guitar-oriented record with little or no keyboard. Since Jim's decision to leave the band, at least for the foreseeable future, we've added another guitar player instead of keyboard. Our new guitar player is Ralph Patlan, originally from Houston, Texas, whom we met a couple of years ago on the *Let The Day Begin* tour. He was our guitar technician on the *Red Moon* tour and we had him come up and play with us on a few songs-people may remember him from that tour. He and Tom really enjoy playing together and it's been inspiring. I will also play guitar and Ralph will play some keyboards. A few songs such as "Let The Day Begin", "Oklahoma", and "Walls Came Down" we'll be doing with 2 guitars instead of keyboards, which is appealing to us because we've done the songs for so many years the new approach is a welcome change. We'll still have keyboards on "I Still Believe", "Jealousy", "I Don't Wanna", and "The Woods", but on the next tour we'll mainly be concentrating on the new record and material from the first 3 albums.

When the Call played at the Hard Rock Cafe in Chicago this past New Year's Eve I remember wishing the show could go on for hours knowing that show might be the last one with Jim for a long time.

In the beginning of the last tour when Jim made it known he may be leaving, I decided to try and make the shows quite long since it might be the last time playing with Jim. So we did as many songs from *Reconciled* and *Woods* as possible. We were playing 21/2 to 3 hour shows and it was great doing all those songs. But we've been doing those songs every year for the last five years and it's difficult to maintain a genuine enthusiasm when you realize you've played the songs hundreds of times. It's not to say I don't enjoy doing those songs, but as a musician and writer it's more exciting for me to be able to do new material, or do the older material, especially songs from the first 2 albums.

Your first 2 albums were more politically bent. We're just come out of a war, are you going back to that in your writing?

Some of the songs on the first two albums were political and some definitely were not. What I've tried to do with each record is, hopefully, express some total life experience which can range from a very intimate, private emotion to an outward, political expression.

Right now, for me, it would be difficult to write an overtly political song. I don't think you are going to change or effect people's opinions in the 90's by appealing to some kind of intellectual social justice rationale. The problem is so much deeper you have to try to change people's hearts, or to touch the heart. So I'm trying to engage people in a much more intimate, immediate way that might awaken a deeper sense of love and compassion. If by politics we mean the complexities of the relationship between each one of us, then I would say all of our records have indeed been political records.

I do hope though that there will continue to be writers and musicians who can shed new light on global, political situations and moral responsibility, and I may again do it myself. But I don't go into writing a song with that specifically in mind at this time. Although, during the Gulf War I did write a few songs that could be construed as political songs and I like them, but I'm not

sure they'll see the light of day on the next record.

Well, during the Gulf War singer Lee Greenwood also wrote a "political" song; albeit an anthemic one. How would you define your politics?

Anyone who has followed the Call knows my general political bent. I'm fundamentally anti-military in the sense that I'm highly suspicious of the military's motives and those in power who believe that military action is the acceptable way to solve problems. I detest the idea of sending the youth of any nation into battle as pawns in a deadly game between rulers of countries who should never have been allowed a position of leadership in the first place.

We put those people into positions of leadership.

Yes, but *how* some of these presidents, prime ministers, and kings came to power is a tragedy in itself. One of the biggest dangers is that the media and journalists seem to be in league with the powers that be and are being used to manipulate public opinion rather than enlighten by giving the people both sides of every story so that people can make intelligent choices.

But, you know, the most interesting aspect of all this is that it doesn't seem to me to be political at all. It seems to be the basic human desire for power and innocence. The political leaders of the world want to feel a sense of power and a sense of righteous innocence which is exactly what every other human being in the world wants, and I believe both of these desires are ultimately the downfall of every one of us.

Perhaps we pass judgement on each other because we feel we are better than the other person, that our goodness justifies our condemnation of another person or country, which is probably the ego that is compensating for some deep-seated feeling of guilt or inferiority.

Or because we have this debilitating need to have someone below us - a need to feel superior to another person or country; be it economically, culturally, militarily, the color of skin, the god we worship, or sexual propensity. We feel better about ourselves by sanctifying our goodness.

Exactly. My own feeling is that no one of us is that *good*. Maybe due to a fortunate upbringing, or a well-balanced chemical makeup in our bodies we may be able to act out of the better part of our human nature, but all of those advantages to me are the luck of the draw. And those unfortunate enough to not have these advantages should be dealt with with compassion and understanding. Because after all if we want to utilize the goodness that we do possess, how better way than through compassion and understanding.

Page 3 of Issue #7 – Notified Newsletter

IT'S A LONG TIME COMING

Mercury-Polygram has just released a compilation CD from the Call's first three albums: *The Call, Modern Romans*, and *Scene Beyond Dreams*. Titled *"The Walls Came Down-The Best Of The Mercury Years"*, the 18-song collection does, of course, include the 1982 hit "Walls Came Down" plus:

"War Weary World"
"There's A Heart Here"
"Doubt"
"Upperbirth"
"Flesh and Steel"
"Waiting For The End"
"Turn A Blind Eye"
"Modern Romans"
"Back From The Front"
"Destination"
"Violent Times"
"All About You"
"Scene Beyond Dreams"
"Tremble"
"Delivered"
"Heavy Hand"
"One Life Leads To Another"

"The Walls Came Down-The Best Of The Mercury Years" is also available on cassette. The compilation's liner notes were written by noted journalist/musicologist Jimmy Guterman.

Michael Been recently finished up a week in the studio with Bruce Cockburn, lending a hand on Bruce's new album due out sometime in the Fall. Along with Michael on bass guitar, Cockburn recruited Jim Keltner on drums, Edgar Myer on stand-up bass, and Booker T. on keyboards. T Bone Burnett had the honor of being behind the boards for this great line-up of musicians. Michael had this to say about working with the group: "We really enjoyed playing together. It turned out we all had a lot of the same musical influences. Booker T. is a living legend and an incredibly sweet guy. Jim Keltner is a great drummer-he and I worked together in 1985 on Rosie Vela's album. Edgar Myer is usually seen playing with a symphony orchestra-he's a very talented musician. And although I was not that familiar with much of Bruce Cockburn's past work, I was very impressed with the songs on this album, especially lyrically. He's a great story-teller. The songs struck me as sounding very new, very fresh, and that's a real compliment to someone who has close to twenty albums."

Also look for the latest release by Sam Phillips. Scott Musick and Jim Goodwin helped out on a few tracks.

NOTIFIED
is published by

The Call Information Service
P.O. Box 7183
Rockford, Il 61126

compiled and edited by
Maria Braden

photo credit:
Robert Specter

Michael Been has some interesting concepts and some very personal thoughts in the following excerpts from a conversation we had recently.

What determines the songs you'll put on an album and their sequence?

With this album we went into the studio with 15 songs, all of which potentially could have been on the album. Of the 15, 11 finally made it and they were, simply, the ones that we played the best. As for the sequencing, the potential singles are usually the first, second or third songs because if it isn't happening in those first three songs, radio DJ's and programmers won't take the time to go looking for them. It's just something you have to do—one of the concessions in this business. "Let The Day Begin" is a good opening song; it sets the mood and the energy is good. It also would be a good song to open a show. Like on *Reconciled*, it was either "Everywhere I Go" or "I Still Believe" for the first song. We went with "Everywhere I Go" because it was a little easier to get into.

When you're writing a song do you ever begin with a finished lyric and let the music flow from there?

It can happen in so many different ways, but it never happens where I have a finished lyric and then put music to it. I go back and forth between lyrics and music. Sometimes I'll have a musical idea, a chord change, and I'll start playing it and singing along, just kind of making it up as I go along, and I might come up with a few good ideas then—just things that spark off other ideas. Other times I will have some lyric ideas and kind of mess around with different musical changes to get the phrasing, so that the words fit into a particular rhythm. I'm always writing lyrics. I'll think of a line and immediately write it down for future reference. Another method is like sometimes when the band is rehearsing Tom may start to create a guitar line, or Scott may start a rhythm pattern, or Jim or I may start just playing something, an improvisation, and through that a song may form. With the last three albums, the new one in particular, I've started writing a lot with Jim. He will play me a certain chord change or keyboard line or he'll send me a tape of things he's come up with. Like today I got a tape of about twenty improvisations lasting from like ten seconds to two minutes. I may hear something that inspires me and maybe create a melody line or chorus or bridge. I think it helps the songwriting, and it certainly helps by taking the weight of writing all the songs off me.

When you spoke about making it up as you go along, wasn't that just what happened recording the song "Oklahoma"?

Yeah, almost all of it. I mean I'd been thinking about the theme and images but the lyrics themselves were totally off the top of my head except for like three lines that were just mumbled because I couldn't articulate what I was thinking quickly enough. One of the lines, "the storm hit and the roof gave way and a man said it ain't easy", was supposed to be "a man swore duty, body and soul", but I couldn't get the last words out coherently because the song was moving so fast. So I went back into the studio to overdub it correctly, to say what I wanted to say. The band was playing and music was coming through my vocal microphone and when the new line came in the whole sound of the track altered because all of a sudden there was this

voice that was like it had been inserted from another planet. So I just kept what was on there.

The lyrics are included on Let The Day Begin. How do you feel about that?

I guess I've had to adjust to the reality that people don't have the time or the inclination to really listen to the words. It reflects the fast pace of life today. When I listen to music I don't like reading the lyrics. I like to get my own impressions. When I was a kid music just seemed to take up so much of my day voluntarily. That's how I wanted to spend my time. Not just having the music playing in the background or dancing to it. I got into what the song was saying, and how it would make me feel or inspire me. I would focus right in on it. I enjoyed just listening and figuring out what they were saying. Now most people want it right away. So it's best to include the lyrics.

Do you ever think, "God, if I have to sing that song one more time"? Do you get tired of playing "Walls Came Down" or any of the old Call tunes?

No, not really. It's just that we don't practice a lot of the old songs anymore so we wouldn't be ready. We would have to go and practice them in order to play them. But our heads are much more into the recent songs. It we did a lot of the old songs we would be like our own cover band.

Would you ever consider doing a cover of someone else's song?

Performing live we've played some covers. We've done some Stones tunes like "Last Time" and "Oh, Carol", the Chuck Berry song the Stones covered, and we've done "Love Will Tear Us Apart" by Joy Division. "Temptation", "Not Fade Away", "Knockin' On Heaven's Door"— we've done quite a few. But as for putting one on an album we wouldn't exactly be opposed to doing it, it's just that the song would have to fit with the other songs. We wouldn't just want a token cover song.

One minute a band can't get played for anything and the next minute it can be overkill. How would you handle that?

You can't really control radio but I don't think that's the main problem. To me the problem is publicity and media overkill which can really only be done with your cooperation. It requires a lot of restraint and taste. You have to control that so that people don't become bored with you. I know that has happened where I've really liked a band and they would be everywhere at once. Enough is enough. Like when I look at Rolling Stone magazine it just stuns me how they can justify that many pictures, articles and interviews with Springsteen, U2 and R.E.M.

"Even Now" was the last song you wrote for Reconciled and there's a line that says, "chased, chased out into the woods". Is that where you got the title for Into The Woods?

When I wrote the song "The Woods" I didn't realize I had written that line in "Even Now" until much later. I wanted to call that album,

Expecting. That was the original title of the album and that's what I wanted it to be. But no one liked it at the record company and the guys in the band didn't like it. When they heard it they thought of somebody being pregnant. I didn't and even then I didn't think there was anything wrong with that. But everyone liked *Into The Woods* better so we went with that.

Is Let The Day Begin your most personal album?

They're all my most personal albums. They reflect what I'm living at the time I write them.

Has it ever been difficult to part with one of your songs, to make it public?

No, not really.

Do you feel you've been labeled an intellectual or something that suggests a dark cerebral attitude and do you have a problem with that?

Well, I don't think of myself as an intellectual. It's just that so many rock lyrics are like bad junior high school poetry that it just seems intellectual by comparison. As far as the dark cerebral thing, I think if you write about and confront the realities of life it's going to include the dark and difficult aspects as well as the positive and joyous ones. Part of our rock and roll culture tends to praise misery. We tend to really like knowing that someone is so miserable that they can write these songs that really expose the black, dark, negative side, but I don't think that's what life's about. It's just part of the story. And I don't think anger and blind intensity are desirable qualities. So what I've tried to do over the years and the way my life has developed is to just find some kind of balance between the two. Not where the light is the absence of the dark and not where the dark is the absence of the light. It's both of them together.

So do you think you've arrived at a meaningful pattern to your existence?

Well, the meaning is slowly being formed in all of us, maybe slower in some than others but it is being done. It's important to give voice to your feelings and questions and doubts and fears, and confront them, but I think it's a terrible place to stay--to be trapped in. I think it's part of a process but I don't think it's the end of the process. But I think some people are so depressed about their lives and have such low self-esteem that they like to hear that hopeless stuff because it validates their own negativity and I don't think that's healthy.

Are you shedding your isolation?

I'm trying to.

Have you experienced everything you write about?

Yes, absolutely. I'll experience it either before or after I write the song.

I understand before--but after?

Yes, and that's the most amazing, mystical thing about the whole creative process. Either I will understand what I've written because it has happened or it will happen. I think it's because often when you write, you're writing from a subconscious place. Something inside you is telling you what's going on before you are conscious it's going on. That's not always the case. Some of the writing is reflective--you reflect back on something or at the present moment that's what

you're feeling or thinking. But a lot of the time I'll start writing a song and it will be alien to me and it will be just imagery but later on it will turn into absolute action or flesh. And I don't believe it's because of suggestion from the song. I believe it's like dreams--dreams will tell you what's going on and later on the dream will make sense. I believe there's a part of us that's so far ahead of where we consciously are. We are so much more formed than we know, and like I said before, we're always being formed. Somewhere inside of us we are far more advanced than we can consciously act out and until those things going on inside of us break through into consciousness we go through doubt, confusion and unawareness. But I think something inside is always talking to us, always trying to tell us something. And I think the minute you start questioning, "Why is this going on?", that's when movement out of the problem can begin. But the problem existed long before and the solution existed long before.

You've explored whole areas of psychology, politics and religion in your songs and you seem to back up everything you sing about with the way you live.

Oh, if only I could. I'm doing better. I'm better off than I used to be. But too often I look at how far I've got to go--not how far I've come, and I think that's a fault with me. I'm just striving to be human, rather than less than human.

Well, it's damn hard, Michael.

Yeah, it's damn hard. And it causes a lot of anger. I think most of my anger is directed at myself for not being the person I want to be. Being sub-human in too many ways; too much of the time.

I feel the central tenet in your songs is hope.

Well, I'm glad that comes through in the songs, now if I could only live it. That's very self-revealing for me because a lot of times in my life the central tenet is wait and see and maybe hope will play a part. I wish I had as firm a grasp on hope in my life as I do in my writing.

The Call have been on the threshold of stardom for a while and it could very well happen with this album. I'm sure you've all thought about how it should be handled. You seem to have the kind of protective community that will deflect some of the madness of stardom. I suspect your family and friends would get on your case pretty quickly if you started 'losing it'.

I do have enough people that would call me on it. I always get a little uncomfortable talking about the 'what-I-will-do-to-handle-stardom', you know. It seems like you're predicting it's going to happen and I don't predict that.

Well, I'll predict it then.

Ok. With me it's I'll cross that bridge when I come to it. I'm certainly not 21 and I don't believe all the hype. I think that I could potentially handle it but that's not saying I'm above it all because if enough people told me how wonderful I am I could probably become pretty cocky and arrogant and walk around thinking how great I am.

You mean enough people haven't told you yet? You mean I haven't succeeded, Michael?

Well, it's nice and flattering and all but I know the whole story.

Well, you are pretty wonderful.

I can be pretty horrible, too.

Granted, but we all can.

— **Maria Braden**

Supplemental Insert to Notified Newsletter Page 2

An Interview with Michael Been (1987)

WHAT DO YOU THINK ATTRACTS PEOPLE TO THE MUSIC OF THE CALL?

We get an amazing cross section of people. I'm sure different people get in on different levels. As many people may like The Call for its rhythm as its lyrical stance. There are certain fans that are extremely passionate about it, and have had traumatic situations in their lives where the music really helped them.

I personally like music that speaks to me about my life - not my fantasies - not my ego. When a band writes a song and I can say "that's how I feel - that's what I think - that's my experience," it creates a kind of community. Loneliness, or better still, aloneness, is a basic emotion we all share to varying degrees, and the music that appeals to me is the type that eases that aloneness.

THE CALL HAS A NUMBER OF WELL-KNOWN FANS; BOB DYLAN, U2, AND OTHERS; ALSO GARTH HUDSON AND ROBBIE ROBERTSON PLAYED ON YOUR ALBUMS, AS WELL AS JIM KERR AND PETER GABRIEL. THIS IS PRETTY IMPRESSIVE STUFF.

It's nice that they appreciate our music and it's nice to get to know these people on a personal level. We toured with Simple Minds in 1983 and again in '86, and we've all become good friends. When we were first asked to tour with Peter

Gabriel, we didn't know too much about him except that he'd been in Genesis. During that tour, though, we all got to know each other very well. Peter is one of the most interesting, unassuming people I've ever met.

The most exciting thing to us was THE BAND - Garth and Robbie and Levon and those people - because THE BAND, to us, was the greatest band that ever was. They were an incredible influence on us. I went to see THE BAND when I was about 18, and I was singing a gut- wrenching version of 'Rockin' Chair', and I remember looking through the crowd and seeing people with tears in their eyes. I'd never seen that before. I knew immediately what I wanted to do.

Incidentally, about two years ago, Scott and I played in California with Richard Manuel, Rick Danko, and Garth Hudson on THE BAND's reunion tour. Levon Helm was doing a movie at the time so Scott filled in on drums. Robbie Robertson was busy with a previous commitment and I played guitar. Scott and I really enjoyed playing all those songs we've loved for so long and playing with THE BAND was an incredible experience.

IT SEEMS THAT MICHAEL BEEN HAS A LOT TO SAY IN HIS SONGS. ARE YOUR LYRICS POLITICALLY ORIENTED?

Our music is interpreted and classified a lot as political or social and I suppose it is in some ways. But rather than being concerned with major political issues, our music is more into personal politics. If it's talking about war, it's more a symbolic reference to wars that are going on inside individual people than on a grand scale confrontation. I think that our most political songs, like "Walls" and "Blood Red", are very personal because they're trying to provoke a passionate response in the listener - a very personal reaction to a universal situation.

DO YOU FEEL THE BAND HAS A COMMON BOND WITH OTHER POLITICAL BANDS?

Some bands have a violent revolutionary attitude. We would be much more inclined toward a non-violent approach. But I think that what they're doing is important because there is too much apathy in this country. As an artist, you have a responsibility to do something.

YOU SAID YOU WROTE "BLOOD RED (AMERICA)" AS A RESPONSE TO THE CURRENT ADMINSTRATION'S APPROACH TO SOLVING THE WORLD'S ILLS -

I think anything's possible with that kind of thinking - we are capable of the worst thing that's ever happened in the history of the world. But I think the thing we've got going for us is that historically the pendulum always swings back - and there's always a reaction to that kind of insanity. I'm very patriotic, but I'm patriotic to the human being rather than the flag they stand under.

YOUR LYRICS SOMETIMES SEEM TO HAVE BIBLICAL REFERENCES -

Well, I try to write about my own life experiences, and I'm a Christian myself, so I write from that point of view. Although it wouldn't be the type of Christianity commonly practiced these days. I believe it's a vain presumption to think that all people in the world should believe what I believe or that it would necessarily be right for them. I only know that it's right for me. I'm not interested in selling religion; Christianity or otherwise.

THE CALL HAS MADE FIVE ALBUMS. IN RETROSPECT, ARE YOU SATISFIED WITH YOUR WORK?

I really like all of our albums, and each one for different reasons. In 1980 we went to England to make some demos and play some gigs and at that time there were emerging some great bands - Joy Division, The Clash, The Pretenders, Gang of Four; and we saw them all. The British punk bands weren't so concerned with technique and orthodox standards, they just played like their lives depended on it. In fact, everyone thought we were an English band. We went back to England later on to record our first album. We were exploring music during that time; trying to determine our own direction. The Call (first album) was a compassionate album, but it probably came out as anger.

Modern Romans is our most political album. There was a great deal happening politically - Granada, Lebanon, or government saying the Russians are evil and the Russian government probably saying the same about us. That kind of thinking inspired me to write the last lines of "Walls Came Down". The album reflected the times.

Scene Beyond Dreams, I call our 'metaphysical' album. It was an abstract parallel of the transitions we were going through. Those were the heaviest of times for us. Some personal tragedies and strained relationships caused a great deal of introspection. Lyrically it was a more poetic approach. We were also in the middle of reforming the band with Jim Goodwin. Musically, the change in instrumentation brought out a different sound.

We did Reconciled in the summer of '85. The band hadn't had the luxury of playing very much together prior to making that album. We had gone through two years of not having a recording contract. We fell into a business hell and the band became lawyers over legal bickering with our former record label and management company. We didn't have anything definite other than the band itself. Then we got the Elektra deal and we started rehearsing, and things started clicking and feeling wonderful again. We believed in the band, and I think that all the adversity that we went through strengthened us.

Into The Woods is my favorite album, without a doubt. There's so much of all of us in the album. I really love it. When we finished the album I didn't want to listen to any of it for awhile, after having heard each song about 200 times in the studio. So I separated myself from it. When I did listen again, it was really wonderful. I was enjoying the album and not concerning myself with studio technicalities.

DO YOU SUPPOSE ANY OF YOU WOULD RATHER BE DOING SOMETHING ELSE?

The Call is "home" for all of us. We absolutely love this band. We have that level of commitment - a mutual respect for each other. The band is very special to us; that's why we do it. We've played in a lot of different bands over the years, and it's a miracle when you can get four or five people together, and their minds are all in the same place, and want to play the same kind of music and get along well. This is just the best thing we've ever had.

From - Notified Newsletter. Profile: Scott Musick (1987)

Scott Musick's drumming is the relentless pulse of The Call's music. Since their early beginnings in California clubs, Scott's solid fills and cohesive beat have been an integral part of The Call's unique style.

MUSICAL ROOTS -

Basically self-taught, Scott's musical education began at an early age. "I've been playing since I was a kid. I grew up in a musical environment. My dad was a musician so we always had music in our home. He played drums, trumpet, guitar and sang in combos. My older brother also sang in local bands around Tulsa. I played in the jazz band at school, and it was about that same time I began drumming for a rock band."

"I listened to a lot of jazz as well as rock and roll. The jazz greats, Buddy Rich, Max Roach, Art Blakey - they all had a tough sound. I was affected early on by Stones, Beatles, Yardbirds, and the Band. Charlie Watts of the Stones is still one of my favorite drummers - - he's straight ahead rock and roll. He and Levon Helm of the Band both had well-honed styles for rock and roll drummers. Being from Oklahoma I suppose I was also influenced by country and western music."

BEGINNINGS -

Scott got his first taste of real musical duty in California. "After school I went out to Los Angeles. I played in a couple of bands and from there went to Las Vegas with a club band. That lasted about six months and I went back to Tulsa. I saw this guy I had known I California who suggested I go back and look up this singer named Michael Been who had this really great voice. I did, and Michael and I have been playing music together since then. We played in a lot of bands but after awhile we settled in the Santa Cruz area to concentrate on developing our own style and writing songs."

Mere coincidence that these two Oklahoma musicians should have such musical compatibility? "A few years after we had been playing together, Michael was sitting on the front porch of my granddad's house talking with him about Oklahoma when Michael mentioned that his grandfather had worked in a pharmacy in Tulsa. As it turned out, our grandfathers had been best friends in college and were apprentices at the same pharmacy in Tulsa. It was an incredible discovery."

THE MUSIC -

"One of the things that makes our music unique is, of course, Michael's lyrics. Overall, the songs have strong melodies and a good grove. Individually we all contribute by bringing in our own ideas. Jim has been the most modern influence on jour music. He plays the synthesizer tastefully and doesn't allow the instrument to dominate a song. Tom's style is very diverse and original - his guitar moods can range from atmospheric and flowing rhythms to basic blues. Michael has an amazingly solid and complex bass line. As for myself, I've always tried to be very open-minded about music, so even though I'm mainly grounded in rock and roll, I fall back on my entire background and try to take an intuitive approach to our music."

TOURING -

Part of the inner dynamic that makes The Call stand out from the crowd in rock music today is the band's intense live performances. "We're a performance band, a live band. We have a lot of power on stage. I guess it's because we really love to play music, and we put everything we've got into it. With a live show, you also get an immediate audience reaction, and we have some great audiences."

Despite their years of collective onstage experience, it's the offstage camaraderie that makes The Call a band. "It's an interesting situation. When you're in a band you spend an incredible amount of time together. You're either sound checking, backstage waiting to go, performing or traveling, or in the studio. You have to enjoy the company or you're in trouble."

THE STUDIO -

The Call's background is substantial - -five studio albums and the sixth in the making. "With the upcoming album we basically represented in the studio what we do live. We wanted to record in a method that most closely resembled a live performance as possible, and we like the way it's turning out. We set up in the studio like we would on stage with the monitors in the room. We went into the studio purposely under-prepared to leave room for as much spontaneity as needed. On this last tour we did a few of the new songs at sound checks, but stopped half way through because they were sounding too good. What I mean by that is you can get into liking a song a certain way, and not see the possibilities of what you can do in the studio."

The Call has done most of the production work on their albums. "My drum sound has been different on each album. There are a lot of techniques you can use to beef up or color your sound and I've used them. But I feel musicians should take responsibility for creating their own sound rather than relying totally on an engineer."

ALBUMS -

The Call has been really quite varied and innovative. "We are all pretty eclectic in our tastes - - we tend to like all kinds of music. With each album we've experimented, so our music has been evolving. We've learned something new on every record and have grown musically."

THE AUDIENCE -

Can you describe the audience you want to reach? "As diverse as possible. It's true, though, you can never please everybody, and that's not our ambition. I think everyone wants their music to be accessible and our albums are a result of thinking about getting our music to a wider audience, but still doing what we like to do. Our audience is largely people whose first Call album was "Reconciled" and who probably never heard our earlier stuff. But now they're going back and finding those albums to see what they've missed."

JIM GOODWIN - the interview Notified Newsletter

From this issue of Notified, it takes a personal look at Jim Goodwin, keyboardist for the Call. The music of the Call reveals Jim's talent for creating moods and nuances. Jim is an insightful and genuinely modest person. And while his musical career is taking off, his feet seem firmly planted on the ground.

WHO WERE YOUR MUSICAL INFLUENCES?

I was very much influenced by the classical rock stuff like Yes, Genesis with Peter Gabriel, Gentle Giant and a lot of jazz like the original Weather Report.

SO THOSE ARE YOUR ROCK ROOTS?

Well, prior to that, I had taken piano lessons when I was about 9 years old and I hated it. One of my very first lessons I learned the I-IV-V progression and it was weird really that the teacher was even teaching theory at all in this small town in Oregon were I was living. But I was to have learned all these songs in order to win these busts of the classical composers. So I learned the I-IV-V progression, but at that time to the I-IV-V was "Louie, Louie" and that's all I wanted to play. I would sort of rock on this thing and my mom would come in and say, "Jim, that's not what you're practicing." So I told her that I wasn't into this thing at all and that I hated it. So she let me quit. I played "Louie, Louie" for show and tell in 3rd grade on this little Sears organ with my best friend who sang and played tambourine. That was my first ever gig. So I guess those are my rock roots. Then when I was about 14 I had this uncontrollable urge (to quote Devo) to play music and to take piano lessons. So I hooked up with my cousin in Portland who was taking lessons from this guy who taught theory more than any style of music. He taught you how to play the piano and have good technique and how to write music.

WAS IT AT THAT POINT THAT YOU DECIDED ROCK AND ROLL WAS WHAT YOU WANTED TO PLAY?

Actually, my sister introduced me to the whole rock and roll thing by taking me to a Chuck Berry concert when I was about 14 or 15. For some reason I can't remember, we arrived really late for the show and I was the only one without a ticket and my sister didn't want to buy me one since there were only about 30 minutes left of the show. So she and her friends left me outside the coliseum in Portland and all I heard was this great, loud rock and roll music when someone would open the doors. It really put the bug in me because it was behind these closed doors and it was just this power, this sound and it didn't have any image. I had also inherited my brother's record collection about that same time and he was really into Jimi Hendrix and Cream and I had loved them so much form the time I was very young.

More than anything though I loved Peter Gabriel and Genesis. Their very eclectic, progressive rock - - how they used flute, oboe, and lots of keyboards - - all this avant-garde instrumentation. They were my favorite band which is ironic because Michael, Tom and Scott never knew who Peter Gabriel was. They had heard Genesis but it wasn't what they were into. So I was into all this classical rock and it's interesting really because I feel it's the one thing that defines my contribution to the Call.

Even though Michael also had a background in classical music, he and Scott were into rock and roll, blues, rhythm and blues, and even psychedelic music - - people like Muddy Waters, Chuck Berry, Dylan, the Band, and Moby Grape. All this straight ahead rock music and country western as well. And Tom played in blues bands from day one. So while I was listening to this classical rock stuff, at the same time in their lives they had been listening to and playing this really unpretentious, down-home music. I never had any of that blues band rock. I'm the complete antithesis of Tom in that regard. I never played the blues until we did the Harry Dean Stanton shows. People have the notion that you can't really play music unless you have those blues roots. But I think you can - - it's just that you end up playing it differently.

ALL MUSICIANS ARE INFLUENCED BY WHAT CAME BEFORE BECAUSE EVERY GENERATION HAS CHRONICLED ITS MUSIC. THAT'S WHAT INSPIRATION IS - THE TORCH BEING PASSED.

Yeah, that's true and I feel this wide range of influence works well for the Call. Like Tom is really pretty traditional with his guitar work although he ends up with these weird sounds because we throw him into these non-traditional situations and he'll add this blues rock thing. Michael and Scott lay down this really honest, but unusual, rhythm section, and I'll add this thing that I grew up with - - a more melodic approach.

A LOT OF TODAY'S MUSIC RELIES TOTALLY ON THE TECHNICALLY SOPHISTICATED SYNTHETIC SOUND. ARE YOU PRETTY STATE-OF-THE-ART?

I try to avoid all that because it's so clichéd and it wouldn't work well with the Call. We go toward more piano and organ sounds. I'm much more interested in the notes that I'm playing than in the sound. I'm not a technical keyboard player. I'm not a programmer. I don't use a computer. I don't sequence my stuff. I don't have state-of-the-art equipment by any means. What I do is play parts and to me melody is more important than the sound. I appreciate the great sounds, but I focus on performance and melody.

IT WAS FIRSTLY ON 1986'S RECONCILED THAT THE COLLABORATIVE SONGWRITING APPROACHES OF MICHAEL BEEN AND JIM GOODWIN WERE BEGINNING TO SHOW THEMSELVES.

The most wonderful thing to me about Reconciled was writing songs with Michael. It was such a surprise when he asked me if I had any songs to submit. I said, "Well, yes, as a matter of fact, I do." So I gave him a couple of keyboard melodies which eventually became "Tore The Old Place Down", and "I Still Believe". To me it was the beginning of the great opportunity of writing with Michael that has blossomed on Let The Day Begin. For me it's the ultimate situation because I'm not a real prolific songwriter and I'm not even really good at writing songs. I'm really good at coming up with a million little chord progressions and melodies. But I never know what to do with them. I just pump them out.

I think Michael is the songwriter I've been trying to find all my life because I've always wanted to collaborate with someone but no one has ever understood or appreciated or been able to hear what I've been doing. Michael is such a talented songwriter that all he needs is a spark of an idea and he'll come up with an entire format for a song out of it. And the band is so good at honing it down into a song that usually all it takes is just one line or chord progression. Scott's drumming is so great and Tom's guitar playing is truly brilliant.

DO YOU WRITE LYRICS WITH MICHAEL?

Not really. With Michael it's only to the extent he'll bounce lines off me and say, "What do you think works better" or "Do you think this is pretentious or vague?" And since we room together on the road, he'll be working on a lyric and he'll say, "What do you think about this?" but mostly I just let him go because he's so good at it. Lyrics are probably the hardest thing to write. I never even have to consider that the lyrics he will put to my music will be anything but great. I'm totally flattered that he can be inspired by my music to come up with the kind of lyrics he writes. I think the lyrics are by far the best on the new album. Michael said at one time he thought the song "When" is the song he's always been trying to write. To me that was the biggest compliment that I could get. I wasn't responsible for it, but in some small way I had contributed to get that song out of him. To be a part of this band is a total honor and a fortunate blessing for me.

People ask me what it's like playing with the Call or writing songs with Michael and I have to say that basically I feel if I had to name the ten best singer /

songwriters in the history of rock and roll, Michael would be one of them. It would be like how you would feel if you had played with Jimi Hendrix or Jim Morrison. It would be the equivalent.

EVEN THOUGH MICHAEL'S LYRICS LEAVE PLENTY OF ROOM FOR INTERPRETATION, MANY OF THE CALL'S SONGS ARE INFUSED WITH RELIGIOUS CONNOTATIONS. WERE YOU BROUGHT UP IN A RELIGIOUS ENVIRONMENT?

My family was Presbyterian but it really wasn't stressed. My grandfather was a lunatic, fundamentalist bible-beating minister. And for a long time my father rejected Christianity because his father represented this Christian faith and to him it was all bull because of the manner in which he was raised. To him it was all just a lie. It was violent and hateful and he totally rejected it. My dad agreed to go with the Presbyterians because my mother insisted we go to church. So we had regular Sunday School and all that. But I was never really into it because of the rigid formality. When I was in high school I had this great philosophy teacher and we read all these philosophies and I sort of believed everything because there was no reason not to believe it and if it works that's great. That's what I liked about the basic ideas of Christianity, which is all my mother ever stressed, that we should forgive each other and be kind to one another.

WHILE DEEPLY CONCERNED WITH THE SPIRITUAL JOURNEY AND WITH THE POLITICAL AND SOCIETAL INEQUITIES, IT SEEMS THE CALL ARE CAREFUL NOT TO GET ON A SOAPBOX - - FEELING RATHER THAT SONGS SHOULD COMMUNICATE MORE IN AN ABSTRACT WAY. BUT IN ALL THE SONGS IT IS OBVIOUS: THE MESSAGE IS LOVE.

It's all about being human and taking care of each other. People need a much more practical approach in living with each other. I think the thing I'm most overwhelmed by in people in general is the fear that everyone lives with. The fear that we have of each other and our intense insecurities breed all this violence, aggression, and machoism, and every kind of hatred and racism. It's always been there and I think it will always be there unless people really start educating themselves to have a higher, elevated spiritual concept of life and living with people. It's part of the natural human condition. We're afraid of each other and so we build these fortresses.

YOU'VE BEEN WITH THE CALL FOR SIX YEARS. WHAT BANDS WERE YOU IN BEFORE JOINING THE CALL?

I toured with Sparks and I recorded and toured with John Cale. It was a strange thing really how I joined the

Call. I happened to run into an acquaintance of mine who played bass who told me he was auditioning for the Call and I asked him if they needed a keyboard player and he said he though they did. I had heard the Call and really liked them. This was 1983 and "Walls Came Down" was having a lot of success. I called their management company and the receptionist said, "Yes. I think they are looking for a keyboard player", and gave me the number of the studio where they were recording Scene Beyond Dreams. When I called they said sorry we aren't looking for a keyboardist right now, but Michael told me to come on over anyway. So I did and we became acquainted and Michael took my number.

Their keyboardist was just temporary and as it turned out they had some difficulty with him and he left the band. They needed someone immediately as they were about to leave for Europe to tour with Peter Gabriel. So I hooked up at the last minute. I was pretty much in heaven on that tour because here I was playing with this great band and opening for Peter Gabriel who had been my favorite for years. We returned from Europe and finished Scene Beyond Dreams. After it was released it became pretty obvious Polygram was burying us, giving us no support whatsoever. So we were left with two years ahead of us without a record label.

We played some shows in California during the legal entanglements with Polygram to keep us alive. It was during one of those shows that a twist of fate dictated a change in the band. We had this date booked in San Francisco and our bass player, Joe Read, who had joined the Call when I did, decided to leave the band. We didn't have time to find a replacement so Michael said he would play bass since no one could learn the songs fast enough. Bass was Michael's first instrument and he and Scott played for years together with Michael playing bass. It was about halfway through the show when we realized that this was the best show ever. We all played better than we had ever played before. Tom played better because he was the only guitar player. Scott played better because he and Michael had played that way together for so long. And it suddenly made me feel like I understood what I was supposed to be doing. It was a lot clearer what I wanted and needed to do. Everyone's role became much more defined somehow and it felt good. So Michael said he would continue playing bass. And it was interesting because he's such a good guitar player, but he had no problem and he seemed to love playing bass and it sounded interesting, and it immediately became apparent that we suddenly had this distinct style because of his bass. He continued to play guitar on the albums as well as bass and now on stage I play keyboard bass when he plays guitar.

I FEEL "LET THE DAY BEGIN" IS PROBABLY THE PUREST EMOTIONAL RECORD THE CALL HAS RECORDED. HONEST, ROMANTIC DECLARATIONS MIXED WITH SOMETIMES UNSETTLING RELIGIOUS IMAGERY. AND WHILE THE CALL HAVE ALWAYS BEEN A LITTLE LEFT OF MAINSTREAM, THE NEW SINGLE, "LET THE DAY BEGIN" IS SO INFECTIOUS. IT'S WITHOUT A DOUBT A GREAT RADIO SONG.

Yes, it is, and we're pleased about that. But it wasn't a flagrantly commercial move to write a radio song - - it just happened. I can just hear some critic now saying something like, "the song is great but I expected more from Michael Been". Some critics have labeled him as a dark, brooding songwriter and while that is definitely a part of him it's not the whole picture. The song is upbeat but the words are very intense. This album is so completely live and recording it was a rejuvenating experience for all of us. We wanted that live sound on Into The Woods but we just came close. "In The River" and "I Don't Wanna" sound pretty live. We realized for this album we didn't need a fancy producer. We just needed someone to set us up in the studio.

We were in a large room with full concert monitors, with side fills and wedges for all of us and we just played loud. We play best loud and powerful. The only thing redone was the vocals. "Surrender" was completely live.

Tom's guitar solos are completely live. I listen to Reconciled now and it's good, but if we could do it over the way we did this one, it would be ten times more powerful. I think Reconciled and Into The Woods led up to this album. For what it's worth, you always tend to look back and think "God, if we could do this and that over", but I don't think we would have gone through those steps to get there. When someone looks over the group's history, it will be an interesting body of work. A real progression.

WHAT ARE YOU LOOKING FORWARD TO RIGHT NOW?

I hope we have success with this album just so we can establish ourselves and work to our full capabilities, our full potential without having to go through these two year nightmares and being screwed around by the record company executives that don't have any idea what's going on. Unfortunately it's a fact of life in this business, but if you have a certain amount of success you can finally transcend some of that dependency on the record label because they become dependent on you. You're left alone. You've proven that what you're doing is successful and so you don't have to audition and you can get past them and just have them there to put out your record and keep your career going. I feel really productive on every level of my life. I'm at the time of my life where if I'm given any opportunity I'll seize it and try to make something out of it. Whereas back in Reconciled time if I'd been given an opportunity via that success I might have squandered the success and money in some kind of unproductive way.

We are all really anxious to get back on the road. It's our career and it's extremely important to us. The thing that has kept us going is how much we believe in this record, but two years is a long time. We all love touring. The people are wonderful, so completely open. And when you reflect back you realize all those moments are so great. Makes you feel good about what you're doing.

A Conversation with Tom Ferrier – Notified Newsletter

The Call have always upheld an intuitive approach to music. They've relied on interaction and have avoided technical excess. The personalities and strengths of the band's members are tantamount to the highly individualistic sound of the Call.

Tom Ferrier's superlative guitar work reflects his early influences of rhythm and blues. At the heart of Tom's playing is feeling and expression, and he has kept his playing very close to its original inspiration

WERE YOU INSPIRED TO TAKE UP THE GUITAR BY OTHER'S EXAMPLES?

I was very influenced by blues guitarists like B.B. King, Freddy King and I loved Ray Charles. I think the fundamental thing that links all music is the blues. When I was about seven years old I got a walkie-talkie for Christmas and I would pretend to have this radio show and play all my favorite music. After I got my first guitar it became an obsession pretty quickly. I was diligent about practicing by playing along with records, playing them over and over so I could hear every little thing the guitarist was doing. I gigged around in different bands growing up in California. Back then surf music was the rage but I played in blues-based bands. I really liked Clapton, Beck and Page - - the white boys interpretation of the blues. When you're learning your craft you copy others, then suddenly there's a time in your growth when you have your own style.

HAVE YOU BEEN WITH THE CALL SINCE ITS BEGINNINGS?

Actually before because we were Motion Pictures before we were the Call. Scott, Michael and I were in different bands playing in bars, doing covers, wanting to do original material. And it was a fluke really that we got together. What happened was Scott and Michael were in a band and their guitarist didn't show up for a gig one night and someone called and asked if I would sit in. We played so naturally together - everything just clicked.

We made some demo tapes and when we were ready to send them out we discovered, after a name check, that there already was a band called Motion Pictures, so we had to come up with another name pretty fast. We thought of all the names in the world and decided on the Call. It was just the obvious choice - - it seemed to fit.

THE CALL ARE SOMETIMES PERCEIVED AS A "SERIOUS" BAND - - ARE THEY?

We're serious about our music and if you want to compete on a high-level you have to be serious. We just do the best we can musically to make ourselves happy and we try to do this as honestly and sincerely as we can. But I think we got labeled a "serious" band during Modern Romans. We had good success with that album, but the downside was that it pidgeonholed us. The social justice message is just one part of the Call. The songs are about many things.

THE CALL MAKES PLAYING MUSIC SEEM SO EFFORTLESS BUT WE KNOW IT ISN'T...

Well, unlike a lot of other bands, we have a respect and natural flow with each other. Creating the songs is effortless in that we each understand what's required of us in terms of playing together and coming up with song ideas. One reason for this is that Michael is always writing songs, so we're never at a loss for new material. And also when you've been playing together as long as we have, you tend to know each other pretty well in the studio. Another reason is that the Call has the best rhythm section there is and if the beats not there, everybody can go home.

EVERYONE'S EMOTIONAL PICTURES OF A SONG ARE DIFFERENT AND THE CALL IS A BAND THAT PEOPLE TEND TO FEEL AN EMOTIONAL BOND WITH THAT GOES BEYOND, "YEAH, GREAT BEAT!".

That's true. We have fans who hang on every word of a song and a particular song will touch them deeply. People are affected by what they hear in our music.

IT'S AN INHERENT THING - - WE TEND TO GRAVITATE TOWARD THOSE PEOPLE WHO POSSESS THE SAME QUALITIES WE POSSESS. WHEN YOU HEAR FROM YOUR FANS TALK TO PEOPLE AFTER SHOWS WHAT FEELINGS ARE EXPRESSED?

We get all sorts of comments really. The pure essence of Michael's lyrics is very spiritual and people get a lot of spiritual images from the songs. But, actually, it runs the full gamut. Some are serious images and some just want to take us out for a beer. We take time to talk because we get a lot out of those conversations, as well.

Especially when we're on the road - - it keeps you going to hear it's not all in vain.

THE CALL SEEMS PRETTY UNAFFECTED BY ALL THE RAZZMATAZZ OF THE ROCK MUSIC WORLD.

We've been in this business long enough to know that fame is erratic. We have a real need to play and that's what we love and do best, and that's enough for us. Of course we'd like to have that hit song but it has to be something we feel comfortable with. We believe in doing songs about the process of living and lot of music today is pretty removed from the real world. We have our own ideas on what makes a song great.

MY IDEA OF A GREAT SONG IS WHEN AFTER YOU'VE LISTENED TO IT TWENTY TIMES IT STILL BOWLS YOU OVER.

I agree. When a song is revealed too easily there's nothing to think about or interpret. We've always been more concerned with making a good record that will stand on its own several years from now.

IF THE CALL WERE TO BE OBSERVED IN THEIR WORKING ENVIRONMENT, THE STUDIO, WOULD THE CHEMISTRY BE UNPREDICTABLE?

It probably would but that's what makes us more creative. None of us is insensitive to the other's ideas. We're musically compatible.

I GUESS THE QUESTION I WAS ALLUDING TO WOULD BE - IS THERE ANY HEALTHY FRICTION IN THE BAND?

Sure, but it doesn't come from ego - it comes from a passion about the music. All great bands have had it. It keeps you from becoming complacent. It's easy for a musician to get in a rut and always play the same. Everyone has blind spots.

WHAT IS THE BIGGEST OBSTACLE THE CALL HAVE HAD TO OVERCOME?

The music has always meant enough to us to stick together through all sorts of adversity. We've tried to maintain the highest musical standards and that's tough in this business and it's real tough when the bills are due. It's a strange profession. Just applying yourself to this thing every day is a struggle. But we have a great time. Some bands get so jaded that they break up because they can't take the road or because of psychological reasons. But we have a lot of fun or we wouldn't be doing it.

THE CALLS' SIXTH ALBUM IS DUE OUT EARLY NEXT YEAR AND YOU HAVE A NEW RECORD LABEL. ANY COMMENTS ON EITHER?

We have some great songs on this album, and the sound we got is very live, with few overdubs. The studio we recorded in had a natural resonance like a big club. I'm really pleased with the guitars on this one. As for the new label - we've signed with MCA records and we're just being cautiously optimistic. The possibilities are wide open.

WHAT MUSIC HAVE YOU BEEN LISTENING TO LATELY?

I got into the Living Colour album for awhile. I like some of their songs; "Open Letter to a Landlord" is a good song, some great choruses. I also like the new Stones record and Dylan's new one. And then late at night I revert back to this record I don't think anybody has - - it's a strictly blues album by this guy Robben Ford.

A FAVORITE MOVIE:

"Kid Creole". That was Elvis at the height of his game.

NAME A SONG YOU WISH YOU HAD WRITTEN:

"The Night They Drove Old Dixie Down" by the Band. Every time I hear that song it makes me kind of well up, almost cry, because it's such a clear picture and emotional message of the Old South and how we destroyed it in one night. The story is as big, and I mean as big as in the hugeness and vastness, as any told in a song.

Michael discusses RED MOON

From the September, 1990 Notified Newsletter.

"Hello fellow Call fans! Talk about timing! This issue of Notified is arriving in your mailboxes just days before the Call's seventh album, Red Moon, hits the stores? and the date to circle on your calendars is September 18 1990!"

"Red Moon is an album that plays directly into the Call's musical roots. Not that the band are waxing nostalgic? Not even near it! This is the Call now, with a decade of record making to their credit, playing in the musical vernacular they grew up with and were inspired by."

"Red Moon covers many musical bases. How's yer blues? (my passion for blues/rock was certainly indulged). There are moments of jazz, some fleeting, some ponderable ? with equal parts of head and heart. Great harmonies; tasteful, well-arranged horns; and some of the best percussion I've heard by anyone. It's all here under this rubric called rock 'n roll, and all within the framework of the Call's own distinctive sound.

This time out, Notified devoted all space to a recent interview with Michael Been. Michael spoke candidly with me about the music of yesterday and today. He also lucidly describes the recording of Red Moon. So consider this issue sort of a companion piece to the album. With that said, read on!"

"P.S. U2's Bono sings on this record. Bono shares vocal harmonies with Michael on the album's first single, "What's Happened to You", which will be released to radio on September 12, 1990."

"Red Moon is a wonderful album and I think it's unique because it seems to be a real studio album."

"Well, these days that's a little misleading. The way most records are recorded today is they'll go in and just have two or three musicians lay down a track, and they'll play with a drum machine or click track and keep recording it until at least one and hopefully more instruments have played it well. Let's say the bass player played great, but they didn't think the guitar player or drummer played that great, so perhaps they'll keep the bass track because the bass will be locked into this consistent clock time. And then the drummer? if, in fact, there even was a real drummer, since most records you hear, especially Top 40, are drum machines and not a human drummer at all. Will go into the studio by himself and play just to that bass guitar and that click track until he plays it the way they want it played. They'll then bring in the guitar player and he'll play to those two people. Usually nobody is really in the studio together playing at the same time."

That sounds rather boring. But what I meant by studio album is that once the basic song is recorded you take advantage of subtle techniques, [and] add lots of interesting things to the song."

"Right. With this album there were more overdubs, more "production". It was exactly the same process as Let the Day Begin: we went in with a P.A., no headphones, and played the basic tracks live. Although, we didn't play loud this time "Let the Day Begin" was played very loud at live volume. But the nature of these songs didn't call for that. We wanted a lot of little subtle interplay, so we set up in this tiny area, a corner really, of this big studio. We were all right next to each other. With Let the Day Begin, we were going for the way it would sound in a live concert; whereas, with this one we were going for the way it would sound if we were playing in your living room for you."

"What the Call does in the studio is we play a song until everyone has played well. Sometimes we've played until three of us have gotten it right, then we'll have the fourth guy fix his part. But we've rarely fixed on entire part. There might be a section where someone didn't play it well or thought he could play it better, and he'll fix that section."

This album is so diverse. It has everything from funky blues to jazz. This is the first Call record that the lyrics are almost secondary to me. Not to say the lyrics are inferior, they certainly aren't, they're incredibly moving but it's a musical album. With each listen the music just washes over me."

"I think we were inspired by the sounds we were using. We used old amps, old drums, keyboards, everything. We intentionally didn't want to use anything made after 1970, except for some synthesizer sounds that we modified to get away from that standard sterile synth sound. There's an inherent quality with the modern sounds. There's a tonal quality that the old records have that the new ones don't have. The new sounds are considered better in a certain way, but I personally question whether or not they're really better. On this album we used Mellotron and Chamberlin, which were sort of the first synthesizers; but they used tapes."

"I'm not a fan of the new technology. I recently saw Steven Spielberg being interviewed, and he was asked whether or not he wanted to use, or looked forward to using, the modern advances in technology in his moviemaking. He said, "I think I have all the tools I need. If I can't make great movies with what's available today, which is basically what they used twenty, thirty, and forty years ago, then I shouldn't really be making movies." He went on and said, "Can you make a better baseball bat? Without cheating?" I liked that."

"I remember Mellotron from the Beatle days. Didn't the Beatles pioneer instruments like Mellotron, and Chamberlin? Companies would make new, innovative instruments, and the Beatles would use them in the studio."

"Yeah, but it wasn't really companies, it was this guy Chamberlin. They're the most incredible instruments you've ever seen, very primitive. Chamberlin, in the early 60's, recorded symphony musicians, not as a group, but individual instruments, like a violin, a cello, french horn, every instrument of an orchestra. He recorded them onto a tape recorder, using quarter inch tape. And he had great microphones, those old 40's tube microphones that are so ambient. He would have, for example, the cello player pick a note or bow across the string forward and back for 8 seconds or so. He did this with each instrument plus other sounds like a dog barking and all kinds of things, but the main thing are these instruments from the orchestra. He then put each tape on some sort of electric pulley system with a weight, so when you hit the key it releases the weight and the weight goes down and pulls the tape over the tape head. So you hit the note and it plays, and when it stops you have to push it down to start the tape again. It's a rather awkward way of playing, and you really have to master the touch of it. Jim played it on this record for the cello and French horn sounds."

"But, regardless of the technology of it, the reason the Call used it is because the sounds are so fantastic. They're the old sounds before digital came in, this beautiful, rich sound of an acoustic instrument."

"The way that most music is going today, technology-wise, is sonically unacceptable to me. If you hear the sound of an actual cello, say a cellist goes out in a room and runs a bow across a cello, and you have a nice microphone on it, compare that to the digitized sound of the cello setting on a synthesizer, and the synth is so inferior. It's the difference between fresh peas out of your garden, and frozen processed peas. And I think it's a good analogy because we're getting so far away from a natural approach that the music is losing it's humanness. I personally feel it would be best to use an actual cello player or whoever."

"But that's not always desirable if you want to keep a band fairly self-contained. But I think you can use an acoustic instrument or Chamberlin-style organ and still create great sounds."

"I think many of today's musicians naturally gravitate toward synthesizers and drum machines because computers and their technology have become so ensconced in our everyday lives."

"Computers and technology are taking over our lives in all kinds of ways. We've been warned about this for years, that the more technology comes in, the less the human being will be involved. It's like the difference between the great old hand-drawn movie cartoons and computer cartoons. How can you compare them? One is wonderful and one is cheesy."

"I guess I'm on a crusade to ask musicians to avoid using drum machines and these tasteless synthesizer sounds that are so sizzly and thin. You can get good sounds out of them, but it's very difficult. Many of the things being recorded now are so synthetic it's destroying our hearing. Synthesizers can create overtones and extreme highs that people are getting used to and our senses are getting dulled to natural tones. Musicians and engineers are saying, "I need more high-end, I need more high-end", it's like a drug, "I need more, I'm not getting off on it anymore." It's like an aural addiction. I think it's best to stay within the acoustic instrument sound range, except for maybe the occasional special effect for dynamics."

"I'll tell you a story. They were recording Elvis Costello's album and they had a synthesizer player in the studio, and he had access to like literally a thousand different sounds through Midiing up all kinds of synthesizers. And they were in there, going through all these squeaks and beeps and blips, trying to find a sound, and they're getting frustrated because none of the sounds are right. And what happened is somebody goes out into the studio and hits a note on a piano and they all go, "What was that? That's fantastic!" True story."

"But, Michael, some people will tell you it's a matter of taste, that these modern sounds are superior to the old ones."

"I don't think so. Those drum sounds of the 40's, 50's, and 60's were so wonderful, so real, they've got a very primitive quality. And a drum set is a primitive thing, there's supposed to be a wildness to it. But instead we have all these synthetic, triggered sounds, a lot of which is just gated white noise. They take that sound and mix it together with the sound of an actual drum and all kinds of digital reverb sounds. I just find it to be abrasive and unmusical."

"I agree. But if you were to ask anyone who frequents a dance club, he or she would tell you that they like dancing to the drum machines."

"Drum machines keep perfect time, it's like dancing to a clock, it's unhuman. But that perfect time is also addictive. People don't even know they're addicted to it, it's very subtle. And I don't think it's good for dancing, it's too inhibiting. I suppose you can do the latest choreographed steps to it, but you can't really lose yourself in it and just move to the music. It's very disco to me. It's self-conscious, posing-type dancing. Real drummers, on the other hand, speed up and slow down continuously, following the dynamics of the song."

"I was driving home today and on the radio they played "Stand!", by Sly and the Family Stone, and oh, it's just brilliant. It has this trashy ass primitive drum feel. And musicians, especially young musicians, here and in Europe, and terribly inspired by this soul feel - Motown, James Brown, Sly and the Family Stone. The drum beat at the end of "Stand!" is the drum beat used by most dance music currently on the radio. It's this high hat playing 16th notes - clanging around, kind of sloppy and flying by the seat of the pants. Now these musicians took this drum machine that reproduced that drum beat in a most clinical way. Instead of it being sloppy ad wild and funky, it became very clean, mechanical and robotic."

"People who use these machines should go back and listen to those old records, and hear how twisted and soulless this interpretation of it has become. Young drummers are even trying to play like drum machines. Think about it. It's ridiculous."

"And it goes through the whole synthesizer spectrum. You know, you should be able to get almost everything out of different organs by adding outboard sound effects, like choruses, flangers, and harmonizers, or the old original analog digital domain it's like, "we went too far guys, let's go back." I've been tempted by it myself. We've experimented with a lot of those sounds on our albums, but it isn't satisfying to me anymore. Now don't get me wrong, I like many of the bands who use this stuff."

"But I know they would be infinitely better if they used real drummers and more natural instruments. I think this equipment being used is ultimately a dead end."

"When you use a real instrument the sound and interpretation of that instrument will depend entirely on the style and soul of the player, so the possibilities are as infinite as the differences between each human being. But these machines take away so much of the style of the player, anyone who sits at them is basically going to sound exactly the same."

"Now someone like Garth Hudson or Jim Goodwin can use synthesizers and create exciting, original sounds because they're aware of these inherent dangers. They know how to EQ all the undesirable tones out of these instruments. But remember these men are professionals, so don't try this at home (laughs). Seriously, though, in the hands of a lesser keyboardist who maybe didn't even learn on an organ or piano, the results can be disastrous."

"Some people, young people in particular, might argue that much of the music of the 60's and 70's sounds exactly the same to them."

"Well, I hated most of the 70's sounds. But if a person would go back and listen to the instruments of the 40's, 50's, and 60's, and actually studied them, I don't believe they would think that. I don't think all the old sounds were great on every record, but far more than now."

"I really liked some of the early 70's heavy metal bands. I thought AC/DC was great."

"Yeah, they were, but I don't think of them as metal. For me it was just a louder, exaggerated version of the blues - bands like Zepplin, Hendrix, Cream, T-Rex - that was a wild, sometimes drug induced, interpretation."

"Talking about drums, I remember in the 60's there was so much cymbal."

"The Beatles did that for effect, they liked it. Another reason for it was that musicians and engineers didn't know miking techniques well enough to keep the high hat and cymbals out of the snare drum and tom tom. But even that I like better than what they've come up with today. For example, this loud overdone bass drum sound, where you have all this music playing and then sitting out on its own is this kick drum to show you where to tap your foot. It's stupid."

"Did you put any effects on the drums for this album or did you record them differently this time? They sound so great."

"Scott used a 1957 Gretsch drum set and an old Ludwig set. The old drum sets were lightweight so that the set would kind of rattle when you hit it. For us it was all very intentional to get back to a real set of drums, no samples. The modern drums are made of really heavy, very thick wood, and the whole reason for that is to get each drum to be such a self-contained sound so that it doesn't ring into another drum. And they are designed for effects to be put on them. But they don't sound like a trap kit, where everything should connect to each other. When you hear them they sound like you've taken each drum and put it in a different part of a gymnasium. So, what we did was we got this old drum set where when you hit one drum the other drums resonate - they're lightweight and they all shake so that you get the sound of a real drum kit."

"You added a lot of additional percussion on this album like wood blocks and maracas and lots of horns and vocal harmonies. How will you duplicate some of the songs live?"

"We really can't totally duplicate it live unless we bring in other players. And for some shows we may bring in a small horn section for a few of the songs."

"I think your first and second albums were more like Red Moon as far as studio albums. After that it was more in the synthesizer vein."

"Yeah, well, Jim brought a lot of that in and it was good because he's very creative with programming. But he's starting to dig the more natural instruments."

"You have a lot of high separation on this album."

"That was really from playing quietly. You can get separation by gating instruments or by putting amplifiers in different rooms, but we got it from just playing quietly. If you turn it up loud on your stereo, that's probably louder than we played it."

"Aren't there double tracked guitars on this record?"

"No, not double tracked exactly, but Tom and I overdubbed quite a few guitars."

"I counted four guitars plus bass on "A Swim In The Ocean". You come in on guitar to start the song, then Tom on slide, and then the wah-wah, and there's also one more guitar."

"There are actually only three guitars on that song. That's not a guitar through a wah-wah - that's Jim playing a clavinet through a wah-wah. Then I overdubbed another guitar playing some licks and fills. Also, that song doesn't have a bass guitar on it. It's just a floor tom, and I think Jim may have added some low piano or clavinet."

"On "The Hand That Feeds You", what is that synthetic crash sound at the beginning of the song?"

"It isn't synthetic. I hit the inside of a grand piano with a drum mallet. I was looking for an ominous kind of sound to set the mood in the introduction. I played percussion and piano on that song. I used the piano as a drum and we put a lot of reverb on it. It was a grand piano with the lid up and I hit the strings and the music stand with a drum mallet."

"You don't usually play bass chords, but in the song "Family" you did."

"I have done it before, but on that song I do it a lot."

"What song has the backward guitar?"

"Floating Back". The solo is Tom. It's actually two different solos playing at the same time. We turned the tape over so that it came out backwards. It was Tom's idea to do that to fit the song "Floating Back". It was a great idea."

"The bass on "What a Day" is so great - you play a lot of high notes. Your bass reminds me of Jack Bruce on that song."

"I played a little Ibanez fretted bass - it felt right for that song. On the rest of the album I use my Ampeg fretless bass."

"What microphones did you use for this album?"

"We used old stuff. We recorded at Oceanway Studios, and they've got one of the best selection of microphones in the world."

"T-Bone Burnett was involved with this record. How did you meet him?"

"Scott and I have known T-Bone for about fifteen years. Last March we started talking with him about music and that we wanted to make a different type of record this time; more natural, more organic. He agreed with our approach, mainly about the things we've been talking about in this interview. We talked about him co-producing the album with me, but he was already producing his wife's, Sam Philips, album and Tonio K's album at the same time. So, we booked Oceanway Studios in L.A., where he was working with Sam and Tonio. Oceanway has about five different studios in one building, so he could at least pop in and be involved. He'd come in from time to time and offer his opinion and suggestions. He had some great ideas; for example, the horn line on "Like You've Never Been Loved" was his idea. He's a very talented guy."

"Bono sang with you on "What's Happened To You". How did that come about?"

"Well, Bono came into town for a vacation, but he wanted to record this song he had written. It's a country song and I think he wrote it with Willie Nelson in mind. He tried recording it a few different times and couldn't get it to feel right with the musicians he was playing with. T-Bone heard the song and suggested to Bono that he have Jim and I play on it. It was during the mixing of the album, so Tom and Scott had gone home. So Bono came in and we did the song. It's a really beautiful song and it sounded quite great. After that he wanted to hear some of the things we were doing. He told us he was "a fan from afar". T-Bone wanted him to hear "Floating

Back". He liked it and wanted to hear more. We played "What's Happened To You" for him and at the time we didn't have the harmonies, only my lead vocal. So I said how about singing on this one and he said sure. So he and I sang the chorus and the la, la's, and the voices sounded really good together."

"Bono doesn't do a lot of harmony singing - his voice is so distinctive. But we wanted the voices to blend like a chorus to create a dreamy effect. And I knew he would be great on the la, la's because it's kind of an Irish melody. He was a very nice man, and it was good to meet him after all these years."

"Did he mention anything about when we can expect a new album from U2?"

"They're working on songs, but from what I gathered they are not going to put anything out until 1992. I think they want to get into different types of music, and if they make a new album now there wouldn't be a big enough difference from what they've done in the past and what they want to do in the future. I know Edge is listening to a lot of different kinds of guitar playing. He's just recently been influenced by many of the old blues players and country players, and I think they want to take their music in a different direction."

"I've loved them since 1980 and I know that they certainly weren't schooled in music."

"That's right. And I think that was a great value because if you're not schooled you come up with something really unique and your own, but it's also a limitation after a while. It's great for a time, but then you can't do much other than that. And if you're a serious musician, and I think they are serious musicians, you'll want to expand your possibilities."

"I read an article around the time the Sun City album was being recorded in which Bono told a story of how one night he was sitting around with Keith Richards and several other musicians playing songs they had been influenced by, songs they had loved in their early days. Bono said that he had felt so removed from that moment because he really had no major influences and no songs to sing from his past. He then decided he would learn all he could about the early music of the blues greats. He also said that he regretted not studying Gaelic, and becoming more proficient in his history through Irish folk songs."

"Yeah, we talked about that. To be able to continue and grow musically you've got to become a student of it, a fan, that sits and listens to it. You've got to study it with the diligence that you study anything else."

"There are some young artists who are going back to the early sounds and instruments. I really love the Lenny Kravitz record. I saw him live and he was incredible. He had these wonderful blues players with him. He's so 60's in his approach to music in the way you've been describing."

"Lenny Kravitz is really getting some wonderful sounds. He's thrown out the modern stuff and I respect that. And I think it's a consciousness. All of a sudden you wake up and go, "Wait a minute. All this modern stuff is weak.""

"Recording has gotten into the hands of computer people, people who get off on technology. They're not musicians, they don't have good ears. They're going more for efficiency and quantity of choices. Rock 'n Roll to me was always about primitive expression and limitation. Limitation in a good way. "Here's the instrument, make something out of it", rather than, "Here's a synthesizer with a thousand sounds, pick one you like.""

"The good things about the digital world, however, are CD's and digital audio tape. Once you record a song using real instruments on analog equipment, the reproduction onto digital is quite good. You lose some of the warmth of vinyl, but it does have great clarity."

"You play an old electric Gretsch hollow body guitar on this album and it sounds so good. Rather than having that short, twangy sound of the Telecaster, the Gretsch is still twangy, but it has more style and body. It sounds better than your Telecaster because it has more tonal value."

"That's right, and tonal value is what we've been talking about."

"You told me a little while back that Red Moon is the kind of record the Call would have made years ago, before you had to concern yourselves with what record companies want and what will sell."

"An interesting thing about Red Moon is that this is the first record that we've made in many years that I did not think one thought about whether it's commercial, whether it will sell. I was talking with our engineer, Jim Scott, and it simultaneously dawned on us that if we don't resurrect this approach, records are not going to be made this way anymore. It will be a forgotten art. We have to do it, because not enough people are doing it. But we're hoping it will create a consciousness. If we can at least get this through to the musicians, if we can get them to hear what we're talking about, I think they'll know it."

"I've always found it so interesting to learn something about each song on an album, such as who played what instrument and who sang on what songs. Tell me about the instrumentation and vocals for the songs on Red Moon."

"Well, on 'What's Happened To You' Jim played Mellotron and electric piano. Tom played guitar and solo. I played the piano and bass and Bono and I sang it. And, of course, Scott played the drums."

'Red Moon' is Jim on a grand piano. Scott played the drums with brushes. Jim and I and Scott sang the harmonies. I played a short bass solo. Jim played Chamberlin and Tom is on guitar."

'You Were There' has Tom playing the guitar solo, one of my all-time favorite solos. Jim played all the horn parts on saxophone. It was so great watching him do it, he's a one-man horn section."

"On 'Floating Back' Scott played drums and overdubbed maracas. Tom Played two tracks of backward guitar and made it work as a solo. I had some chorusing effect on the bass. And Jim and Scott and I sang the vocals. Jim also played an old ARP string ensemble."

"'On 'A Swim In The Ocean', Tom and I played guitars. Tom played slide guitar and I overdubbed another guitar. Jim played piano and overdubbed a clavinet. I changed the sound of my voice on this song. Scott played drums. I really love the feel of that song."

'Like You've Never Been Loved' has Jim on saxophones and electric piano through a Lesley speaker. Scott overdubbed wood blocks. Other than that, it's pretty much straight ahead. T-Bone sang background vocals with us."

'Family' was recorded basically like "Red Moon", bass, drums, guitar and grand piano. Jim then overdubbed Chamberlin and Mellotron. The pedal steel sound is the Chamberlin. Jim also played a KX-88 synthesizer, but we eliminated all those tones that are equated with that sizzly synth sound. We EQ'd it all out to create a flute-like organ sound, and ran it through a Lesley. It's Jim and Scott and me singing once again."

"'This Is Your Life' is the next one. Recording it was fun. We had a lot of our friends in the studio that night and everybody was screaming and yelling and having a good time. It was just the kind of energy we needed, a celebration-type song. I overdubbed a twelve-string guitar and Tom played the solo."

"On 'The Hand That Feeds You' Jim and I played piano. I played bass and percussion by using the piano as a drum. I wanted the song to sound kind of jazzy and dark.

Jim played saxophone just beautifully, it reminds me of Chet Baker. Tom played guitar and that's me on the short guitar solo. Jim also played organ. Scott played the tom tom drum pattern."

"The basic track for 'What a Day' was recorded during the Let The Day Begin sessions. Tom really liked the guitar, so I was busy writing words as I was singing them, Jim overdubbed a Chamberlin playing trombones."

"One last question, Michael. Much of music now is very short term-one trend after another. How have the Call maintained a philosophy of seriousness in their music, an attitude of credibility as a band, in today's musical climate?"

"We play according to a tradition. It's a tradition where music is not a fad, or a trend, or a style. It isn't theatre, or a beauty contest, or a fashion show. It can be used, or rather abused, to serve those things because music can't defend itself. But musicians can."

****

You have been "Notified."

Chapter Eleven:

The Tours / Concert Dates

(While it is impossible to have a complete list this is the best we could compile with the help from fans and the band. I apologize if we missed a show that you attended.)

Jan 21, 1982 - Crow's Nest, Santa Cruz, CA [billed as The Call – per Greg Freeman's records]

Feb 20, 1982 – The Call at Veteran's Hall, Santa Cruz, CA ["official" live debut as The Call, AFAIK – Greg Freeman]

Mar 22, 1982 – The Call at Crow's Nest, Santa Cruz CA

April 30, 1982 – The Call at Country Club, Reseda, CA (opening for Pete Shelley)

May 1, 1982 – The Call at Perkins Palace, Pasadena, CA (opening for Pete Shelley)

May 7th, 1982 - The Call at The Old Waldorf, San Francisco, CA, USA

May 8, 1982 – The Call at Campbell Hall, UC Santa Barbara, Santa Barbara, CA (opening for Split Enz)

May 14, 1982 – The Call at Orange Pavilion, National Orange Show, San Bernardino, CA (opening for Joan Jett and the Blackhearts)

May 17th, 1982 - The Call at Bakersfield Memorial Auditorium, Bakersfield, CA w/ Joan Jett

*Sep 16, 1982 - The Oz, Monterey, CA (Cancelled?)

Oct 29, 1982 – The Call at The Beat, Santa Cruz, CA

Nov 12, 1982 – The Call at Sacramento (opening for Translator)

Nov 13th, 1982 - The Call at Keystone Berkeley, Berkeley, CA, USA (opening for Translator)

Nov 14th, 1982 - The Call at Keystone, Palo Alto, CA, USA (opening for Translator)

Nov 16, 1982 – The Call at Modesto (opening for Translator)

Nov 20th, 1982 - The Call at Kabuki Theater, San Francisco, CA, USA (opening for Iggy Pop)

Nov 26th, 1982 - The Call at Berkeley Square, Berkeley, CA

Dec 3, 1982 – The Call at Lord Beaverbrooks, Sacramento, CA

Dec 17, 1982 – The Call at Berkeley Square, Berkeley, CA (opening for 3 O'Clock)

Feb 8th, 1983 - The Call at Keystone, Palo Alto, CA, USA

Feb 11th, 1983 - The Call at Berkeley Square, Berkeley, CA, USA

Feb 12th, 1983 - The Call at Beaverbrook's North, Sacramento, CA, USA

Feb 26th, 1983 - The Call at The Old Waldorf, San Francisco, CA, USA

*Mar 4, 1983 - The Spirit, San Diego, CA (Cancelled?)

Mar 7th, 1983 - Club Lingerie w/ Shadow Minstrels

Mar 8th, 1983 - The Call at Graham Central Station, Phoenix, AZ, USA

Mar 9, 1983 – The Call at 321, Santa Monica, CA

Mar 10, 1983 – The Call at Catalyst, Santa Cruz, CA

*Mar 11, 1983 - Star Palace, Fresno, CA (Cancelled?)

*Mar 25, 1983 - Buena Park, CA (with Felony) (Cancelled?)

*Mar 26, 1983 - Costa Mesa, CA (Cancelled?)

*Mar 27, 1983 - Long Beach, CA (Cancelled?)

Apr 7th, 1983 - The Call at Galactica 2000, Sacramento, CA, USA

Apr 9, 1983 – The Call at Country Club, Reseda, CA

Apr 12, 1983 – The Call at Kabuki Theater, San Francisco, CA (opening for Simple Minds)

Apr 13, 1983 – The Call at Kabuki Theater, San Francisco, CA (opening for Simple Minds)

Apr 15, 1983 – The Call at Beverly Theater, Los Angeles, CA (opening for Simple Minds)

Apr 16, 1983 – The Call at Perkins Palace, Pasadena, CA (opening for Simple Minds)

*Apr 18, 1983 - UCSD

*Apr 19, 1983 – Phoenix (Cancelled?)

Apr 22, 1983 – The Call at Tower Theatre, Houston, TX (opening for Simple Minds)

*Apr 23, 1983 – Austin (Cancelled?)

Apr 24, 1983 – The Call at Agora Ballroom, Dallas, TX (opening for Simple Minds)

May 2, 1983 – The Call at Rainbow, Denver CO

May 6th, 1983 - The Call at 688 Club Atlanta, GA USA

May 7, 1983 – The Call at The Pier, Raleigh, NC

May 8, 1983 – The Call at Much More, Richmond, VA

May 10, 1983 – The Call at Ripley's, Philadelphia, PA

May 11, 1983 – The Call at Seagull Inn, Essex, Baltimore, MD

May 11th, 1983 – The Call at Le Palladium, Montreal, QC, Canada [Per Greg Freeman one of these May 11th incorrect]

May 13, 1983 – The Call at Wax Museum, Washington, DC

May 14, 1983 – The Call at Metrone, Harrisburg, PA

May 15th, 1983 - The Call at My Father's Place (Roslyn, NY)

May 17, 1983 – The Call at Toad's Place, New Haven, CT

May 18th, 1983 - The Call at The Paradise Boston, MA USA

May 20th, 1983 – The Call at The Ritz (NY, NY)

May 21, 1983 – The Call at Agora, Hartford, CT

May 22, 1983 – The Call at Blondie's, Atlantic City, NJ

May 24, 1983 – The Call at Lost Horizon, Syracuse, NY

May 25, 1983 – The Call at Casablanca, Rochester, NY

Mar 26, 1983 – The Call at Continental, Buffalo, NY

May 28th, 1983 – The Call at Saint Andrew's Hall, Detroit, MI, USA

May 31, 1983 – The Call at Fantasy, Lakewood, OH

June 2nd, 1983 – The Call at Park West (322 W. Armitage), Chicago, IL

June 4th, 1983 – The Call at Cantrell's Nashville, TN USA

June 7, 1983 – The Call at Rumors, Decatur, GA

June 9, 1983 – The Call at Playground South, Jacksonville, FL

June 10, 1983 – The Call at Rockin' Crown, Tampa, FL

June 11th, 1983 – The Call at Summers on the Beach – Fort Lauderdale, FL USA

June 12, 1983 – The Call at Plaza Hotel, Ft. Lauderdale, FL

June 13, 1983 – The Call at Destin, FL

June 15, 1983 – The Call at Bell Theater, Univ. of Alabama, Birmingham, AL

June 16, 1983 – The Call at Madison House, Memphis, TN

June 17, 1983 – The Call at Hall of Industry, Arkansas State Fairgrounds, Little Rock, AR (with Stevie Ray Vaughan)

June 19, 1983 – The Call at The Bowery, Oklahoma City, OK

June 21, 1983 – The Call at 6th Street Live, Austin, TX

June 22nd, 1983 - The Call at Numbers, Houston, TX, USA

June 23, 1983 – The Call at Daddy's, San Antonio, TX

June 24th, 1983 - The Call at Tango, Dallas, TX, USA

June 27, 1983 – The Call at Graham Central Station, Albuquerque, NM

June 28, 1983 – The Call at Rox-Z, Lubbock, TX

June 30, 1983 – The Call at PanAmerican Center, Las Cruces, NM

July 3, 1983 – The Call at River Raft Race, El Paso, TX

July 4th, 1983 The Call at Midnight Express, Tucson, AZ, USA

July 5, 1983 – The Call at Gold Rush, Tempe, AZ

July 7, 1983 – The Call at Country Club, Reseda, CA

July 8, 1983 – The Call at Magic Mountain, Valencia, CA

July 9, 1983 – The Call at Golden Bear, Huntington Beach, CA

*July 15th, 1983 - The Call at Keystone, Palo Alto, CA, USA (Peter Gabriel) [possibly wrong date? We were in PA on this day getting ready for the Peter Gabriel tour, May not have happened – Greg Freeman]

July 16th, 1983 - The Call at Agora Ballroom, West Hartford, CT, USA (Peter Gabriel)

July 18, 1983 - The Call at CNE Bandshell, Toronto, ONT (Peter Gabriel)

July 20th, 1983 - The Call at Place des Nations, Montreal, QC, Canada (Peter Gabriel)

July 22, 1983 – The Call at Garden State Arts Center, Holmdel, NJ (Peter Gabriel)

July 23rd, 1983 - The Call at Mann Music Center, Philadelphia, PA, USA (Peter Gabriel)

July 24th, 1983 - The Call at Saratoga Performing Arts Center, Saratoga Springs, NY, USA (Peter Gabriel)

July 27, 1983 – The Call at E.M. Loew's Theatre, Worcester, MA (Peter Gabriel)

July 29, 1983 – The Call at Forest Hills Tennis Stadium, Forest Hills, NY (Peter Gabriel)

July 30, 1983 – The Call at Merriweather Post Pavilion, Columbia, MD (Peter Gabriel)

July 31, 1983 – The Call at Pine Knob Theatre, Pine Knob, MI (Peter Gabriel)

Aug 2nd, 1983 - The Call at Poplar Creek Music Theater, Hoffman Estates, IL, USA (Peter Gabriel)

Aug 3, 1983 – The Call at Blossom Music Center, Cuyahoga Falls, OH (Peter Gabriel)

Aug 10, 1983 – The Call at Paramount Theatre, Seattle, WA (Peter Gabriel)

Aug 12th, 1983 - The Call at William Randolph Hearst Greek Theatre, Berkeley, CA, USA (Peter Gabriel)

Aug 13th, 1983 - The Call at William Randolph Hearst Greek Theatre, Berkeley, CA, USA (Peter Gabriel)

Aug 16, 1983 – The Call at Greek Theatre, Los Angeles, CA (Peter Gabriel)

Aug 17, 1983 – The Call at Greek Theatre, Los Angeles, CA (Peter Gabriel) *[my last show! – Greg Freeman]*

Oct 1st, 1983 – The Call – Hamburg, Gmy (Peter Gabriel)

Oct 4th, 1983 – The Call – Frankfurt, Gmy (Peter Gabriel)

Oct 6th, 1983 – The Call – Munich, Gmy (Peter Gabriel)

Oct 7th, 1983 – The Call – Vienna, Austria (Peter Gabriel)

Oct 10th, 1983 – The Call – Hannover - (Peter Gabriel)

Oct 11th, 1983 – The Call – Berlin, Gmy (Peter Gabriel)

Oct 12th, 1983 - The Call at Sporthalle, Böblingen, (Stuttgart) Germany (Peter Gabriel)

Oct 14th, 1983 – The Call – Geneva, Switzerland (Peter Gabriel)

Oct 15th, 1983 – The Call – Clermont-Ferrand, France (Peter Gabriel)

Oct 16th, 1983 – The Call – Toulousse, France (Peter Gabriel)

Oct 17th, 1983 – The Call – Bordeaux, France (Peter Gabriel)

Oct 18th, 1983 – The Call – Avignon, France (Peter Gabriel)

Oct 20th, 1983 – The Call – Grenoble, France (Peter Gabriel)

Oct 21st, 1983 – The Call – Dijon, France (Peter Gabriel)

Oct 22nd, 1983 – The Call – Strausbourg, France (Peter Gabriel)

Oct 24th, 1983 – The Call – Lille, France (Peter Gabriel)

Oct 25th, 1983 – The Call – Paris, France (Peter Gabriel)

Oct 27th, 1983 – The Call – Nantes, France (Peter Gabriel)

Oct 28th, 1983 - The Call at Petite Salle de Penfeld, Brest, France (Peter Gabriel)

Nov 8th, 1983 - The Call at The Venue (Auto De Fe')

Nov 9th, 1983 - *The Call*, BBC *Paris* Studios , *London*

April 5th, 1984 - The Call at Keystone Berkeley, Berkeley, CA, USA

April 6th, 1984 - The Call at The Stone, San Francisco, CA, USA

July 12th, 1984 - The Call at The Stone, San Francisco, CA, USA

July 14th, 1984 - The Call at Keystone, Palo Alto, CA, USA

Aug 16th, 1984 - The Call at Greek Theatre, Los Angeles, CA, USA

Aug 20th, 1984 - The Call at Greek Theatre, Los Angeles, CA, USA

Sept 10th, 1984 - The Call at The I-Beam, San Francisco, CA, USA

Mar 9th, 1985 - The Call at Berkeley Square, Berkeley, CA, USA

Aug 24th, 1985 - The Call at Gaslamp Quarter, San Diego, CA, USA

Feb 21st, 1986 – The Call – Santa Cruz, CA – Catalyst

Feb 22nd, 1986 – The Call – San Jose, CA – Cabaret

Mar 1st, 1986 - The Call at Berkeley Square, Berkeley, CA, USA

Mar 3rd, 1986 – The Call – Santa Rosa, CA – Cotati Cabaret

Mar 4th, 1986 - The Call at Oasis, San Francisco, CA, USA

Mar 7th, 1986 - The Call at New George's, San Rafael, CA

Mar 25th, 1986 - The Call at James L. Knight Center, Miami, FL, USA (Simple Minds)

Mar 26th, 1986 – The Call – Tampa, FL – Curtis Hixon Hall (Simple Minds Tour)

March 28th, 1986 – The Call – Charleston, SC – Galliard Auditorium (Simple Minds Tour)

Mar 29th, 1986 – The Call at Miami Knight Center – Miami, FL USA (Simple Minds)

Mar 31st, 1986 – The Call – Memphis, TN – Orpheum Theatre (Simple Minds)

Apr 1st, 1986 – The Call – Nashville, TN – Vanderbilt University (Simple Minds)

Apr 3rd, 1986 - The Call at Cajun dome, Lafayette, LA, USA (Simple Minds)

Apr 4th, 1986 - The Call at Lakefront Arena – New Orleans, LA USA (Simple Minds)

Apr 5th, 1986 - The Call at Southern Star Amphitheatre, Houston, TX, USA (Simple Minds)

Apr 7th, 1986 – The Call – Austin, TX (Simple Minds)

Apr 8th, 1986 – The Call – San Antonio, TX – Majestic Theatre (Simple Minds)

Apr 9th, 1986 - The Call at Bronco Bowl, Dallas, TX, USA (Simple Minds)

Apr 11th, 1986 – The Call – Lacruzes, TX – Pan Am Center (Simple Minds Tour)

Apr 12th, 1986 - The Call at McKale Memorial Center, Tucson, AZ, USA (Simple Minds)

Apr 13th, 1986 – Phoenix, AZ – Mesa Amphitheatre (Simple Minds Tour)

Apr 15th, 1986 - The Call at Greek Theatre, Los Angeles, CA, USA (Simple Minds)

Apr 16th, 1986 - The Call at Greek Theatre (Simple Minds)

Apr 19th, 1986 - The Call at SDSU Open Air Theatre, San Diego State Univ., CA, USA (Simple Minds)

Apr 22nd, 1986 - The Call Pacific Amphitheatre – Costa Mesa, CA USA (Simple Minds)

Apr 23rd, 1986 - The Call at UC Santa Barbara Events Center, Isla Vista, CA, USA (Simple Minds)

Apr 25th, 1986 – The Call – Berkeley, CA – Greek Theatre (Simple Minds Tour)

Apr 26th, 1986 - The Call at William Randolph Hearst Greek Theatre, Berkeley, CA, USA (Simple Minds)

Apr 27th, 1986 - The Call at Recreation Hall, Davis, CA, USA (Simple Minds)

Apr 29th, 1986 - The Call at Pacific Coliseum, Vancouver, BC, Canada (Simple Minds)

May 1st, 1986 - The Call at Northlands Coliseum, Edmonton, AB, Canada (Simple Minds)

May 2nd, 1986 – The Call – Edmonton, Canada (Simple Minds Tour)

May 3rd, 1986 - The Call at Olympic Saddledome, Calgary, AB, Canada (Simple Minds)

May 5th, 1986 – The Call – Winnipeg, Canada (Simple Minds Tour)

May 6th, 1986 - The Call at Winnipeg Arena, Winnipeg, MB, Canada (Simple Minds)

May 9th, 1986 - The Call at Starlight Theater, Kansas City, MO, USA (Simple Minds)

May 10th, 1986 – The Call – St. Louis, MO – Fox Theatre (Simple Minds Tour)

May 12th, 1986 - The Call at Veterans Memorial Auditorium, Columbus, OH, USA(Simple Minds)

May 13th, 1986 - The Call at Richfield Coliseum, Richfield, OH, USA (Simple Minds)

May 15th, 1986 – Ontario, Canada (Simple Minds)

May 16th, 1986 - The Call at Ottawa Civic Centre, Ottawa, ON, Canada (Simple Minds)

May 17th, 1986 - The Call at Forum de Montréal, Montreal, QC, Canada (Simple Minds)

May 19th, 1986 - The Call at Cumberland Co. Civic Center – Portland Maine USA (Simple Minds)

May 20th, 1986 – The Call – Troy, NY – RPI Field House (Simple Minds Tour)

May 22nd, 1986 – Rochester, NY (Simple Minds Tour)

May 23rd, 1986 - The Call at New Haven Coliseum – New Haven, CT USA (Simple Minds)

May 24th, 1986 - The Call at Stabler Arena – Bethlehem, PA USA (Simple Minds)

May 27th, 1986 - The Call at Radio City Music Hall, NY – NY, USA (Simple Minds)

May 28th, 1986 - The Call at Radio City Music Hall, New York, NY, USA (Simple Minds)

May 29th, 1986 - The Call at The Ritz (NY, NY)

June 5th, 1986 - The Call at Paradise Rock Club (Boston, MA) (Wrote: " I Don't Wanna" the night before)

June 7th, 1986 - The Call at Agora Ballroom – West Hartford, CT USA

June 18th, 1986 - The Call at The Ritz, Roseville, MI, USA

June 20th, 1986 - The Call at Alpine Valley Music Theatre – East Troy, WI USA (ZZ Top)

June 21st, 1986 - The Call at Alpine Valley Music Theatre – East Troy, WI USA (ZZ Top)

June 22nd, 1986 - The Call at Roberts Municipal Stadium – Evansville, IN USA (ZZ Top)

June 28th, 1986 - The Call at Legend Valley, Thornville, OH, USA (ZZ Top)

Aug 1st, 1986 - The Call at Omni Club, Oakland, CA, USA

Aug 2nd, 1986 - The Call at Party on the Bay, San Francisco, CA, USA

Aug 4th, 1986 - The Call at Wolfgang's, San Francisco, CA, USA

Aug 5th, 1986 - The Call at One Step Beyond, Santa Clara, CA, USA

Aug 30th, 1986 - The Call at East Village, San Diego, CA, USA

Oct 10th, 1986 - The Call at Melbourne Auditorium, Melbourne, FL, USA

July 26th, 1987 - The Call at Bob Carr Performing Arts Center – Orlando, FL USA (Psychedelic Furs)

July 28th, 1987 - The Call at Park Center, Charlotte, NC

July 31st, 1987 - The Call at Fox Theater, Atlanta, GA

Aug 8th, 1987 - The Call at Syria Mosque, Pittsburgh, PA, USA (Psychedelic Furs)

Aug 14th, 1987 - The Call at Sandstone Amphitheater, Bonner Springs, KS, USA

Aug 19th, 1987 - The Call at Orpheum Theatre, Minneapolis, MN, USA

Aug 20th, 1987 - The Call at Riverside Theatre – Milwaukee, WI, USA (Psychedelic Furs)

Aug 21st, 1987 - The Call at Riverside Theater, Milwaukee, WI, USA (Psychedelic Furs)

Aug 28th, 1987 - The Call at William Randolph Hearst Greek Theatre, Berkeley, CA, USA (Psychedelic Furs)

Aug 30th, 1987 - The Call at Santa Cruz Civic Auditorium, Santa Cruz, CA, USA (Psychedelic Furs)

Sept 3rd, 1987 – The Call – London, Town & Country Club

Sept 5th, 1987 – The Call – Amsterdam – Paradiso

Sept 7th, 1987 – The Call – Hamburg - Markethalle

Sept 8th, 1987 - The Call at Tor 3, Düsseldorf, Germany

Sept 10th, 1987 – The Call – Munich, Germany

Sept 11th, 1987 – The Call – Zurich, Switzerland

Sept 13th, 1987 – The Call – Reggio Emilia – Reggio Festival - Italy

Sept 15th, 1987 - The Call at Rolling Stone, Milan, Italy

Sept 17th, 1987 - The Call at La Cigale, Paris, France

Sept 20th, 1987 – The Call – Oklahoma City – Fritzies

Sept 21st, 1987 – The Call – Dallas Alley

Sept 22nd, 1987 – The Call – Houston, TX – Xcess

Sept 23rd, 1987 – The Call – Austin, TX – The Backroom

Sept 25th, 1987 – The Call – Phoenix, AZ

Sept 26th, 1987 – The Call – San Juan Cap – Coach House

Sept 27th, 1987 – The Call – San Diego, CA – Bachanal

Sept 28th, 1987 – The Call – Los Angeles, CA – Roxy

Sept 30th, 1987 – The Call – Santa Clara, CA – 1 Step Beyond

Oct 2nd, 1987 - The Call at Trocadero Transfer (San Francisco, CA) w/ Tonio K

Jan 22nd, 1988 – The Call – San Juan Cap – Coach House

Jan 23rd, 1988 – The Call – Phoenix / Tempe - Chuys

Jan 24th, 1988 - The Call at Tucson Gardens, Tucson, AZ

Jan 25th, 1988 - The Call – Albuquerque, NM - L'Parc

Jan 29th, 1988 – The Call – Norman, OK – Ozone Club

Jan 30th, 1988 - The Call at Cain's Ballroom, Tulsa, OK

Feb 1st, 1988 – The Call – Dallas Alley – Boiler Room

Feb 2nd, 1988 – The Call – San Antonio, TX – Rockwave

Feb 3rd, 1988 – The Call – Houston, TX – NRG Club

Feb 4th, 1988 – The Call – Austin, TX – Backroom

Feb 6th, 1988 – The Call – Phoenix, AZ – Chuys

Feb 7th, 1988 - The Call – San Diego, CA – Bachanal

May 8th, 1988 - The Call at Bogart's, Long Beach, CA USA

June 1st, 1988 – The Call – Neptune – Broadway

June 2nd, 1988 – The Call – Maxime

June 3rd, 1988 – The Call – Park Hotel

June 4th, 1988 - The Call at De Røde Sjøhus - Stavanger, Norway

June 5th, 1988 – The Call – Caledonien

June 6th, 1988 – The Call – Daily News

June 8th, 1988 – The Call – Arbeiderforeninga

June 9th, 1988 – The Call – Studentersamfundet

June 10th, 1988 – The Call – Alta Hotel

June 11th, 1988 – The Call – Ungdommens Hus, Denmark

June 12th, 1988 – The Call – Sinus

June 14th, 1988 – The Call – Messeparken

June 15th, 1988 – The Call – Sardine's

June 17th, 1988 – The Call - Copehagen – Alexandra

June 18th, 1988 – The Call – Draupner

June 19th, 1988 – The Call – Club Melody

Aug 6th, 1988 - The Call at Municipal Stadium, San Jose, CA, USA

Sept 26th, 1988 - The Call at Anderson's Fifth Estate, Scottsdale, AZ, USA

Oct 20th, 1988 - The Call at Graffiti – Pittsburgh, PA USA

Oct 23rd, 1988 - The Call at Toad's Place – New Haven, CT, USA

July 18th, 1989 – The Call – Sacramento – Crest Theatre

July 19th, 1989 – The Call – San Jose, CA – One Step Beyond

July 21st, 1989 – The Call – Santa Cruz, CA - Catalyst

July 22nd, 1989 - The Call at The Fillmore, San Francisco, CA, USA

July 23rd, 1989 - The Call at Raven Theater, Healdsburg, CA, USA

July 25th, 1989 – The Call – San Juan, CA – Coach House

July 26th, 1989 – The Call – Los Angeles, CA – Palace

July 28th, 1989 – The Call – San Diego, CA – Theatre

July 29th, 1989 – The Call – Ventura, CA – Ventura Thtr

July 30th, 1989 – The Call – Tempe, AZ – After the Gold Rush

Aug 1st, 1989 – The Call – Albuquerque, NM – The Beach

Aug 3rd, 1989 – The Call – Houston, TX – Rockefellers

Aug 4th, 1989 – The Call - Dallas, TX – Tommy's

Aug 5th, 1989 - The Call at Oklahoma State Fairgrounds, Oklahoma City, OK, USA

Aug 7th, 1989 – The Call – Tulsa, OK

Aug 8th, 1989 - The Call at London's, Kansas City, MO

Aug 10th, 1989 – The Call – St. Louis, MO – Mississippi Nights

Aug 11th, 1989 – The Call – Springfield, MO – Regency

Aug 12th, 1989 – The Call – Columbia, MO – Blue Note

Aug 14th, 1989 – The Call – Omaha, NB

Aug 15th, 1989 – The Call – Minneapolois, MN – Cabooze

Aug 16th, 1989 – The Call – Madison, WS – Headliner Club

Aug 17th, 1989 – The Call – Chicago, IL – Cabaret Metro

Aug 22nd, 1989 - The Call at The Ritz, Roseville, MI, USA

Sept 9th, 1989 - The Call at Berklee Performance Center, Boston, MA, USA

Sept 14th, 1989 - The Call at Toad's Place, New Haven, CT, USA

Sept 18th, 1989 - The Call at The Lost Horizon, Syracuse, NY, USA

Sept 24th, 1989 - The Call at Lackawanna County Stadium, Moosic, PA, USA

Oct 14th, 1989 - The Call at The Boathouse, Norfolk, VA

Nov 8th, 1989 – The Call – Lancaster, PA – Chameleon

Nov 11th, 1989 – The Call – Kansas City, MO – Wm Jewel

Nov 13th, 1989 – The Call – Lexington, KY – Breedings

Nov 14th, 1989 – The Call – Bloomington, IN – Stardust

Nov 15th, 1989 – The Call – Indianapolis, IN – Vogue

Nov 17th, 1989 – The Call – Chicago – Cabaret Metro

Nov 18th, 1989 - The Call at Newport Music Hall, Columbus, OH, USA

Nov 20th, 1989 – The Call – Ann Arbor, MI - Nectarine

Nov 21st, 1989 - The Call at The PLC, Madison, WI, USA

Nov 22nd, 1989 – The Call – Omaha, NE – Ranch Bowl

Nov 24th, 1989 – The Call – Springfield, MO – Regency

Nov 25th, 1989 – The Call – Tulsa, OK – Cain's Ballroom

Nov 27th, 1989 – The Call – Houston, TX - Rockefellers

Nov 29th, 1989 – The Call at Liberty Lunch, Austin, TX

Nov 30th, 1989 - The Call at Arcadia Theatre, Dallas, TX

Dec 1st, 1989 – The Call – Wichita, KS – Coyote Club

Dec 3rd, 1989 – The Call – Boulder, CO – Univ. of CO

Dec 4th, 1989 – The Call – Albuquerque, NM – Confetti's

Dec 5th, 1989 – The Call – Tucson, AZ – Univ. of AZ

Dec 6th, 1989 – The Call – Phoenix, AZ – Celebrity Thtr

Dec 9th, 1989 – The Call – San Diego, CA - Bacchanal

Dec 10th, 1989 - The Call at KROQ Christmas Bash! 1989 – Universal Amphitheatre – Universal City, CA

Dec 12th, 1989 – The Call – San Francisco, CA – Stone

Dec 14th, 1989 - The Call at Starry Night, Portland, OR, USA

Dec 16th, 1989 – The Call – Vancouver, BC

Dec 17th, 1989 – The Call – Santa Cruz, CA - Catalyst

Dec 18th, 1989 – The Call – Santa Clara – 1 Step Beyond

Dec 19th, 1989 - The Call at Omni Club, Oakland, CA, USA

May 25th, 1990 - The Call at Concord Pavilion, Concord, CA, USA

May 26th, 1990 - The Call at Santa Barbara Bowl, Santa Barbara, CA, USA

May 27th, 1990 - The Call at Irvine Meadows Amphitheatre, Irvine, CA, USA

Aug 25th, 1990 - The Call at Greenbelt 1990 - Castle Ashby House, Castle Ashby, England

Oct 17th, 1990 - The Call at The Coach House, San Juan Capistrano, CA, USA

Oct 19th, 1990 - The Call at The Hop Riverside Concert Club, Riverside, CA, USA

Oct 26th, 1990 - The Call at Boston Garden, Boston, MA

Oct 27th, 1990 – The Call – Poughkeepsie, NY – Chance

Oct 28th, 1990 – The Call – New Haven, CT – Toads

Oct 29th, 1990 – The Call – Washington D.C. – Bayou

Oct 31st, 1990 – The Call – Baltimore, MD – Hammerjacks

Nov 1st, 1990 - The Call at The Bottom Line, New York, NY, USA

Nov 2nd, 1989 – The Call – Ardmore, PA – 23rd St. E.

Nov 3rd, 1990 – The Call – Norfolk, VA – Boathouse

Nov 5th, 1990 – The Call – Lancaster, PA – Chameleon

Nov 7th, 1990 – The Call – Cleveland, OH – Empire Rm

Nov 8th, 1990 – The Call – Columbus, OH – Newport MH

Nov 9th, 1990 – The Call – Detroit – Ritz

Nov 10th, 1990 – The Call – Indianapolis, IN – Ritz

Nov 12th, 1990 – The Call – Cincinnati, OH – Bogart's

Nov 13th, 1990 – The Call – Grand Rapids, MI – Club Eastbrook

Nov 15th, 1990 – The Call – Chicago, IL – The Vic

Nov 16th, 1990 – The Call – Milwaukee, WS – Presidents

Nov 17th, 1990 – The Call – Minneapolis – First Avenue

Nov 18th, 1990 - The Call at Barrymore Theatre, Madison, WI, USA

Nov 19th, 1990 – The Call – Champaign, IL – Mabel's

Nov 21st, 1990 – The Call – Omaha, NE – Peony Park

Nov 22nd, 1990 - The Call at The Shadow, Kansas City, MO, USA

Nov 23rd, 1990 – The Call – Springfield, MO – Regency

Nov 24th, 1990 – The Call – Tulsa, OK – Cain's Ballroom

Nov 25th, 1990 – The Call – Norman, OK – The Rome

Nov 27th, 1990 – The Call at Rockefeller's Houston, TX

Nov 28th, 1990 – The Call – San Antonio, TX - Rockwave

Nov 29th, 1990 - The Call at Sneakers, Kansas City, MO

Nov 30th, 1990 – The Call – Dallas, TX – Metroplex

Dec 3rd, 1990 – The Call – Tempe, AZ – After the Gold

Dec 4th, 1990 - The Call at Calamity Jayne's Nashville Nevada, Las Vegas, NV, USA

Dec 5th, 1990 – San Diego, CA – The Bacchanal

Dec 7th, 1990 - The Call at Ventura Concert Theatre, Ventura, CA, USA

Dec 8th, 1990 - The Call at The Coach House, San Juan Capistrano, CA, USA

Dec 9th, 1990 - The Call at The Coach House, San Juan Capistrano, CA, USA

Dec 10th, 1990 - The Call at The Roxy, West Hollywood

Dec 11th, 1990 - The Call at Bogart's, Long Beach, CA

Dec 13th, 1990 - The Call at Slim's, San Francisco, CA

Dec 14th, 1990 - The Call at The Catalyst, Santa Cruz, CA

Dec 15th, 1990 – The Call – San Jose, CA - Cabaret

Oct 24th, 1992 - The Call at Nightstage, Cambridge, MA

June 4th, 1994 - The Call at KTCL's Big Adventure 1994 - Fiddler's Green, Greenwood Village, CO, USA

****

July 2nd, 1994 – Aug 9th, 1994 – Michael Been Tour Shows "On the Verge of a Nervous Breakthrough"

- **Total of 30 – Michael Been "Solo" Shows**

****

July 6th, 1994 - The Call at The Vogue, Indianapolis, IN

July 2nd, 1997 - The Call at Cornerstone 1997 - Cornerstone Farm, Bushnell, IL, USA

Aug 6th, 1997 - The Call at Boston Common, Boston, MA

Aug 29th, 1997 – The Call at Madison's – Seattle

Sept 21st, 1997 - The Call at The Coach House, San Juan Capistrano, CA, USA

Oct 5th, 1997 - The Call at Steamroller Blues – Tulsa, OK

March 14th, 1998 – The Call at Madison's – Seattle

March 15th, 1998 – The Call at Madison's – Seattle

May 4th, 1998 - The Call at The Bottom Line, NY,NY

July 4th, 1998 - The Call at Cornerstone 1998

July 17th, 1999 – The Call – Soul Festival - MA

July 18th, 1999 – The Call – Soul Festival - MA

April 18th, 2013 - The Call at Slim's, San Francisco, CA (Featuring Robert Been on Vocals & Bass)

April 19th, 2013 - The Call at Troubadour, West Hollywood, CA (Featuring Robert Been on Vocals & Bass)

Apr 22nd, 2017 - The Call at Siberia (New Orleans, LA) w/ guest vocalist Michael Divita, Ray Ganucheau & J.D. Buhl

Apr 20th, 2018 - Scott Musick & Tom Ferrier (of The Call) w/ guest vocalist Michael Divita at Cain's Ballroom – Tulsa, OK (Benefit Show – Played some Call songs)

****

Courtesy of Mark Brittell collection

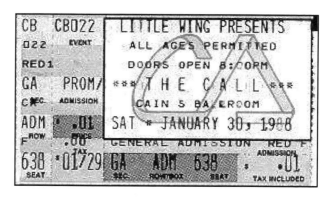

(For me this Cain's show was one of the most memorable and amazing concerts I have ever been to. They were at the top of their game and tore the ole place down!)

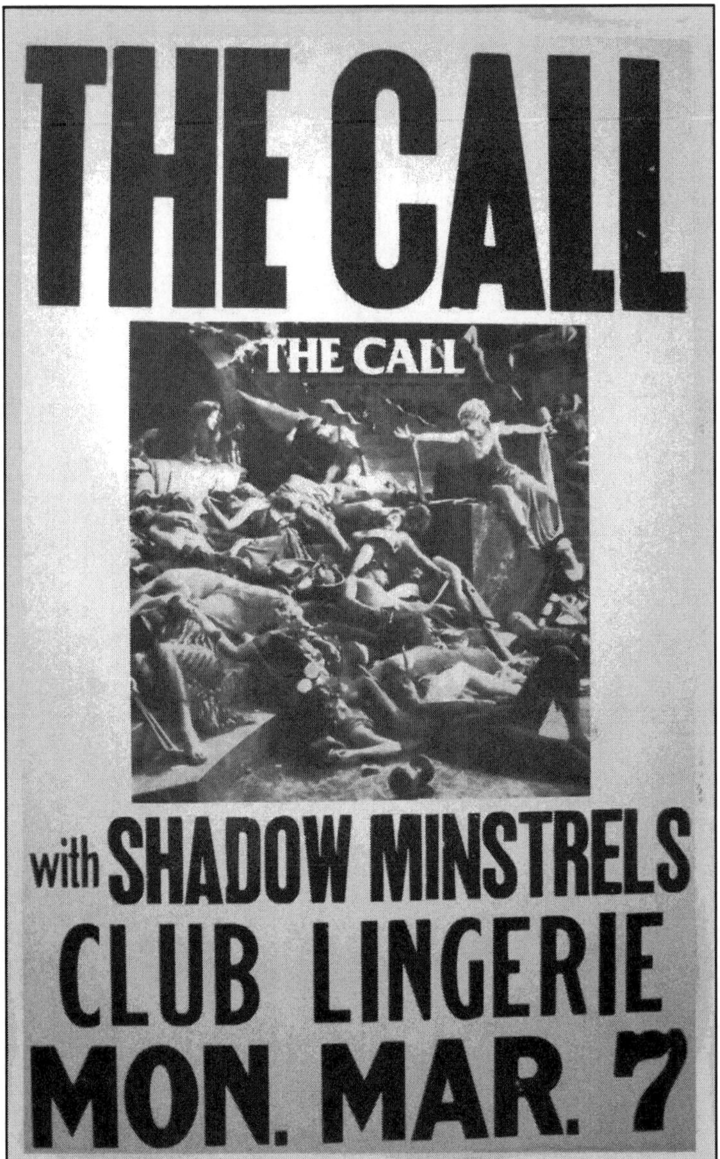

THE CALL
THE CALL
with SHADOW MINSTRELS
CLUB LINGERIE
MON. MAR. 7

Ticket courtesy of Eric Feil – March 14, 1998 show

Ticket courtesy of Eric Feil – March 15, 1998 show

Autographs on back of ticket courtesy Eric Feil.

Ticket courtesy of Eric Feil – August 29, 1997 show

Oct 2nd, 1987 - The Call at Trocadero Transfer
(San Francisco, CA) w/ Tonio K

Newspaper ad from 1983 – Club Lingerie - Sunset Blvd

Mar 7th, 1983 - Club Lingerie w/ Shadow Minstrels

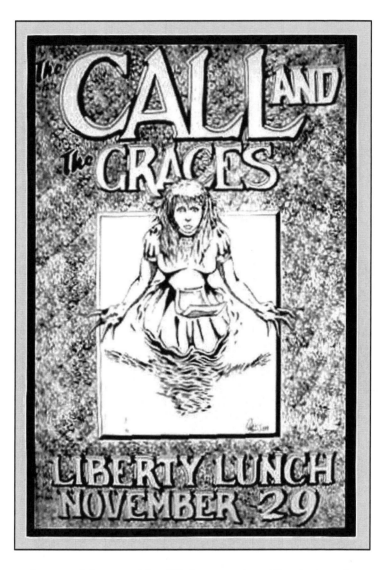

A very elaborate 11 x 17 show poster. Liberty Lunch
Austin, TX, November 29th, 1989

Courtesy Knoel & Wendy Honn collection

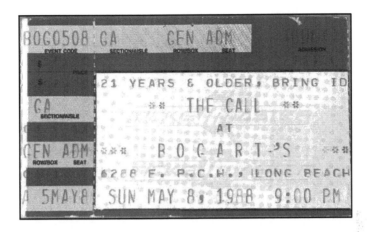

The Call - $15.00 at Bogart's May 8th, 1988

The Call - $10.00 at Wolfgang's Aug 4th, 1986

The Call w/ Psychedelic Furs - $21.75 Aug 20th, 1987

Advertisement – The Call at The Venue Nov 8th, 1983

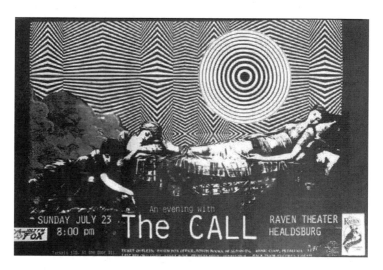

July 23rd, 1989 - The Call - Raven Theater, Healdsburg, CA

cavallo, ruffalo & fargnoli

MANAGEMENT

THE CALL-PETER GABRIEL EUROPEAN TOUR

DATE:	NIGHTS:	HOTEL:	CITY:	PHONE NO.:
OCT. 1	3	PLAZA	HAMBURG	35.20.35
OCT. 4	2	PLAZA	FRANKFURT	68.00.11
OCT. 6	1	PENTA	MUNICH	448.55.55
OCT. 7	3	HILTON	VIENNA	75.26.52
OCT. 10	1	INTERCONTINENTAL	HANNOVER	16.911
OCT. 11	1	INTERCONTINENTAL	BERLIN	26.02.01
OCT. 12	2	ROYAL	STUTTGART	62.50.50
OCT. 14	1	BRISTOL	GENEVA	32.44.00
OCT. 15	1	FRANTEL	CLERMONT-FERRAND	93.05.75
OCT. 16	1	FRANTEL	TOULOUSSE	21.21.75
OCT. 17	1	TERMINUS	BORDEAUX	92.71.58
OCT. 18	2	EUROPE	AVIGNON	32.66.92
OCT. 20	1	LES DIGUIERES	GRENOBLE	96.55.36
OCT. 21	1	FRANTEL	DIJON	72.31.13
OCT. 22	2	SOFITEL	STRAUSBOURG	32.99.30
OCT. 24	1	CARLTON	LILLE	52.24.11
OCT. 25	2	HOLIDAY INN	PARIS	53.37.463
OCT. 27	1	FRANTEL	NANTES	47.10.58
OCT. 28	1	OCEANIA	BREST	30.66.66

***EUROPEAN HOTELS - ALL ACCOMODATIONS ARE 4 TWINS AND 1 SINGLE.

THIS SCHEDULE AS OF SEPTEMBER 30, 1983

PER GENE VANO

/jw

11340 w. olympic blvd. suite 357 los angeles california 90064 (213) 473-1564
cable: arccomplex lsa · twx: 9103427581

Original Peter Gabriel tour document.
Tour dates and city – September 1983

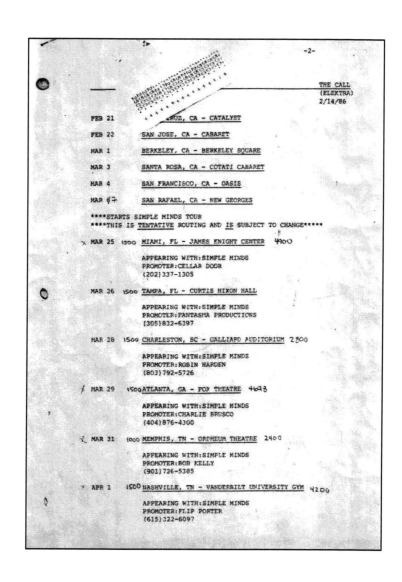

THE CALL
(ELEKTRA)
2/14/86

FEB 21   ~RUZ, CA - CATALYST

FEB 22   SAN JOSE, CA - CABARET

MAR 1   BERKELEY, CA - BERKELEY SQUARE

MAR 3   SANTA ROSA, CA - COTATI CABARET

MAR 4   SAN FRANCISCO, CA - OASIS

MAR 67   SAN RAFAEL, CA - NEW GEORGES

****STARTS SIMPLE MINDS TOUR
****THIS IS TENTATIVE ROUTING AND IS SUBJECT TO CHANGE*****

X MAR 25 1500 MIAMI, FL - JAMES KNIGHT CENTER   4900

          APPEARING WITH:SIMPLE MINDS
          PROMOTER:CELLAR DOOR
          (202)337-1305

  MAR 26 1500 TAMPA, FL - CURTIS HIXON HALL

          APPEARING WITH:SIMPLE MINDS
          PROMOTER:FANTASMA PRODUCTIONS
          (305)832-6397

  MAR 28 1500 CHARLESTON, SC - GALLIARD AUDITORIUM 2800

          APPEARING WITH:SIMPLE MINDS
          PROMOTER:ROBIN HARDEN
          (803)792-5726

/ MAR 29 1500ATLANTA, GA - FOX THEATRE   4673

          APPEARING WITH:SIMPLE MINDS
          PROMOTER:CHARLIE BRUSCO
          (404)876-4300

X MAR 31 1000 MEMPHIS, TN - ORPHEUM THEATRE   2400

          APPEARING WITH:SIMPLE MINDS
          PROMOTER:BOB KELLY
          (901)726-5385

+ APR 1   1500 NASHVILLE, TN - VANDERBILT UNIVERSITY GYM 4200

          APPEARING WITH:SIMPLE MINDS
          PROMOTER:FLIP PORTER
          (615)322-6097

Original Simple Minds tour document page 1.
Tour dates and city – 1986

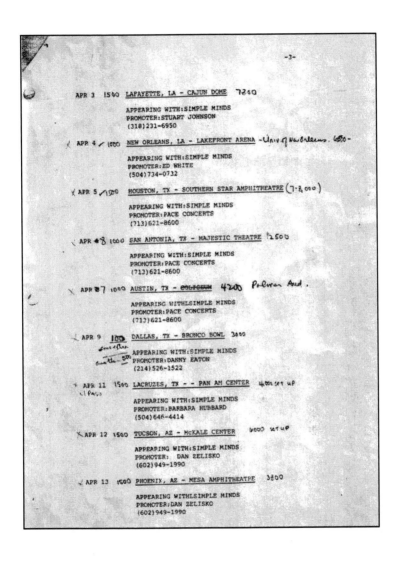

APR 3 1500 LAFAYETTE, LA - CAJUN DOME 7260

    APPEARING WITH:SIMPLE MINDS
    PROMOTER:STUART JOHNSON
    (318)231-6950

✗ APR 4 ✓ 1000 NEW ORLEANS, LA - LAKEFRONT ARENA -Univ.of New Orleans. 6000-

    APPEARING WITH:SIMPLE MINDS
    PROMOTER:ED WHITE
    (504)734-0732

✗ APR 5 ⟋1500 HOUSTON, TX - SOUTHERN STAR AMPHITHEATRE (7-8 000)

    APPEARING WITH:SIMPLE MINDS
    PROMOTER:PACE CONCERTS
    (713)621-8600

✓ APR #8 1000 SAN ANTONIA, TX - MAJESTIC THEATRE 2500

    APPEARING WITH:SIMPLE MINDS
    PROMOTER:PACE CONCERTS
    (713)621-8600

✗ APR #7 1000 AUSTIN, TX - COLISEUM 4200 Palmer Aud.

    APPEARING WITHSIMPLE MINDS
    PROMOTER:PACE CONCERTS
    (713)621-8600

✓ APR 9 100 DALLAS, TX - BRONCO BOWL 3000
    on the
    on the - 500 APPEARING WITH:SIMPLE MINDS
            PROMOTER:DANNY EATON
            (214)526-1522

+ APR 11 1500 LACRUZES, TX - - PAN AM CENTER 4000 set up
  el Paso
                APPEARING WITH:SIMPLE MINDS
                PROMOTER:BARBARA HUBBARD
                (504)646-4414

✗ APR 12 1500 TUCSON, AZ - McKALE CENTER 6000 set up

    APPEARING WITH:SIMPLE MINDS
    PROMOTER: DAN ZELISKO
    (602)949-1990

✓ APR 13 1500 PHOENIX, AZ - MESA AMPHITHEATPE 3800

    APPEARING WITHLSIMPLE MINDS
    PROMOTER:DAN ZELISKO
    (602)949-1990

Original Simple Minds tour document page 2.
Tour dates and city – 1986

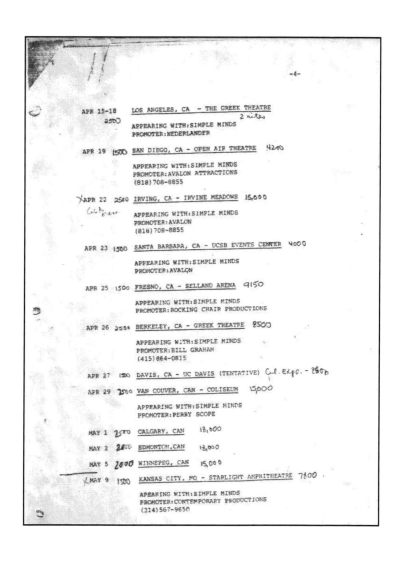

APR 15-18   LOS ANGELES, CA - THE GREEK THEATRE
   2500   2 nites
            APPEARING WITH:SIMPLE MINDS
            PROMOTER:NEDERLANDER

APR 19 1500 SAN DIEGO, CA - OPEN AIR THEATRE   4200
            APPEARING WITH:SIMPLE MINDS
            PROMOTER:AVALON ATTRACTIONS
            (818)708-8855

APR 22 2540 IRVING, CA - IRVINE MEADOWS 15,000
            APPEARING WITH:SIMPLE MINDS
            PROMOTER:AVALON
            (818)708-8855

APR 23 1500 SANTA BARBARA, CA - UCSB EVENTS CENTER 4000
            APPEARING WITH:SIMPLE MINDS
            PROMOTER:AVALON

APR 25 1500 FRESNO, CA - SELLAND ARENA 9150
            APPEARING WITH:SIMPLE MINDS
            PROMOTER:ROCKING CHAIR PRODUCTIONS

APR 26 2560 BERKELEY, CA - GREEK THEATRE 8500
            APPEARING WITH:SIMPLE MINDS
            PROMOTER:BILL GRAHAM
            (415)864-0815

APR 27 1500 DAVIS, CA - UC DAVIS (TENTATIVE) Cal. Expo. - 2600
APR 29 2500 VAN COUVER, CAN - COLISEUM   15,000
            APPEARING WITH:SIMPLE MINDS
            PROMOTER:PERRY SCOPE

MAY 1 2500 CALGARY, CAN   18,600
MAY 2 2800 EDMONTON,CAN   12,000
MAY 5 2000 WINNEPEG, CAN   15,000
MAY 9 1500 KANSAS CITY, MO - STARLIGHT AMPHITHEATRE 7800
            APPEARING WITH:SIMPLE MINDS
            PROMOTER:CONTEMPORARY PRODUCTIONS
            (314)567-9650

Original Simple Minds tour document page 3.
Tour dates and city – 1986

MAY 10 (5:0) ST. LOUIS, MO - FOX THEATRE 4800

    APPEARING WITH:SIMPLE MINDS
    PROMOTER:CONTEMPORARY PRODUCTIONS
    (314)567-9650

MAY 12 1250 CLEVELAND, OH - RICHFIELD COLISEUM THEATRE gove and up

    APPEARING WITH:SIMPLE MINDS
    PROMOTER:JULES BELKIN
    (216)464-5990

MAY 13 453 1577 BATTLECREEK, MI OR GRAND RAPIDS, MI 5600

MAY 15 ONTARIO, CAN Hamilton (?) - U.S in states

MAY 16 1250 OTTAWA, CAN - CIVIC CENTER 10,000

    APPEARING WITH:SIMPLE MINDS
    PROMOTER:TBA

MAY 17or18 1000 MONTREAL, CAN - FORUM 16,000 (deal not set)
    Hockey
    APPEARING WITH:SIMPLE MINDS
    PROMOTER:RUBER FOGEL
    (514)288-7500

MAY 19 1500 PORTLAND, ME - CUMBERLAND COUNTY CIVIC 8450

    APPEARING WITH:SIMPLE MINDS
    PROMOTER:TBA

MAY 20 1250 TROY, NY - RPI FIELD HOUSE 4,200

    APPEARING WITH:SIMPLE MINDS
    PROMOTER:TBA

MAY 22 1500 ROCHESTER, NY (TENTATIVE) 6000 -

MAY 23 1250 NEW HAVEN, CT - COLISEUM (TENTATIVE) 6100

MAY 24 ALLENTOWN, PA OR BETHLEHEM, PA 6,000 (no deal set)

MAY 26-29 2500 NEW YORK, NY - RADIO CITY MUSIC HALL 5,000 (don't have offer)

Original Simple Minds tour document page 4.
Tour dates and city – 1986

The Call's first three albums have
been re-released on the Mercury/
Polygram label.

The Call - 1982
Modern Romans - 1983
Scene Beyond Dreams - 1984

Lyrics from previous Call albums
will be included with Notified.

The Call is in Europe headlining
the Elektra Caravan '87 tour.
Upon their return to the States-
they begin a tour of the Southwest:

Sep 20 - Oklahoma City - Fritzies
      21 - Dallas Alley - free!
      22 - Houston - Xcess
      23 - Austin - The Backroom
      25 - Phoenix - TBA
      26 - San Juan Cap - Coach House
      27 - San Diego - Bachanal
      28 - Los Angeles - Roxy
      30 - Santa Clara - 1 Step Beyond
-TBA - San Francisco and Sacramento-

In The River" has been released as
a single to album oriented radio
stations. If you get the chance-

This appears to be dates for late 1987 after coming back
from the European Elektra Caravan '87 tour.

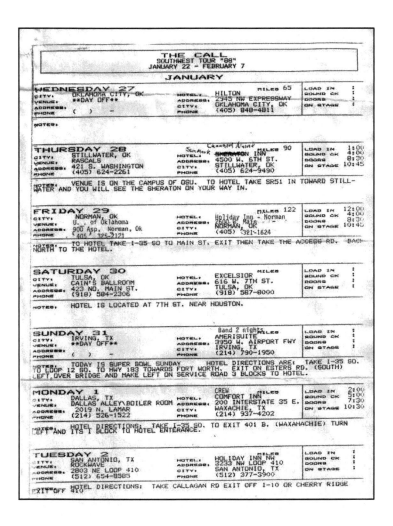

THE CALL
SOUTHWEST TOUR "88"
JANUARY 22 - FEBRUARY 7

JANUARY

WEDNESDAY 27 · MILES 65
CITY: OKLAHOMA CITY, OK · **DAY OFF**
VENUE: · HOTEL: HILTON
ADDRESS: · ADDRESS: 2345 NW EXPRESSWAY
PHONE ( ) - · CITY: OKLAHOMA CITY, OK · PHONE (405) 848-4811
LOAD IN : · SOUND CK : · DOORS : · ON STAGE :

NOTES:

THURSDAY 28 · MILES 90
CITY: STILLWATER, OK · HOTEL: SHERATON INN · SunHawk Conned Point
VENUE: RASCALS · ADDRESS: 4500 W. 6TH ST.
ADDRESS: 421 S. WASHINGTON · CITY: STILLWATER, OK
PHONE (405) 624-2261 · PHONE (405) 624-9490
LOAD IN 1:00 · SOUND CK 4:00 · DOORS 8:30 · ON STAGE 10:45

NOTES: VENUE IS ON THE CAMPUS OF OSU. TO HOTEL TAKE SR51 IN TOWARD STILL-
WATER AND YOU WILL SEE THE SHERATON ON YOUR WAY IN.

FRIDAY 29 · MILES 122
CITY: NORMAN, OK · HOTEL: Holiday Inn - Norman
VENUE: U. of Oklahoma · ADDRESS: NORMAN, OK
ADDRESS: 900 Asp, Norman, Ok · CITY: NORMAN, OK
PHONE (405) 325-2121 · PHONE (405) 321-1624
LOAD IN 12:00 · SOUND CK 4:00 · DOORS 8:30 · ON STAGE 10:45

NOTES: TO HOTEL TAKE I-35 SO TO MAIN ST. EXIT THEN TAKE THE ACCESS RD. BACK
NORTH TO THE HOTEL.

SATURDAY 30 · MILES
CITY: TULSA, OK · HOTEL: EXCELSIOR
VENUE: CAIN'S BALLROOM · ADDRESS: 616 W. 7TH ST.
ADDRESS: 423 NO. MAIN ST. · CITY: TULSA, OK
PHONE (918) 584-2306 · PHONE (918) 587-8000
LOAD IN : · SOUND CK : · DOORS : · ON STAGE :

NOTES: HOTEL IS LOCATED AT 7TH ST. NEAR HOUSTON.

SUNDAY 31 · MILES
CITY: IRVING, TX · HOTEL: AMERISUITE · Band 2 nights
VENUE: **DAY OFF** · ADDRESS: 3950 W. AIRPORT FWY
ADDRESS: · CITY: IRVING, TX
PHONE ( ) - · PHONE (214) 790-1950
LOAD IN : · SOUND CK : · DOORS : · ON STAGE :

NOTES: TODAY IS SUPER BOWL SUNDAY   HOTEL DIRECTIONS ARE: TAKE I-35 SO.
TO LOOP 12 SO. TO HWY 183 TOWARDS FORT WORTH. EXIT ON ESTERS RD. (SOUTH)
LEFT,OVER BRIDGE AND MAKE LEFT ON SERVICE ROAD 3 BLOCKS TO HOTEL.

MONDAY 1 · MILES
CITY: DALLAS, TX · HOTEL: COMFORT INN · CREW
VENUE: DALLAS ALLEY\BOILER ROOM · ADDRESS: 200 INTERSTATE 35 E.
ADDRESS: 2019 N. LAMAR · CITY: WAXAHACHIE, TX
PHONE (214) 526-1522 · PHONE (214) 937-4202
LOAD IN 2:00 · SOUND CK 5:00 · DOORS 7:30 · ON STAGE 10:30

NOTES: HOTEL DIRECTIONS: TAKE I-35 SO. TO EXIT 401 B. (WAXAHACHIE) TURN
LEFT AND ITS 1 BLOCK TO HOTEL ENTERANCE.

TUESDAY 2 · MILES
CITY: SAN ANTONIO, TX · HOTEL: HOLIDAY INN NW
VENUE: ROCKWAVE · ADDRESS: 3233 NW LOOP 410
ADDRESS: 2803 NE LOOP 410 · CITY: SAN ANTONIO, TX
PHONE (512) 654-8585 · PHONE (512) 377-3900
LOAD IN : · SOUND CK : · DOORS : · ON STAGE :

NOTES: HOTEL DIRECTIONS: TAKE CALLAGAN RD EXIT OFF I-10 OR CHERRY RIDGE
EXIT OFF 410

The Call Southwest Tour 1988

Page 1

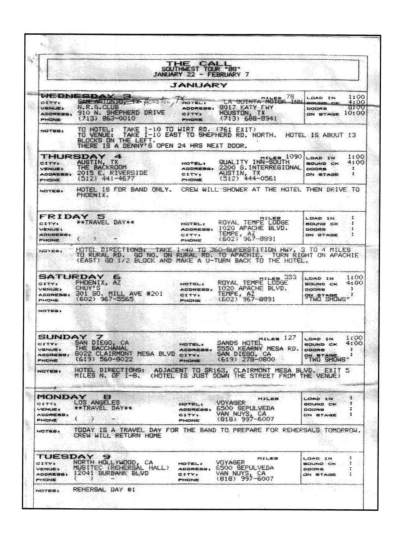

THE CALL
SOUTHWEST TOUR "88"
JANUARY 22 - FEBRUARY 7

JANUARY

WEDNESDAY 3
				MILES 78	
CITY:	SAN ANTONIO, TX *Houston*	HOTEL:	LA QUINTA MOTOR INN	LOAD IN	1:00
VENUE:	N.R.G.CLUB	ADDRESS:	8017 KATY FWY	SOUND CK	4:00
ADDRESS:	910 N. SHEPHERD DRIVE	CITY:	HOUSTON, TX	DOORS	8:00
PHONE:	(713) 863-0010	PHONE:	(713) 688-8941	ON STAGE	10:00

NOTES: TO HOTEL: TAKE I-10 TO WIRT RD. (761 EXIT)
TO VENUE: TAKE I-10 EAST TO SHEPHERD RD. NORTH. HOTEL IS ABOUT 13
BLOCKS ON THE LEFT.
THERE IS A DENNY'S OPEN 24 HRS NEXT DOOR.

THURSDAY 4
				MILES 1090	
CITY:	AUSTIN, TX	HOTEL:	QUALITY INN-SOUTH	LOAD IN	1:00
VENUE:	THE BACKROOM	ADDRESS:	2200 S. INTERREGIONAL	SOUND CK	4:00
ADDRESS:	2015 E. RIVERSIDE	CITY:	AUSTIN, TX	DOORS	:
PHONE:	(512) 441-4677	PHONE:	(512) 444-0561	ON STAGE	:

NOTES: HOTEL IS FOR BAND ONLY. CREW WILL SHOWER AT THE HOTEL THEN DRIVE TO
PHOENIX.

FRIDAY 5
				MILES	
CITY:	**TRAVEL DAY**	HOTEL:	ROYAL TEMPE LODGE	LOAD IN	:
VENUE:		ADDRESS:	1020 APACHE BLVD.	SOUND CK	:
ADDRESS:		CITY:	TEMPE, AZ	DOORS	:
PHONE:	( ) -	PHONE:	(602) 967-8891	ON STAGE	:

NOTES: HOTEL DIRECTIONS: TAKE I-40 TO 360-SUPERSTITION HWY. 3 TO 4 MILES
TO RURAL RD. GO NO. ON RURAL RD. TO APACHIE. TURN RIGHT ON APACHIE
(EAST) GO 1/2 BLOCK AND MAKE A U-TURN BACK TO THE HOTEL.

SATURDAY 6
				MILES 353	
CITY:	PHOENIX, AZ	HOTEL:	ROYAL TEMPE LODGE	LOAD IN	1:00
VENUE:	CHUY'S	ADDRESS:	1020 APACHE BLVD.	SOUND CK	4:00
ADDRESS:	301 SO. MILL AVE #201	CITY:	TEMPE, AZ	DOORS	:
PHONE:	(602) 967-5565	PHONE:	(602) 967-8891	ON STAGE	: "TWO SHOWS"

NOTES:

SUNDAY 7
				MILES 127	
CITY:	SAN DIEGO, CA	HOTEL:	SANDS HOTEL	LOAD IN	1:00
VENUE:	THE BACCHANAL	ADDRESS:	5550 KEARNY MESA RD.	SOUND CK	4:00
ADDRESS:	8022 CLAIRMONT MESA BLVD	CITY:	SAN DIEGO, CA	DOORS	:
PHONE:	(619) 560-8022	PHONE:	(619) 278-0800	ON STAGE	: "TWO SHOWS"

NOTES: HOTEL DIRECTIONS: ADJACENT TO SR163, CLAIRMONT MESA BLVD. EXIT 5
MILES N. OF I-8. (HOTEL IS JUST DOWN THE STREET FROM THE VENUE)

MONDAY 8
				MILES	
CITY:	LOS ANGELES	HOTEL:	VOYAGER	LOAD IN	:
VENUE:	**TRAVEL DAY**	ADDRESS:	6500 SEPULVEDA	SOUND CK	:
ADDRESS:		CITY:	VAN NUYS, CA	DOORS	:
PHONE:	( ) -	PHONE:	(818) 997-6007	ON STAGE	:

NOTES: TODAY IS A TRAVEL DAY FOR THE BAND TO PREPARE FOR REHERSALS TOMORROW.
CREW WILL RETURN HOME

TUESDAY 9
				MILES	
CITY:	NORTH HOLLYWOOD, CA	HOTEL:	VOYAGER	LOAD IN	:
VENUE:	MUSITEC (REHERSAL HALL)	ADDRESS:	6500 SEPULVEDA	SOUND CK	:
ADDRESS:	12041 BURBANK BLVD	CITY:	VAN NUYS, CA	DOORS	:
PHONE:	( ) -	PHONE:	(818) 997-6007	ON STAGE	:

NOTES: REHERSAL DAY #1

The Call Southwest Tour 1988
Page 2

```
                    --THE CALL--

7/18  SACRAMENTO-Crest Theatre      8/04  DALLAS-Tommy's
7/19  SAN JOSE-One Step Beyond      8/05  OKLA CITY-The Katt's(100.5FM)
7/21  SANTA CRUZ-Catalyst                 Beach Party
7/22  SAN FRANCISCO-Fillmore        8/07  TULSA-to be announced
7/23  HEALDSBURG-Raven Theatre      8/08  KANSAS CITY,MO-London's
7/25  SAN JUAN-Coach House          8/10  ST LOUIS-Mississippi Nights
7/26  LOS ANGELES-Palace            8/11  SPRINGFIELD,MO-The Regency
7/28  SAN DIEGO-Calif. Theatre      8/12  COLUMBIA,MO-Blue Note*
7/29  VENTURA-Ventura Theatre       8/14  OMAHA-to be announced
7/30  TEMPE,AZ-After The            8/15  MINNEAPOLIS-Cabooze*
              Gold Rush             8/16  MADISON,WIS-Headliner Club*
8/01  ALBUQUERQUE-The Beach         8/17  CHICAGO-Cabaret Metro
8/03  HOUSTON-Rockefeller's               *Not Confirmed

      DATES SUBJECT TO CHANGE--CALL VENUE OR CALL INFORMATION HOTLINE
      815-399-5553.


          --THE CALL - LET THE DAY BEGIN TOUR 1989--

11/08 LANCASTER,PA-The Chameleon     11/30 DALLAS-The Arcadia
11/11 KANSAS CITY,MO-William Jewel   12/01 WICHITA-Coyote Club
            College                  12/03 BOULDER-U. of Colorado
11/13 LEXINGTON,KY-Breedings               Glenn Miller Ballroom
11/14 BLOOMINGTON,IN-Stardust Club   12/04 ALBUQUERQUE-Confetti's
11/15 INDIANAPOLIS-The Vogue         12/05 TUCSON-U. of Arizona
11/17 CHICAGO-Cabaret Metro          12/06 PHOENIX-Celebrity Theatre
11/18 COLUMBUS,OH-Newport Music Hall 12/09 SAN DIEGO-Bacchanal
11/20 ANN ARBOR,MI-Nectarine Ballrm  12/10 LOS ANGELES-KROQ's Xmas
11/21 MADISON,WI-Headliners                Bash-Univ. Amphitheatre
11/22 OMAHA,NE-Ranch Bowl           12/12 SAN FRANCISCO-The Stone
11/24 SPRINGFIELD,MO-The Regency     12/14 PORTLAND,OR-Starry Nights
11/25 TULSA,OK-Cain's Ballroom       12/16 VANCOUVER,BC-TBA
11/27 HOUSTON-Rockefeller's          12/17 SANTA CRUZ-The Catalyst
11/29 AUSTIN-Liberty Lunch           12/18 SANTA CLARA-One Step Beyond

*DATES SUBJECT TO CHANGE**CALL VENUE OR THE CALL HOTLINE 815-399-5553!
```

Original tour date documents sent out from Notified Newsletter about the *Let the Day Begin* tour 1989.

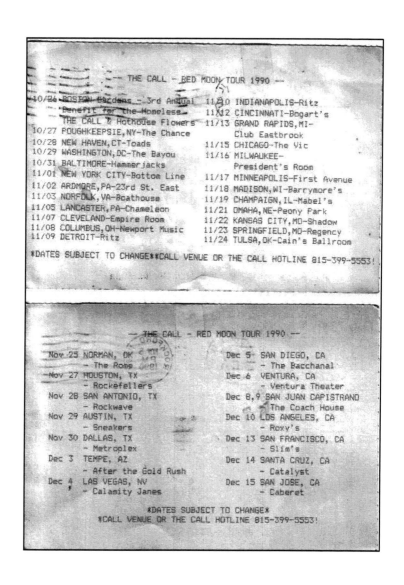

```
                    -- THE CALL - RED MOON TOUR 1990 --

10/26 BOSTON-Gardens - 3rd Annual     11/10 INDIANAPOLIS-Ritz
      Benefit for the Homeless        11/12 CINCINNATI-Bogart's
      THE CALL & Hothouse Flowers     11/13 GRAND RAPIDS,MI-
10/27 POUGHKEEPSIE,NY-The Chance             Club Eastbrook
10/28 NEW HAVEN,CT-Toads              11/15 CHICAGO-The Vic
10/29 WASHINGTON,DC-The Bayou         11/16 MILWAUKEE-
10/31 BALTIMORE-Hammerjacks                 President's Room
11/01 NEW YORK CITY-Bottom Line       11/17 MINNEAPOLIS-First Avenue
11/02 ARDMORE,PA-23rd St. East        11/18 MADISON,WI-Barrymore's
11/03 NORFOLK,VA-Boathouse            11/19 CHAMPAIGN,IL-Mabel's
11/05 LANCASTER,PA-Chameleon          11/21 OMAHA,NE-Peony Park
11/07 CLEVELAND-Empire Room           11/22 KANSAS CITY,MO-Shadow
11/08 COLUMBUS,OH-Newport Music       11/23 SPRINGFIELD,MO-Regency
11/09 DETROIT-Ritz                    11/24 TULSA,OK-Cain's Ballroom

*DATES SUBJECT TO CHANGE**CALL VENUE OR THE CALL HOTLINE 815-399-5553!
```

```
                    -- THE CALL - RED MOON TOUR 1990 --

Nov 25 NORMAN, OK                     Dec 5  SAN DIEGO, CA
       - The Rome                            - The Bacchanal
Nov 27 HOUSTON, TX                    Dec 6  VENTURA, CA
       - Rockefellers                        - Ventura Theater
Nov 28 SAN ANTONIO, TX                Dec 8,9 SAN JUAN CAPISTRANO
       - Rockwave                            - The Coach House
Nov 29 AUSTIN, TX                     Dec 10 LOS ANGELES, CA
       - Sneakers                            - Roxy's
Nov 30 DALLAS, TX                     Dec 13 SAN FRANCISCO, CA
       - Metroplex                           - Slim's
Dec 3  TEMPE, AZ                      Dec 14 SANTA CRUZ, CA
       - After the Gold Rush                 - Catalyst
Dec 4  LAS VEGAS, NV                  Dec 15 SAN JOSE, CA
       - Calamity Janes                      - Caberet

           *DATES SUBJECT TO CHANGE*
     *CALL VENUE OR THE CALL HOTLINE 815-399-5553!
```

Original tour date documents sent out from Notified
Newsletter about the *Red Moon* tour 1990.

Michael Been
ON THE VERGE OF A NERVOUS BREAKTHROUGH TOUR

DATE	CITY	STATE	VENUE
7/2/94	CHICAGO	IL	METRO
7/3/94	LOUISVILLE	KY	STAGE DOOR JOHNNIES
7/4/94	E. LANCING	MI	THE SMALL PLANET
7/6/94	INDIANAPOLIS IN		THE VOGUE
7/7/94	CINCINNATI	OH	BOGART'S
7/8/94	COLUMBUS	OH	LULOWS
7/9/94	DETROIT	MI	THE MAJESTIC
7/11/94	LANCASTER	PA	CHAMELEON
7/12/94	PROVIDENCE	RI	THE STRAND
7/13/94	POUGHKEEPSIE NY		THE CHANCE
7/14/94	NEW YORK	NY	WETLANDS PRESERVE
7/16/94	ASBURY PARK NJ		FAST LANE
7/17/94	CAMBRIDGE	MA	MIDDLE EAST
7/19/94	WASHINGTON	DC	9:30 CLUB
7/20/94	NORFOLK	VA	BOATHOUSE
7/22/94	ATLANTA	GA	COTTON CLUB
7/23/94	NASHVILLE	TN	EXIT INN
7/24/94	ST. LOUIS	MO	MISSISSIPPI NIGHTS
7/26	HOUSTON	TX	ROCKEFELLER'S
7/27	SAN ANTONIO TX		ROCK ISLAND
7/28	DALLAS TX		TREES
7/29	SPRINGFIELD	MO	THE REGENCY
7/31/94	OMAHA NB		RANCH BOWL
8/1/94	BOULDER	CO	BOULDER THEATER
8/3/94	PHOENIX	AZ	THE ROXY
8/4/94	SAN DIEGO	CA	CHILLER'S
8/5/94	HOLLYWOOD	CA	TROUBADOUR
8/6/94	SAN JUAN CAPIST.	CA	COACH HOUSE
8/8/94	SANTA CRUZ	CA	CATALYST
8/9/94	SAN FRANSISCO	CA	GREAT AMERICAN

1994 – Michael Been's – *On the Verge of a Nervous Breakthrough* tour, 30 cities in 6 weeks.

Date: SAT, JUL 17, 1999 Artist: THE CALL   Miles To Next Gig
City: LINCOLN, NH Venue: INSIDE OUT SOUL FESTIVAL ()

PROMOTER: DAN RUSSELL Tel: 978 346 4577
Promoter Company: NEW SOUND CONCERTS Fax: 978 346 7608
Promoter Address: PO BOX 197 Settle With: MARY SLAVIN
Promoter City: MERRIMAC MA, 01860
Guarantee: $4000.00 Additionally: LODGING, GROUND TRAVEL, MEALS PASSES, BACKLINE
Deposit $ Due: $2000.00 Deposit Due Date: 6/30/99 Amount Received: $2,000.00
Ticket Prices Adv.: $25.00 $45.00 $55.00 Door: $30.00 $60.00 Tx Info
Bonuses: BALANCE DUE IS $2,000.
Catering: MEAL PASSES Lodging: PROMOTER PROVIDES Travel: GROUND

VENUE Type: FESTIVAL Venue Cap 10000 Ages: ALL AGES
Venue INSIDE OUT SOUL FESTIVAL Tel 508 878 5706 Fax
Venue Contact HARV HALLAS Tel 617 308 6162 Fax
Venue Address RT 112 LINCOLN, NH
Prod. Contact DAN HALLAS Tel 617 510 6353 Fax
Back Stage Tel: Fax
Dress Rm Qty TEMPORARY YES Towel Info YES
Directions RUNNERS WILL TAKE YOU TOO AND FROM THE HOTEL.
BACK STAGE PHONE # - 603 745 6261 X 5691 OR 5699, FAX 603 745 2381 IF YOU NEED A LIFT, CALL
THE BACK STAGE # AND AX FOR HARV OR SOMEONE WHO MIGHT BE ABLE TO HELP YOU. I'LL ALSO
GIVE MICHAEL MY CAR TO COLLECT YOU WHEN POSSIBLE
Parking Info

GIG Load In: 6 PM Sound Check Time: NONE Doors: ALL DAY Show Time: 9:10
THE CALL On At: 9:10 Set Length: 45 min
Billing: 1 OF 10 Support: JARS OF CLAY CLOSE
Set Info: Sc Info: LINE CHECK ONLY
Load In Point: STAGE RIGHT
Loaders Qty: 2
Load In Info: BRING INSTRUMENTS TO BACK STAGE Load Out Info:
Merch Info: 25%, VENUE SELLS Sellers/ Tables 1 TABLE, ALL 3 DAYS
Catering: 2 MEAL PASSES ON SAT & SUNDAY PER BAND MEMBER
FOH engineer festival LD festival

PUBLICITY NEED YOU TO BE AVAILABLE FOR THE WMSJ ARTIST SIGNING TENT 30 MINUTES FOLLOWING
PERFORMANCE

DEAR ARTIST, MICHAEL IS STAYING THURSDAY NIGHT @ THE HIGHLANDER 603 625 6246, SHUTTLE AVAILABLE
LOOK AFTER YOURSELF TO GET TO THE HOTEL. AT NOON, MICHEAL WILL BE COLLECTED AND
BROUGHT TO THE MILL HOUSE AT LOON WHERE YOU WILL STAY FOR FRI, SAT & SUN NIGHTS.

DALE AND TOM AND SCOTT ARE STAYING AT THE WOODWARD, WHICH IS JUST AS CLOSE AT THE MILL.
UNFORTUNATELY, DUE TO A MISTAKE...HUMAN ERROR, WE LOST OUR ROOMS AND HAD TO SPLIT YOU
UP.

HOTEL MILL HOUSE 800 654 6183 Tel: 803 625 6426 Single: X rooms
Hotel contact DEBI LOMBARDI Fax: 603 745 9790 Double: X rooms
Hotel address P O BOX 696 Misc Charge For
Hotel city LINCOLN state NH zip 03251 Tax: %
Hotel directions SHUTTLE TO AND FROM Total Tax
Doubles
Singles
Hotel parking Total:
Distance to venue 2 MILES Confirmation #
Hotel notes

July 17, 1999 – Soul Festival
Michael, Dale Ockerman, Scott and Dicky

Date: **SUN, JUL 18, 1999**
City: **LINCOLN, NH**

Artist: **THE CALL**
Venue: **INSIDE OUT SOUL FESTIVAL**

Miles To Next Gig
( )

PROMOTER: DAN RUSSELL
Promoter Company: NEW SOUND CONCERTS
Promoter Address: PO BOX 197
Promoter City: MERRIMAC MA , 01860
Guarantee:
Deposit $ Due:
Ticket Prices Adv.: $25.00 $45.00 $55.00   Door: $30.00 $60.00
Bonuses: LOTS OF LOVE, NEW FANS,
Catering: MEAL PASSES

Tel: 978 346 4577
Fax: 978 346 7608
Settle With: MARY SLAVIN
Additionally: LODGING, GROUND TRAVEL, MEALS PASSES, BACKLINE
Deposit Due Date:
Amount Received:
Tx Info
Lodging: PROMOTER PROVIDES
Travel: GROUND

VENUE Type: FESTIVAL
Venue: INSIDE OUT SOUL FESTIVAL
Venue Contact: DALE RICHER
Venue Address: INSIDE OUT STAGE   LINCOLN , NH
Prod. Contact: DALE   Tel
Back Stage Tel:

Venue Cap 10000   Ages: ALL AGES
Tel 508 878 5706   Fax
Tel 603 654 5756   Fax
Fax
Fax

Dress Rm Qty: TEMPORARY YES   Towel Info YES
Directions: REVIVAL STAGE = SATURDAY (MAIN STAGE) DALE RICHER IS THE PRODUCTION MGR AND ENGINEER
INSIDE OUT STAGE = 6 PM ON SUNDAY. SHOW UP AT THE STAGE ROUND 4:30 MICHAEL WILL BE DRIVING YOU?? OR A RUNNER?
Parking Info

GIG Load In: 4:30 PM   Sound Check Time: NONE   Doors: ALL DAY   Show Time: 6 & 6:45
THE CALL   On At: 6 & 6:45   Set Length: 45 min / 60 min
Billing: 1 OF 10   Support:
Set Info: Sc Info: LINE CHECK ONLY
Load In Point:
Loaders Qty: 2
Load In Info: BRING INSTRUMENTS TO BACK STAGE   Load Out Info:
Merch Info: 25%, VENUE SELLS   Sellers/ Tables 1 TABLE, ALL 3 DAYS   @
Catering : 2 MEAL PASSES ON SAT & SUNDAY PER BAND MEMBER
FOH engineer: festival   LD festival

PUBLICITY   SOUL CAFE DETAILS !! AFTER THE 6 PM PERFORMANCE GET TO THE SOUL CAFE BY 7:45PM
MARK POPADIC IS THE PRODUCTION MANAGER. THIS PERFORMANCE WILL BE RECORDED

DEAR ARTIST,   YOU'RE PLAYING 2 SETS TODAY ON 2 DIFFERENT STAGES. CHECK IN 3 HOURS PRIOR FOR THE FIRST PERFORMANCE AND 90 MINUTES PRIOR FOR THE SECOND PERFORMANCE.

MARK POPADIC IS THE PRODUCTION CHIEF FOR THE SOUL CAFE (THE 2ND PERFORMANCE)

SCOTT, DALE, TOM, DON'T FORGET TO SORT OUT YOUR OWN AIRPORT SHUTTLE ON MONDAY AM

HOTEL   MILL HOUSE & HIGHLANDER/AIRPORT
Hotel contact
Hotel address
Hotel city   state   zip
Hotel directions

Hotel parking
Distance to venue
Hotel notes

Tel:
Fax:

Single: X   rooms
Double: X   rooms
Misc Charge   For
Tax: %
Total Tax
Doubles
Singles
Total:
Confirmation #

July 17, 1999 – Soul Festival
Michael, Dale Ockerman, Scott and Dicky

Chapter Twelve:
Discography

The Call - *The Call* – 1982 – Mercury / Polygram

Recorded at Basing Street Studios, London, England and

The Manor, Shipton on Cherwell, England

Band: Michael Been, Scott Musick, Tom Ferrier, Greg Freeman and Garth Hudson.

Image used with permission: The Call

Album: The Call – *The Call*

<u>Tracks:</u>

War Weary World	4:18
There's a Heart Here	2:56
Doubt	4:19
This is Life	3:06
Fulham Blues	3:13
Who's that Man	3:05
Upperbirth	3:38
Bandits	3:28
Flesh and Steel	4:54
Unbearable	2:37
Waiting for the End	5:15

2nd Album – *Modern Romans*

Released 1983 – Mercury / Polygram

Recorded at Indigo Studio, July – August, 1982

Band: Michael Been, Scott Musick, Tom Ferrier, Greg Freeman, Steve Huddleston, Garth Hudson.

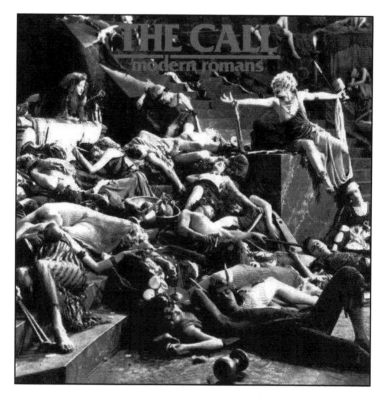

Image used with permission: The Call

Album: The Call – *Modern Romans*

<u>**Tracks:**</u>

The Walls Came Down	3:35
Turn a Blind Eye	3:48
Time of Your Life	3:27
Modern Romans	3:24
Back from the Front	4:02
Destination	4:32
Violent Times	4:28
Face to Face	4:05
All About You	4:20

"While recording **Modern Romans** in Malibu at Indigo Studio, the A&R man would come by, hang out and listen to what we were doing. He could not stand "**The Walls Came Down.**" He said we should take the song off of the album and replace it with anything else. His dislike for the song spread through the record company and executives. They wanted the song canned, as well, but our contract stated we had artistic rights, so we included the song on **Modern Romans**. Due to our defiance, the record label wouldn't help us promote the album and shelved it. Our good friend, Barry Albright, stepped up and financed the video, filmed by Video Caroline, in a subterranean pump station in San Francisco. That song and video is what really put us on the map. Thanks to Barry Albright, and MTV we finally broke out, people [finally] knew about us, and we became popular." – *Scott Musick*

So, it seems perhaps one song and one video made all the difference.

3rd Album – *Scene Beyond Dreams*

Released 1984 – Mercury / Polygram

Recorded at El Dorado Studio, Los Angeles

Band: Michael Been, Scott Musick, Tom Ferrier, Joe Read, Jim Goodwin (Steve Huddleston & Garth Hudson).

Image used with permission: The Call

Album: The Call – *Scene Beyond Dreams*

<u>**Tracks:**</u>

Scene Beyond Dreams	3:47
The Burden	3:34
Tremble	4:01
Delivered	4:03
Heavy Hand	3:23
Promise and Threat	4:30
One Life Leads to Another	4:38
Apocalypse	1:46
Notified	2:58

* Steve Huddleston on *Scene Beyond Dreams*
* Garth Hudson on *The Burden*

"The warehouse in Scene beyond Dreams was in Oakland, I believe. Once a biplane factory, or who knows. Whatever it was, the building had been sold and was going to be turned into a mall. Someone got into trouble because we flooded it for the video."

- Scott Musick - January 24th, 2021

4th Album – *Reconciled*

Released 1986 – Elektra

Recorded at the Power Station, NYC - 1985

Band: Michael Been, Scott Musick, Tom Ferrier, Jim Goodwin. With guests Jim Kerr (Sanctuary & Everywhere I Go), Peter Gabriel (Everywhere I Go) & Robbie Robertson (Guitar on The Morning).

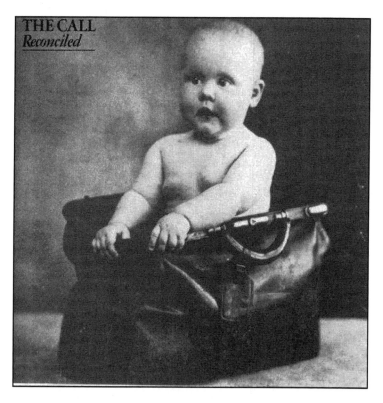

Image used with permission: The Call

Album: The Call – *Reconciled*

Tracks:

Everywhere I Go	4:18
I Still Believe (Great Design)	5:30
Blood Red (America)	3:42
The Morning	4:40
Oklahoma	4:18
With or Without Reason	4:02
Sanctuary	3:57
Tore the Old Place Down	4:12
Even Now	4:32

* *Everywhere I Go* - Jim Kerr & Peter Gabriel – Backing Vocals

* *The Morning* - Robbie Robertson (of The Band) - Guitar

Referred to as "The Baby in a Bag" album by the band.

Trivia Note: According to the band, no one knows who the baby in the bag actually is. The photo was discovered by accident, while searching for tornado photos, which ended up being bumped to the back of the album.

5th Album – *Into the Woods*

Released 1987 – Elektra

Recorded at A&M, One on One & Rumbo and Conway Studios – Los Angeles - 1987

Band: Michael Been, Scott Musick, Tom Ferrier, Jim Goodwin.

Image used with permission: The Call

Album: The Call – *Into the Woods*

<u>**Tracks:**</u>

I Don't Wanna	5:15
In the River	4:04
It Could Have Been Me	4:38
The Woods	5:10
Day or Night	4:12
Memory	4:05
Too Many Tears	4:24
Expecting	4:52
Walk Walk	3:50

* In the River – written by Michael Been & Scott Musick

* Day or Night – written by Michael Been & Tom Ferrier

* The Woods – written by Michael Been & Jim Goodwin

6th Album – *Let the Day Begin*

Released 1989 – Elektra

Recorded at American Recording and The Complex – Los Angeles, CA, and the Power Station, NYC - 1989

Band: Michael Been, Scott Musick, Tom Ferrier, Jim Goodwin. (With guest Harry Dean Stanton – Harmonica)

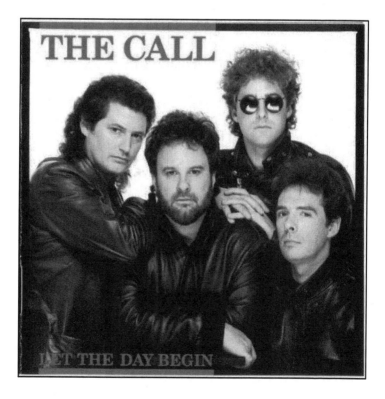

Image used with permission: The Call

Album: The Call – *Let the Day Begin*

<u>**Tracks:**</u>

Let the Day Begin	3:52
You Run	5:33
Surrender	4:08
When	5:18
Jealousy	5:39
Same Ol' Story	3:36
For Love	6:14
Closer	5:04
Communication	5:38
Watch	4:19
Uncovered	2:24

* Harry Dean Stanton – harmonica on *"For Love"*

7th Album – *Red Moon*

Released 1990 – MCA

Recorded at Ocean Way Recording and American Recording – Los Angeles, CA - 1990

Band: Michael Been, Scott Musick, Tom Ferrier, Jim Goodwin. (With guests Bono & T-Bone Burnett)

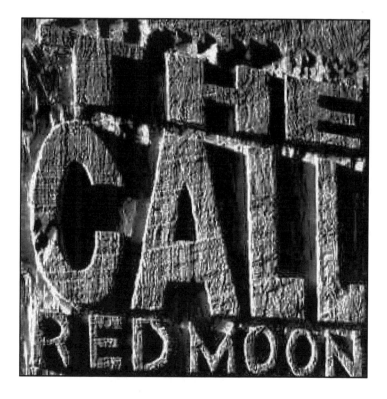

Image used with permission: The Call

Album: The Call – *Red Moon*

<u>**Tracks:**</u>

What's Happened to You	4:18
Red Moon	3:46
You Were There	4:04
Floating Back	3:25
A Swim in the Ocean	3:51
Like You've Never Been Loved	4:14
Family	3:41
This is Your Life	4:09
The Hand That Feeds You	3:33
What a Day	4:12

* What's Happened to You – Bono – Backing Vocals

* Like You've Never Been Loved – T-Bone Burnett – Backing Vocals

* What a Day – Written by Michael Been & Jim Goodwin

8th Album – *The Walls Came Down:*
The Best of the Mercury Years

Released 1991 – Mercury / Polygram

Compilation recording - 1991

Band: Michael Been, Scott Musick, Tom Ferrier, Jim Goodwin, Greg Freeman, Steve Huddleston, Garth Hudson, Joe Read.

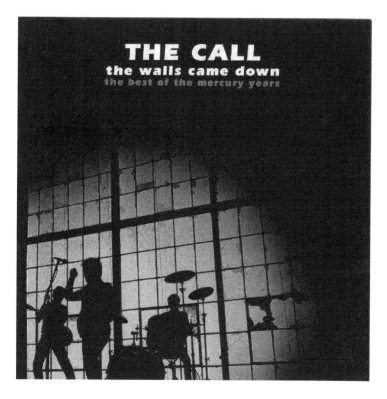

Image used with permission: The Call

Album: The Call – *The Walls Came Down:*
The Best of the Mercury Years

Tracks:

War Weary World	4:17
There's a Heart Here	2:55
Doubt	4:20
Upperbirth	3:38
Flesh and Steel	4:54
Waiting for the End	5:15
The Walls Came Down	3:42
Turn a Blind Eye	3:48
Modern Romans	3:25
Back from the Front	4:02
Destination	3:45
Violent Times	4:29
All About You	4:23
Scene Beyond Dreams	3:48
Tremble	3:59
Delivered	4:03
Heavy Hand	3:23
One Life Leads to Another	4:36

Michael Been Solo Album – *Light Sleeper Soundtrack*

Released 1992 – Red Dot Records / Warner Music U.K.

Band: Michael Been, Scott Musick, Tom Ferrier

Image used w/permission:
Neeb Music & Red Dot Records

Album: Michael Been – *Light Sleeper (Soundtrack)*

<u>Tracks:</u>

World on Fire	5:30
To Feel This Way	5:01
World on Fire (John's Theme)	5:43
Anxious (Pt. 1)	0:47
Without You (Marianne's Theme)	2:03
To Feel This Way (Film Version)	3:59
Beloved	3:30
Loss	0:53
Anxious (Pt. 2)	0:54
Abandoned	4:18
Marianne's Fall	3:14
Jumpoffs	4:04
Betrayed or not Betrayed	1:01
Suspicious (Tis' Theme)	3:49
Fate	6:39
Embrace	4:40

* There was another bootleg version of this album released in 1999, which had 7 additional tracks but is not considered an official release.

Michael Been Solo Album #2 –

On the Verge of a Nervous Breakthrough

Released 1994 – Qwest Records

Recorded at: Studio D, Sausalito, CA

Key Band Members: Michael Been, Scott Musick, Tom Ferrier, Ralph Patlan, Robert Been

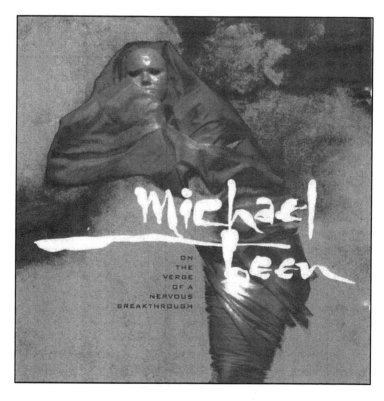

Image used w/permission:
Neeb Music & Qwest Records.

Album: Michael Been –
On the Verge of a Nervous Breakthrough
<u>**Tracks:**</u>

Us	3:47
When You're With Me	4:47
Nearly Fell	3:54
This World	4:43
In My Head	5:03
This Way	6:57
Luminous	5:35
She	4:12
Worried	4:15
For Your Love	3:17
Invitation	3:54
Now I Know High (Part 2)	7:42
To Feel This Way	4:54

9th Album – *The Best of The Call*

Released 1997 – Warner Bros.

Compilation Recorded: 1983 - 1997

Primary Band on tracks: Michael Been, Scott Musick, Tom Ferrier, Jim Goodwin.

Additional: Jim Keltner – Drums & Bruce Cockburn – guitar on "Become America" and "All You Hold On To."

Image used w/permission: The Call

Album: The Call – *The Best of The Call*

<u>**Tracks:**</u>

Let the day Begin	3:51
Everywhere I Go	4:20
I Still Believe	5:32
I Don't Wanna	5:06
Memory	4:05
What's Happened to You	4:11
You Were There	4:02
Become America	3:19
To Feel This Way	5:59
Us	3:45
All You Hold On To	3:19
We Know too Much	5:50
The Walls Came Down	3:40
Uncovered	2:22

10th Album – *To Heaven and Back*

Released 1998 – Fingerprint Records

Recorded at Brilliant Studio, San Francisco, CA - 1997

Band: Michael Been, Scott Musick, Tom Ferrier, Jim Goodwin. (Addt'l Background Vocals – Daniel Presley)

Image used with permission: Dan Russell & Fingerprint Records.

Album: The Call – *To Heaven and Back*

<u>Tracks:</u>

Soaring Bird	4:06
Criminal	4:20
Love is Everywhere	4:42
World on Fire	5:11
Think it Over	5:09
Musta Been Outta My Mind	3:28
All You Hold On To	3:25
Compromise	3:55
Becoming America	3:38
What Are You Made Of	4:25
Confession	5:55

6 Song Maxi-Single (EP) – *Love is Everywhere*

Released 1998 – Fingerprint Records

Recorded at Brilliant Studio, San Francisco, CA - 1997

Band: Michael Been, Scott Musick, Tom Ferrier, Jim Goodwin.

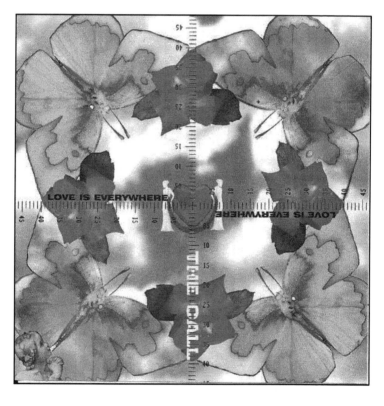

Image used with permission: Dan Russell & Fingerprint Records.

EP Album: The Call – *Love is Everywhere*

<u>**Tracks:**</u>

Love is Everywhere (Single Mix)   4:14

Love is Everywhere (Remix)   4:13

Spring Bird (2.0 Version)   4:02

World on Fire (Soundtrack Mix)   5:44

Love is Everywhere (Love Mix)   5:05

To Feel This Way (Soundtrack Mix)   4:02

Image used courtesy of Ken Hawkins

11th Album – *Live Under the Red Moon*

Released 2000 – Conspiracy Music

Recorded at Coach House, San Juan Capistrano - 1990

Band: Michael Been, Scott Musick, Tom Ferrier, Jim Goodwin. (Addt'l on "You Run" Ralph Patlan)

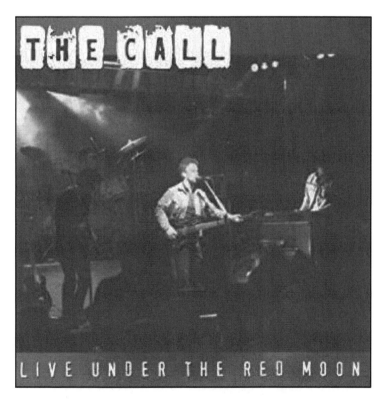

Image used with permission: The Call & Conspiracy Music.

Album: The Call – *Live Under the Red Moon*

Tracks:

Floating Back	4:17
A Swim in the Ocean	7:27
This is Your Life	4:02
I Don't Wanna	5:19
You Run	7:32
Family	4:16
Same Old Story	3:52
Even Now	5:01
Red Moon	3:15
Oklahoma	5:29
You Were There	4:29
I Still Believe (Great Design)	5:30
Let the Day Begin	4:25

12th Album – *20th Century Masters –*
The Millennium Collection: The Best of The Call

Released 2000 – Hip-O Records – Universal Music

Compilation: Recorded 1982 - 1997

Band Members: Michael Been, Scott Musick, Tom Ferrier, Jim Goodwin, Greg Freeman, Steve Huddleston, Garth Hudson.

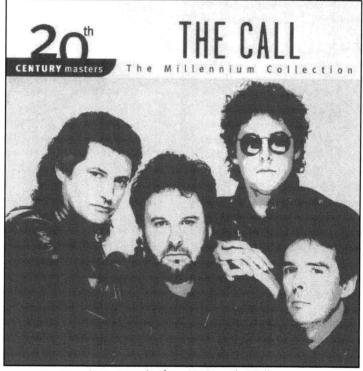

Image used w/permission: The Call

Album: The Call – *20th Century Masters –*
The Millennium Collection: The Best of The Call
<u>**Tracks:**</u>

Let the Day Begin	3:51
The Walls Came Down	3:44
War Weary World	4:18
Turn A Blind Eye	3:49
Modern Romans	3:25
Scene Beyond Dreams	3:50
Everywhere I Go	4:22
I Don't Wanna	5:05
You Run	5:36
Surrender	4:10
What's Happened to You	4:20
I Still Believe (Great Design)	5:33

13th Album – *The Call - A Tribute to Michael Been* featuring Robert Levon Been (BRMC)

Released 2014 – Lightyear Entertainment

Compilation: Recorded 2013 at Troubadour

Band Members: Robert Been, Scott Musick, Tom Ferrier, Jim Goodwin.

Image used w/permission: The Call & Lightyear Entertainment.

Album: The Call - *A Tribute to Michael Been*
featuring Robert Levon Been (BRMC)

<u>**Tracks:**</u>

Everywhere I Go	5:15
I Still Believe	5:45
I Don't Wanna	5:36
Floating Back	3:59
Into the Woods	4:57
Turn A Blind Eye	4:17
Oklahoma	6:55
You Were There	4:22
Red Moon	3:46
Let the Day Begin	4:30
Modern Romans	4:22
You Run	5:46
The Morning	6:11
Same Old Story	4:19
The Walls Came Down	4:17
Uncovered	3:11

* There were multiple versions of this album on CD, Vinyl and a DVD video. Some versions were released autographed by Scott, Tom, Jim and Robert Been.

Scott Musick – Solo Album – *Americana Gold*

Recorded / Released – 2013 - Lagoon Studio, Santa Cruz, CA and The Penthouse, Tulsa, OK.

Musicians – Scott Musick, Jim Lewin, Danny Timms, Randy Ess, Alan Ransom.

Image used with permission: Copyright Scott Musick .

Album: Scott Musick – *Americana Gold*

Tracks:

Manana	3:48
This Love For You	3:30
Blue Highway	3:46
The Crossing	3:48
Olden Days	4:06
Foolish Thangs	3:02
Comin' to You	3:18
The Promise	3:18

* Danny Timms – Former Keyboard and Backing Vocalist for the group The Highwaymen and Kris Kristofferson.

* Randy Ess – Guitar and vocals from The Rogues 5.

Scott subsequently recorded an album *Americana Gospel* in 2016 with a cover of The Call's – "You Run" but it was never officially released.

14th Album – *The Call – Collected* (3CD or 2 Colored LP)

Released 2019 – Universal Music in association with Lightyear / Label / New Sound / Warner Music

Band Members: Michael Been, Scott Musick, Tom Ferrier, Jim Goodwin, Greg Freeman, Steve Huddleston, Garth Hudson, Joe Read and Robert Been.

The 2 LP vinyl version was a limited numbered release of 1000 on Orange Vinyl Records.

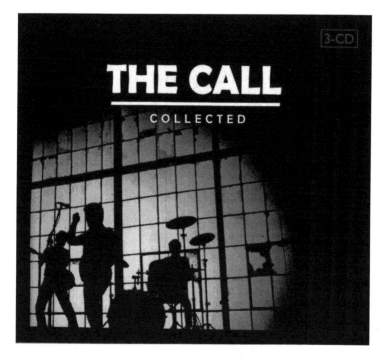

Image used w/permission: The Call

Album: *The Call – Collected* **(3CD Version)**

<u>Tracks:</u>

CD – Disc 1

War Weary World	4:17
There's a Heart Here	2:57
Upperbirth	3:47
Waiting for the End	5:17
The Walls Came Down	3:41
Modern Romans	3:25
Time of Your Life	3:30
Turn a Blind Eye	3:49
Heavy Hand	3:25
Scene Beyond Dreams	3:49
Delivered	4:02
Tremble	4:00
Everywhere I Go	4:21
I Still Believe (Great Design)	5:34
The Morning	4:44
Oklahoma	4:22
Tore the Old Place Down	4:16
In the River	4:02
I Don't Wanna	5:13

Album: *The Call – Collected* (3CD Version)

Tracks:

CD – Disc 2

Walk Walk	5:00
The Woods	5:11
Memory	4:06
Let the Day Begin	3:53
You Run	5:36
When	5:20
Same Ol' Story	3:38
Surrender	4:09
What's Happened to You	4:14
You Were There	4:06
Like You've Never Been Loved	4:15
Floating Back	3:23
What a Day	4:13
Love is Everywhere (Single Mix)	4:14
Become America	3:41
World on Fire	5:10
Soaring Bird	4:07
All You Hold On To	3:24

Album: The Call – *Collected* (3CD Version)

<u>**Tracks:**</u>

CD – Disc 3

I Still Believe – Live 1986	5:48
Oklahoma – Live 1986	5:06
Everywhere I Go – Extended Remix	4:20
To Feel This Way (Michael Been)	5:00
Jumpoffs (MB)	4:05
Us (MB)	3:47
This World (MB)	4:43
For Your Love (MB)	3:17
We Know Too Much (MB)	5:49
Love is Everywhere – Remix	4:12
Soaring Bird – 2.0 Version	4:04
World On Fire – Sound track Mix	5:43
Love is Everywhere – Love Mix	5:03
To Feel This Way – Sound Track Mix	3:58
Even Now – Live 1990	5:02
I Don't Wanna – Live 1990	5:12
Let the Day Begin – Live 2013 (RB)	4:16

(Tribute to Michael Been – Ft. Robert Been)

* 2 LP Orange colored vinyl version had fewer tracks.

Discography Part B:

The Singles / 45's

"The Walls Came Down" (*Modern Romans*) - 1983

Side A – "The Walls Came Down" (*Modern Romans*)

Side B – "Upperbirth" (From the album *The Call*)

Rank #17 on Billboard US Mainstream Rock Music Chart

Special one sided release in Trouser Press
Blue Flexi – Disc 33 RPM Magazine Insert

"The Walls Came Down" – 12" Single on London

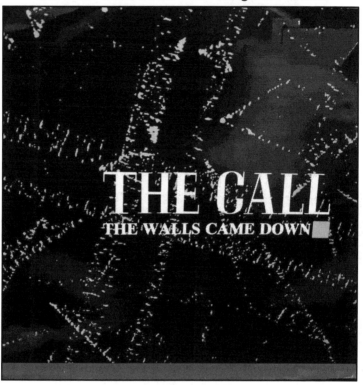

Side A: "The Walls Came Down"

Side B: "Upper Birth" / "War Weary World"

Band Members: Michael Been, Scott Musick, Tom Ferrier, Greg Freeman, Steve Huddleston, Garth Hudson

Back side of "The Walls Came Down" 12" Single

45 RPM – 12" Single – London / Polygram - 1983

London – LONX 28 – ZPMSC 10375 / 10376 / 10377

"Upper Birth" / "War Weary World" from the *The Call*

"Everywhere I Go" (*Reconciled*) – 1986

Side A: "Everywhere I Go"

Side B: "Tore the Old Place Down"

Band Members: Michael Been, Scott Musick, Tom Ferrier, Jim Goodwin

Rank #38 on Billboard US Mainstream Rock Music Chart

Back Side of "Everywhere I Go" - 7" Single

45 RPM – 7" Single – Elektra / Asylum – 1986

Elektra – ST-E-69546-A / ST-E-69546-B

"Everywhere I Go" (By Michael Been)

"Tore the Old Place Down" (By Michael Been / Jim Goodwin)

"I Still Believe (Great Design)" – (*Reconciled*) – 1986

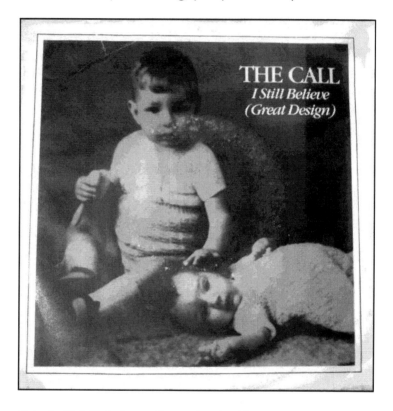

Side A: "I Still Believe (Great Design)"

Side B: "Blood Red (America)"

Band Members: Michael Been, Scott Musick, Tom Ferrier, Jim Goodwin

Rank #17 on Billboard US Mainstream Rock Music Chart

Back Side of "I Still Believe (Great Design)" - 7" Single

45 RPM – 7" Single – Elektra / Asylum – 1986

Elektra – 7-69521 US / 969 548-7 Europe

"I Still Believe (Great Design)" - (By Been & Goodwin)

"Blood Red (America)" - (By Michael Been)

"I Don't Wanna" – (*Into the Woods*) – 1987

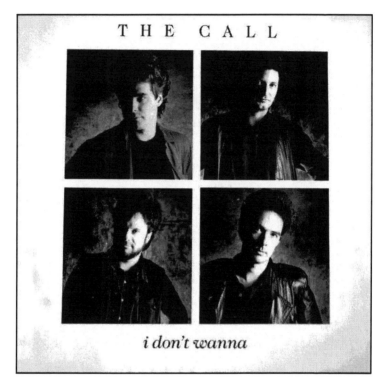

Side A: "I Don't Wanna" (Edit of LP Version)

Side B: "Day or Night" (LP Version)

Band Members: Michael Been, Scott Musick, Tom Ferrier, Jim Goodwin

Rank #38 on Billboard US Mainstream Rock Music Chart

Back Side of "I Don't Wanna" - 7" Single

i don't wanna (EDIT OF LP VERSION) b/w day or night (LP VERSION)

Produced by Michael Been and The Call and Don Smith

from the elektra album "into the woods"

AVAILABLE ON LP 60739-1, CASSETTE 60739-4 COMPACT DISC 60739-2

ELEKTRA/ASYLUM RECORDS, A Division of Warner Communications Inc., ●° 75 Rockefeller Plaza, New York, New York 10019 9229 Sunset Boulevard, Los Angeles, California 90069. ℗ © 1987 Elektra/Asylum Records for the United States and WEA International Inc. for the world outside of the United States. All Rights Reserved. Printed in U.S.A. Warning: Unauthorized reproduction of this recording is prohibited by Federal law and subject to criminal prosecution.

0 7559-69461-7 9

7-69461
45 RPM
STEREO

45 RPM – 7" Single – Elektra / Asylum – 1987

Elektra – 7-69461 US / EKR 60 UK / 96 9461-7 Italy

"I Don't Wanna" (Edit of LP Version) - (By M. Been)

"Day or Night" - (By Michael Been & Tom Ferrier)

"Let the Day Begin" – (*Let the Day Begin*) – 1989

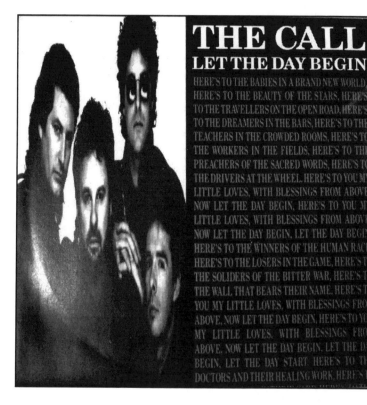

Side A: "Let the Day Begin"

Side B: "Uncovered"

Band Members: Michael Been, Scott Musick, Tom Ferrier, Jim Goodwin

Rank #1 on Billboard US Mainstream Rock Music Chart

Back Side of "Let the Day Begin" - 7" Single

45 RPM – 7" Single – MCA – 1989

MCA – MCA1362A / MCA1362B

"Let the Day Begin" - (By Michael Been)

"Uncovered" - (By Michael Been & Jim Goodwin)

"You Run" – (*Let the Day Begin*) – 1989

Side A: "You Run"

Side B: "Watch"

Band Members: Michael Been, Scott Musick, Tom Ferrier, Jim Goodwin

Rank #29 on Billboard US Mainstream Rock Music Chart

Back Side of "You Run" - 7" Single

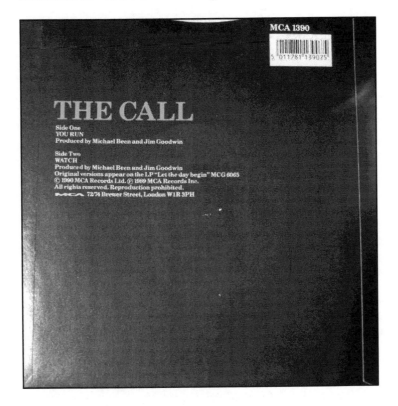

45 RPM – 7" Single – MCA – 1989

MCA – MCA1390A / MCA1390B

"You Run" - (By Michael Been)

"Watch" - (By Michael Been & Harry Dean Stanton)

"What's Happened To You" – (*Red Moon*) – 1990

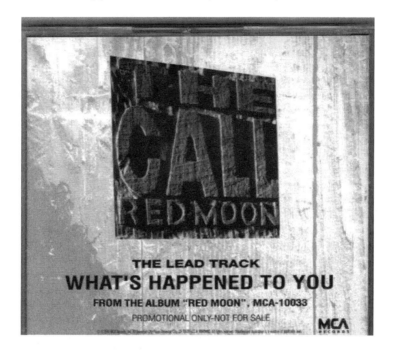

Promotional CD Single Only

Track: "What's Happened To You"

Band Members: Michael Been, Scott Musick, Tom Ferrier, Jim Goodwin

Rank #39 on Billboard US Mainstream Rock Music Chart

Promo CD Single Disc "What's Happened To You"

CD Promo Single – MCA – 1990

MCA – CD45-1008

"What's Happened To You" - (By Michael Been)

*Featuring Bono of U2 on backing vocals.

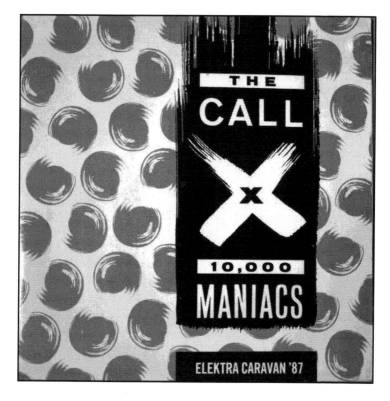

The Call / X / 10,000 Maniacs

Side A – Track 1 – "What's the Matter Here" (10,000 Maniacs)

Side A – Track 2 – "See How We Are" (X)

Side AA – Track 3 – "In the River" (The Call)

Band Members: Michael Been, Scott Musick, Tom Ferrier, Jim Goodwin

Back Side of Elektra Caravan '87 - 7" & 12" Single

33 RPM – 7" & 12" Single – Elektra – 1987

Elektra – SAM 390

"In The River" - (By Michael Been & Scott Musick)

Gatefold cover opens and has the history / bio of the 3 bands… X, The Call and 10,000 Maniacs – Promo Only.

Chapter Thirteen:

Songs, Pictures & Stories

<u>LET THE DAY BEGIN</u>

Here's to the babies in a brand new world
Here's to the beauty of the stars
Here's to the travelers on the open road
Here's to the dreamers in the bars
Here's to the teachers in the crowded rooms
Here's to the workers in the fields
Here's to the preachers of the sacred words
Here's to the drivers at the wheel

Here's to you my little loves
With blessings from above
Now let the day begin
Here's to you my little loves
With blessings from above
Now let the day begin, let the day begin

Here's to the winners of the human race
Here's to the losers in the game
Here's to the soldiers of the bitter war
Here's to the wall that bears their name

Here's to you my little loves
With blessings from above
Now let the day begin

Here's to you my little loves
With blessings from above
Now let the day begin, Let the day begin, Let the day start.
Here's to the doctors and their healing work
Here's to the loved ones in their care
Here's to the strangers on the street tonight
Here's to the lonely everywhere
Here's to the wisdom from the mouths of babes
Here's to the lions in the cage
Here's to the struggles of the silent poor
Here's to the closing of the age

Here's to you my little loves
With blessings from above
Now let the day begin
Here's to you my little loves
With blessings from above
Now let the day begin
Let the day begin
Let the day start

Let The Day Begin
written by Michael Been
published by Neeb / Tarka Music
all rights reserved

Reprinted w/ permission: The Call

In a post after our phone conversation Jim Kerr posted the following on Simple Minds FB page. Aug. 21, 2020

"KINDRED SPIRITS : THE CALL and SIMPLE MINDS"

"We didn't know that we were on the same path until somehow we met at a junction. The junction was music and the mystery that lay at the heart of it. It allowed Simple Minds and The Call to come together, then go crisscrossing North America, giving heart and soul night after night, in doing so we would become kindred spirits. Least that was how it felt to me."

"Many of the bands who Simple Minds toured/performed with would go on to become more than mere acquaintances. I'm thinking in particular of Skids, Icehouse, China Crisis, U2, Silencers, Pretenders, Stranglers, Deacon Blue, and plenty others. All of whom we would become friends with - and there really was no better feeling than being out on tour and experiencing friendships develop - and in some cases go on to become very long lasting."

"Such was the case in early to mid 80's when we toured together, getting to know Michael Been and all the other (wonderful) guys in The Call - including Scott Musick, Tom Ferrier and Jim Goodwin."

"In a world where no one seemingly owes you anything, the spirit and sound of The Call certainly managed to have an effect on many of those who experienced it. For this the guys should be proud."

"In a much fairer world however? The Call, in my opinion, merited a bigger success than much of the stuff that hovered around the top of the Billboard charts both then and now."

"And had it been the other way around? Simple Minds would have been proud to be the opening act for The Call. Such was the level of esteem we had for Michael and his band."

"Michael Been may have left this earth ten years ago this week. However, somewhat like an older brother, I still feel his effect on me both as a songwriter and in other ways more personal. Finding his songs to be as relevant now as they were almost four decades ago, coincidentally it is the music of Michael and the band, The Call, that I have found myself listening mostly over these last few weeks. Yesterday however gave me a chance to also relive some of those memories of when Simple Minds first hooked up with The Call - as I spoke to Knoel Honn in Oklahoma - who is currently writing a book about The Call and the life and times of Michael Been."

"As a measure of how much he is valued still, many who knew and loved Michael are keen on preserving his legacy. Simple Minds have contributed to that in our way and aim to continue further still."

****

"When we were on tour with Simple Minds, Michael would go out at the end of the night to sing with them. They would leave one of their flowing outfits for Michael to wear, if he wanted to. He never wore it... (laughter)" – Tom Ferrier

Michael Been in the early days playing guitar.
Photo by Joe Piccorossi 1982 Destin, FL
Used with permission R. George Inness III

Photo by Joe Piccorossi 1982 Destin, FL
Used with permission R. George Inness III

Drawing by and compliments of Scott Musick.

"This drawing tells the story of the Call performing at the semi acoustic, 150 capacity cafe at SoulFest (circa 1999). The band had tiny amps, appropriate to the tiny room. Michael insisted on using his large Ampeg bass amp."

"I believe, as the story goes, within the first song alone the electricity was blown. Fuses popped. After the first three black outs, we kept someone at the panel to flip the breaker switches back quicker."

- Scott Musick -

Scott drew the previous picture poking fun of Michael and his need for volume, even in the smaller venues. Scott clearly labeled the controls on Michael's amp "Mo Me, Les Dem".

Many fans recalled similar moments:

Greg Netter said, "The same thing happened at Phoenix Hill in Louisville, when The Call played there. I got to meet and chat with them while the fuses were being fixed."

Robert Tate, also remarking on the Louisville show said, "The power at the Phoenix Tavern was blown several times. Still one of the best concerts I have ever seen."

Scott later revealed that the next day on the flight, he made additional drawings for each of the band members and crew, secretly placing them in their seats for them to find.

For me, this speaks volumes to Michael's larger-than-life personality and wanting to give a big show, even to a smaller crowd of 150 people at SoulFest.

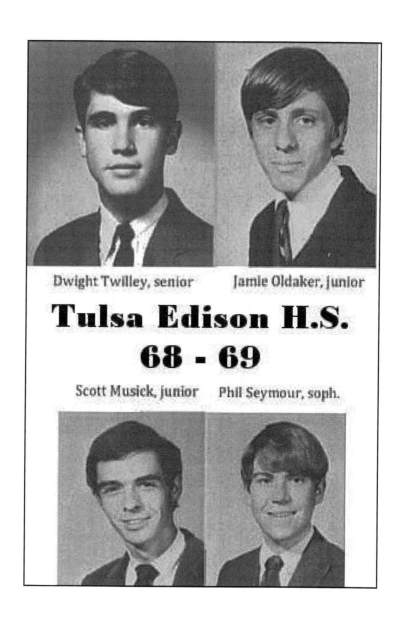

Dwight Twilley, senior — Jamie Oldaker, junior

Tulsa Edison H.S.
68 - 69

Scott Musick, junior — Phil Seymour, soph.

1969 Tulsa Edison High School yearbook

The Call's singer: Walls come down

By PAUL WILLISTEIN
Entertainment Editor

Michael Been takes rock music seriously. No dance fever, get down and boogie or freakazoid nonsense for him.

That's not to say that the lead vocalist and songwriter for one of America's most promising up and coming new rock bands, The Call, doesn't think music should be fun. It's just that when you're writing songs with titles like "The Walls Came Down," there are other things on your mind.

"Scott, the drummer, and I are avid Band fans. Robbie Robertson's lyrics and Bob Dylan influenced us when we were teen-agers. They were a real turning point for us. That was really when we decided we didn't want to do standard pop music. You can do so much more with rock 'n' roll. You don't have to keep it in that adolescent sense, at least not lyrically."

Been spoke recently in a telephone interview prior to tonight's Electric Factory concert at Stabler Arena, Bethlehem, where The Call opens for Peter Gabriel. In addition to Been, who sings lead vocals and plays guitar and synthesizer, The Call includes Greg Freeman, bass; Scott Musick, drums, percussion and vocals, and Tom Ferrier, guitar and vocals.

Robertson led The Band which, originally as The Hawks, backed rockabilly star Ronnie Hawkins during the early '60s, made the legendary "Basement Tapes" with Bob Dylan and toured with him, recorded critically acclaimed LPs of its own, and had its final tour documented in the film, "The Last Waltz." So, one can appreciate Been's enthusiasm when Garth Hudson, organist for The Band, agreed to play on The Call's first two albums, including its latest Mercury Records release, "Modern Romans."

"Playing with Garth is a dream come true. I started to listen to The Band and Dylan at 19," said Been, 31. "Two of my favorite writers are Dylan and Robertson. Garth was so important for setting the mood of those songs.

"About four years ago, we were in the studio doing demos. A Capitol Records company representative asked me, 'If you could play with anybody in the world, who would it be?' I said, 'Garth Hudson.' Well, he knew Garth. He played him the tapes, and Garth called us the next day."

Hudson is seen in the video of "The Walls Came Down" on MTV, and has toured with The Call. Hudson will not appear with The Call tonight because he is rehearsing with The Band for a planned reunion tour (sans Robertson), according to Been.

Friday July, 15 1983 – The Morning Call
By Paul Willistein

"The Call's singer: Walls come down"

"Michael Been takes rock music seriously. No dance fever, get down and boogie or freakazoid nonsense for him. That's not to say that the lead vocalist and songwriter for one of America's most promising up and coming new rock bands, The Call, doesn't think music should be fun. It's just that when you're writing songs with titles like "The Walls Came Down," there are other things on your mind."

"Scott, the drummer, and I are avid Band fans. Robbie Robertson's lyrics and Bob Dylan influenced us when we were teen-agers. They were a real turning point for us. That was really when we decided we didn't want to do standard pop music. You can do so much more with rock 'n roll. You don't have to keep it in that adolescent sense, at least not lyrically."

"Been spoke recently in a telephone interview prior to tonight's Electric Factory concert at Stabler Arena, Bethlehem, where The Call opens for Peter Gabriel. In addition to Been, who sings lead vocals and plays guitar and synthesizer, The Call includes Greg Freeman, bass, Scott Musick, drums, percussion and vocals and Tom Ferrier, guitar and vocals."

"Robertson led The Band which, originally as The Hawks, backed rockabilly star Ronnie Hawkins during the early 60's, made the legendary "Basement Tapes" with Bob Dylan and toured with him, recorded critically acclaimed LP's of its own, and had its final tour documented in the film, "The Last Waltz." So, one can appreciate Been's enthusiasm when Garth Hudson, organist for The Band, agreed to play on The Call's first two albums, including its latest Mercury Records release, "Modern Romans."

"Playing with Garth is a dream come true. I started to listen to The Band and Dylan at 19," said Been, 31. Two of my favorite writers are Dylan and Robertson. Garth was so important for setting the mood of those songs."

"About four years ago, we were in the studio doing demos. A Capital Records company representative asked me, 'If you could play with anybody in the world, who would it be?' I said, 'Garth Hudson.' 'Well, he knew Garth. He played him the tapes and Garth called us the next day.'"

"Hudson is seen in the video of 'The Walls Came Down' on MTV and has toured with The Call. Hudson will not appear with The Call tonight because he is rehearsing with The Band for a planned reunion tour (sans Robertson), according to Been."

1982 – Scott, Greg, Michael, Steve and Tom.
Photo used with permission from The Call.

Jim Goodwin – 1989 – Courtesy Ken Hawkins

When once asked about the other members of the band, Michael replied, "They're extraordinary people. Very unshowbusiness, very bright and extremely talented, and all very different in their approaches. Jim is the youngest, he's full of life, loves life. Scott's very intense, but he's also the funniest guy I've ever known. And Tom, a.k.a. Dicky, is an original - indescribable - there's nobody like him."

Michael, Scorsese and "The Last Temptation of Christ."

Based on the novel Nikos Kazantzakis. Director: Martin Scorsese. Screenplay: Martin Scorsese and Jay Cocks. Producer: Barbara De Fina. Director of Photography: Michael Ballhaus. Music: Peter Gabriel. A Universal Pictures Release.

Cast: Willem Dafoe (Jesus), Barbara Hershey (Mary Magdeline), Harry Dean Stanton (Saul/Paul), Harvey Keitel (Judas Iscariot), Victor Argo (Peter), Michael Been (John), John Lurie (James), Andre Gregory (John the Baptist), Verna Bloom (Mary, Mother of Jesus), David Bowie (Pontius Pilate), Juliette Caton (Angel).

The movie took three months to film. It began in October of 1987, in Morocco, and was completed in late December. It was released to theaters in September, 1988.

Michael gave the following synopsis. "The movie is a fictional account of the life of Jesus, not the biblical story - although, they certainly interweave. I think the purpose of the movie is to show Christ's struggle with his humanness - feeling all the joy and pain, and struggling with the same confusion and temptation we all go through. The movie never denies Jesus' divinity, but it focuses on His human side."

"I have been a fan of his for years," Michael said of Scorsese. "He was like my favorite director from when I saw Mean Streets."

Likewise a longtime "Call" fan, Scorsese invited Michael to screen test and offered him the role of the disciple John. Michael said of their first meeting, "I met him a few years back when he came to hear us play in New York. I found out he followed the group, knew the songs, and liked the music. He felt there was a similarity in what the band was singing about and the purpose of his movies."

Michael recalled his time in Morocco as an, "amazingly intense, loving experience." Attributing the overall success of the casting and filming to Martin Scorsese's technique as a director. "He's an extremely intense filmmaker. He elicits such convincing performances from his actors simply by choosing people who would naturally fit the role. He's not an acting coach, but rather he sets the mood and level of drama. The ultimate sin to him is overacting - he likes real drama but not overdone. He's very concerned that movement and facial expression not be exaggerated, since he expects the content of the dialogue to put the scene across."

"And Willem Dafoe I cannot say enough about. He's a brilliant and intuitive actor. All the actors and crew were extraordinary people - very serious about their work, but at the same time very humorous and real. I made some close friendships during the filming. All the actors were very musical. If we weren't acting we were together making music. Harry Dean Stanton and I became great friends and wrote a song together called 'Watch,' which is on the new album. All these gifted people confined together for three months - a very creative atmosphere, so much passion and expression. It was one of the greatest times of my life."

****

Feeling a strong connection and having written "Watch" together with Michael, Harry Dean Stanton went on the road briefly, playing harmonica at several shows with the guys.

Michael, Harry Dean Stanton and Jim at McCabe's.

Jim, and Michael, with Harry Dean Stanton at Club
Lingerie in Los Angeles. Photos courtesy Jim Goodwin.

Chapter Fourteen:

Memorabilia & Rare Items

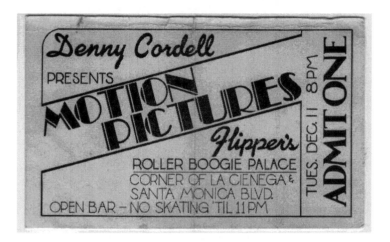

From the collection of Greg Freeman. This is an original ticket from a (Pre-Call) Motion Pictures show December 11th, 1979 at 8pm. Venue was Flipper's Roller Boogie Palace on Santa Monica Blvd. Denny Cordell put together this private invite show to promote the band. It was around this same time Motion Pictures became Phil Seymour's backup band playing shows for Phil and recording some demos with him.

Greg Freeman, as the bass player for Motion Pictures, and subsequently, The Call, has a collection of many rare one of a kind items, and hand written documents from touring and the studio.

MICHAEL BEEN & *Airtight*

DALE
OCKERMAN

GARY
RODA

MICHAEL
BEEN

SCOTT
MUSICK

LOVE WILL LIVE FOREVER
IF YOU EVER WORRIED ABOUT ME
(M. BEEN) DOBUMI PUB. ASCAP. 1979

A rare pressing of Airtight (Pre-Call) Been / Musick

Sleeveless t-shirt *Modern Romans* US tour 1983

Courtesy of the Scott Musick collection

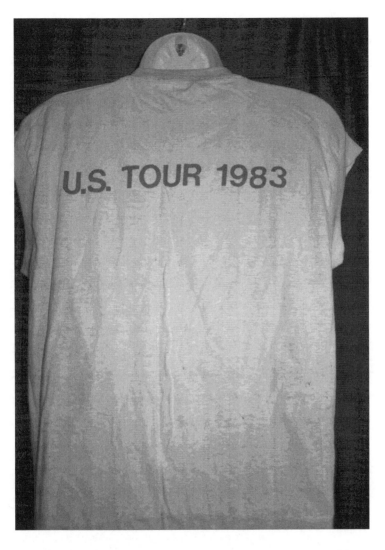

Original *Modern Romans* sleeveless 1983 US tour shirt

Courtesy Scott Musick collection

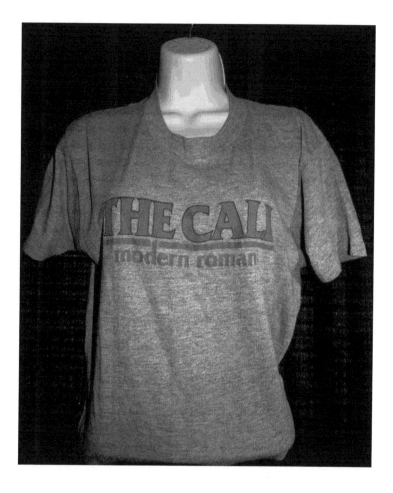

Modern Romans 1983 US tour grey t-shirt

Courtesy Scott Musick collection

Front of original The Call concert security t-shirt from
Oct 10, 1986, in Florida.

Courtesy of Knoel & Wendy Honn collection

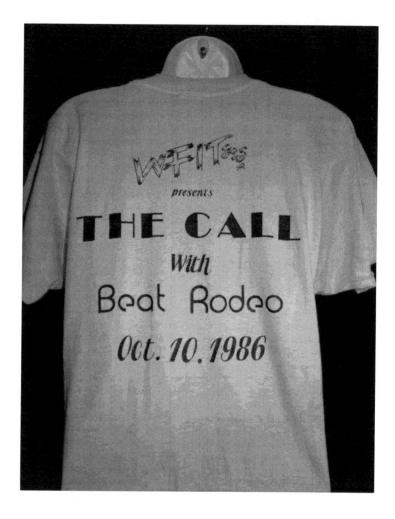

Back of original The Call concert security t-shirt from
Oct 10, 1986, in Florida. WFIT 89.5 FM with Beat Radio.

Courtesy of Knoel & Wendy Honn collection

Original 1986 – The Call – *Reconciled* tour shirt

Possibly the hardest shirt to find and the most popular
with The Call t-shirt collectors. Scott Musick collection.

Front of the very hard to find *Into the Woods* shirt.
Courtesy Scott Musick collection.

Back of The Call – *Let the Day Begin* – World tour shirt
from the 1989 world tour. Someone went all punk and
removed the sleeves, still a great shirt.

Courtesy of Knoel and Wendy Honn collection

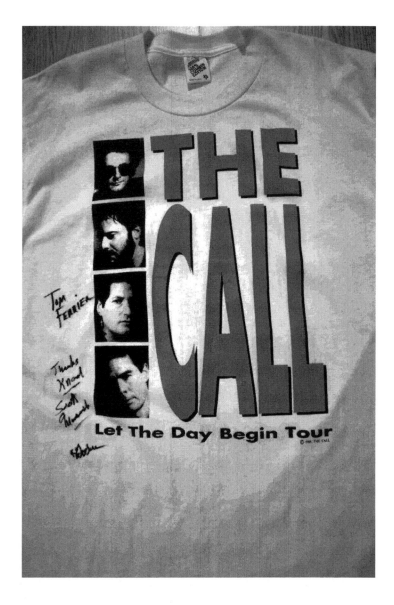

Signed - Let the Day Begin - tour shirt – 1989
Part of the Knoel and Wendy Honn collection

Original –The Call – *Red Moon* - tour t-shirt 1990

Part of the Knoel and Wendy Honn collection

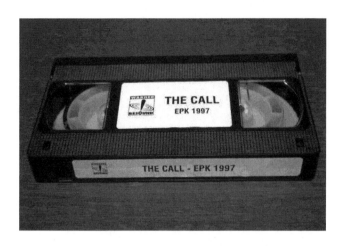

1997 Promo Video Tape – Knoel and Wendy Honn collection

Scott Musick and Tom Ferrier business cards

PW0602E FLOOR GEN ADM L = 6.50
6.50

FLOOR
GA   1X
GEN ADM
JAM1643
L 2JUN3

MILLER HIGH LIFE/JAM
THE CALL
21 YEARS OF AGE OR OLDER
PARK WEST
322 W. ARMITAGE
THU JUN 2 1983 8:00 PM

NP1118 G.A. GEN ADM C .00 ENP1118
EVENT CODE SECTION/AISLE ROW/BOX SEAT ADMISSION EVENT CODE
.00 18 & OLDER PRICE

QFM-96 LISTENER
APPRECIATION CONCERT
QFM-96 LISTENERS ONLY
THE CALL
NEWPORT MUSIC HALL
SAT NOV 18 1989 7:00 DOORS

CN 58327
G.A.
COMP
GEN
CA .00
ADM

G.A.
SECTION/AISLE
CA 1X
GEN ADM
NEW1153
C 2NOV9

TICKETMASTER

Your ticket
to the Best
Seats in Town!

NO REFUND
NO EXCHANGE
SERVICE CHARGE
NOT REFUNDABLE

TICKETFLY

Sec:GA*
VIP*

K.C.H. Promotions Presents
ALARM58 to benefit Leon Russell
Monument Fund
Cain's Ballroom
423 N Main St. Tulsa, OK
Fri Apr 20, 2018 7:00 PM (Doors: 6:30 PM)
Price:$0.00
All Ages; ALARM58.com Preservemusic.org

Order:093149293276 Purchased By:Monument Fund

Sec:GA Apr 20 2018 7:00 PM $0.00
00982817983176

Top two tickets are vintage Call tickets from the 1980's.
The Bottom ticket is from the 2018 benefit concert that
Scott Musick, Tom Ferrier, Matt Martin and Michael
Divita played at to raise money for the Leon Russell
Monument in Tulsa, Oklahoma. Scott and Tom played a
few Call songs with Michael Divita singing. This was the
2nd time Michael Divita filled in on vocals. He was also
the primary vocalist in 2017 for The Call in New Orleans.

Most of the autographed items shown were signed at
the New Orleans, LA rehearsals in 2017

November 27th, 1990 – Rockefeller's Houston, TX
Part of the Knoel and Wendy Honn collection

Signed stick, card, cymbal and drum head by Scott

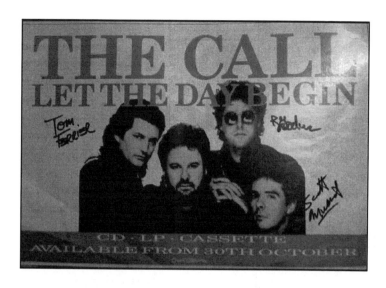

Reconciled signed by Michael, Scott, Tom & Jim

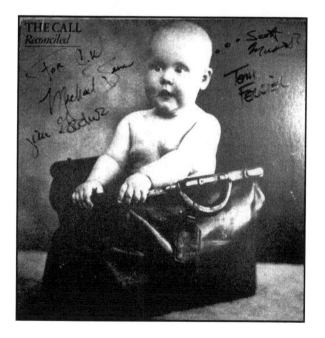

THE CALL

"Peter Gabriel has hailed them as the future of American music, and I wouldn't contradict him for a moment," says Britain's *Melody Maker*. *Time* magazine named the band's **Into The Woods** one of the 10 best albums of 1987; *Bam* tagged **Reconciled** as among the top 10 of 1986. *Rolling Stone* calls Michael Been one of the most literate lyricists in rock 'n' roll today. The *Los Angeles Times* says that The Call is "able to deliver what U2 only skirts: an integration of spiritual yearning with blues-based grit."

This group has been hailed as "one of the best new bands of the '80s" every year of the '80s. And now it's almost the '90s and have you even heard of these guys? Maybe you've heard of some of their fans: Gabriel (who asked The Call to open his 1983 world tour), actor Harry Dean Stanton (who plays harmonica on **Let the Day Begin**'s "For Love"), and director Martin Scorsese (who cast Michael Been as the apostle John in *The Last Temptation of Christ*).

"We never asked for music to give us a free ride or make us big shots," says Been. "All we ever asked was to be working musicians."

Nearly a decade of work has led to the strongest album to date for The Call. **Let the Day Begin**, their MCA debut, delivers all that its predecessors promised, capturing fully the power and passion of Northern California's most uncompromising foursome. "This is the way the band sounds live," says singer/songwriter/producer Been. "And for that reason I'm happiest with this album. We went into the studio with a p.a., not headphones; I sang the songs while we did them."

The songs -- from the driving rock 'n' roll of the title cut (and the lead single) to the hymn-like gentleness of "Uncovered" -- are hewn from the soul, tempered in the heart, and performed from the gut. "Lyrically," says Been, "it's about our inability to communicate, our attempt to run away from ourselves...and others. It's about self-realization, about healing."

The story of The Call began in Santa Cruz, California, in 1980 when Michael Been moved north from Los Angeles with drummer Scott Musick and joined forces with guitarist Tom Ferrier and bassist Greg Freeman. The musical roots of The Call go back further.

Michael Been was raised in Oklahoma City, which, he says "has a particular cultural mindset that I didn't fit into and I knew it...early." By age 7, he was performing Elvis Presley and Buddy Holly tunes for a Hank Williams and Patsy Cline crowd on the television show *Big Red Shindig*. At 16, he was able to escape to Chicago, where he thrived on the indigenous blues scene and briefly performed as a stand-up comedian with his high school buddy, the late John Belushi.

Inspired by Bob Dylan, The Band and the political turmoil of the day, Been moved to California in the early '70s to make his musical statement. After continual rejection by a disco-dominated record industry, the group was brought to England to record **The Call** for producer Hugh Padgham (Phil Collins, XTC, the Police). Garth Hudson, keyboardist for Been's heroes, The Band, asked to play on the 1982 release.

Hudson also played on 1983's **Modern Romans**, shining on the alternative radio hit "The Walls Came Down," and again on 1984's **Scene Beyond Dreams**. **Scene Beyond Dreams** first introduced keyboardist/composer/co-producer Jim Goodwin to the line-up. Bassist Freeman left soon after, and Been switched from six strings to four.

By now, The Call were touring the world with Peter Gabriel and Simple Minds, and both Gabriel and Jim Kerr made appearances on 1986's **Reconciled**. (Been returned the favor, singing on

Page one promo information from 1989.

both their albums as well.) Robbie Robertson also guested -- his first record project in 10 years. Reconciled produced two strong singles: "I Still Believe" and "Everywhere I Go."

While 1987's Into the Woods was a critical success for The Call, other projects demanded their time. Been made his acting debut in the stunning and controversial *Last Temptation of Christ*, and performed nationally with newfound buddy Harry Dean Stanton. He also contributed to the soundtrack for the Paul Newman/Tom Cruise film *Color of Money*, working with Robbie Robertson and the late jazz great Gil Evans.

"We all had offers to do other things, to play with other people," says Been. "But when the four of us play together, it's better than any one of us and more than the sum of the parts. That's why we do it."

The chemistry peaks when the band is onstage, as thousands of concert-goers will attest. With a major summer tour upcoming and a strong commitment from a new record company, The Call is a band whose time has come.

Discography

The Call - 1982
Modern Romans - 1983
Scene Beyond Dreams - 1984
Reconciled - 1986
Into the Woods - 1987
Let the Day Begin - 1989

Personnel

Michael Been - Bass guitar/guitar,/lead vocals
Tom Ferrier - Guitar and vocals
Jim Goodwin - Keyboards and vocals
Scott Musick - Drums and vocals

May, 1989

Page two promo information from 1989.

Document released by MCA Records.

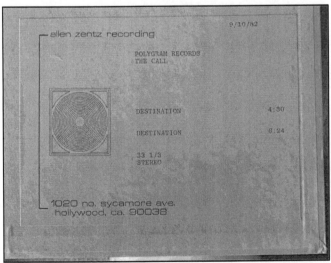

Rare one of a kind remix acetate 9/10/82

Extended mix side of rare The Call acetate
image provided from Greg Freeman collection.

This rare acetate is of two alternate mixes of
"Destination" off of the *Modern Romans* album. Greg
Freeman, and Producer / Engineer Dave Jerden, worked
on these and they were never released. The B side is an
extended remix that is 6:24 almost two minutes longer
than the original track.

This is an original, one of a kind, 1982 test pressing of "War Weary World," which was eventually released as a 12" promo for radio play. It has been autographed by Scott Musick, Tom Ferrier, and Steve Huddleston.

Next is an Elektra white label promotional 12" single of "Oklahoma," "I Still Believe (Great Design)," and "Oklahoma" live vs. This album has been autographed by Jim Goodwin, Scott Musick, and Tom Ferrier. This album and the test pressing above are both part of the Knoel and Wendy Honn collection.

Signed "War Weary World" - 12" promo single.

"Oklahoma" promotional 12" single

Signed by Jim, Scott, and Dicky Dirt.

12" 45 rpm single of "The Walls Came Down" on Mercury label. A promotional copy w/ LP version of "Destination" on B side. Signed by Scott, Tom, and Jim. Part of the Knoel and Wendy Honn collection.

Autographed envelope - Jim, Michael and Scott.

Signed show poster from 2017,

New Orleans, LA - show at club Siberia.

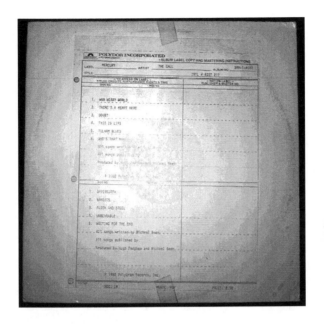

Original test press of the first album *The Call* 1982.

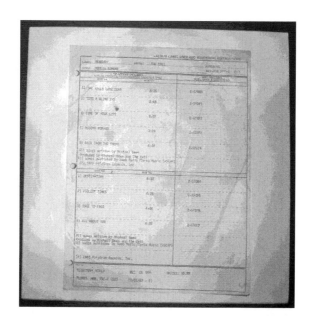

Original test press of *Modern Romans* 1983.

Original test press of the fourth album *Reconciled* 1986.

March On! t-shirt was only available at the New Orleans, LA, show at Club Siberia April 22nd, 2017.

June 26, 1983 – King Biscuit Flower Hour LP

Sept 21, 1986 - King Biscuit Flower Hour LP

Chapter Fifteen:

Documents

In my efforts to do thorough research into the band and its members, I came across a lot of great historical documents; some of them telling fascinating stories and others just cool, because of how they represent what occurred back then.

The first document I came across presents an interesting question... **Was The Call a Christian band?**

The letter Michael wrote on the next page clearly was meant to appeal to Christian rock radio stations. However, in the first issue of the Notified newsletter, Michael paints a little different picture when asked about his lyrics and biblical references in The Call's songs.

"I try to write about my own life experiences, and I am a Christian myself, so I write from that point of view. Although it wouldn't be the type of Christianity commonly practiced these days. I believe it's a vain presumption to think that all people in the world should believe what I believe or that it would necessarily be right for them. I only know that it's right for me. I'm not interested in selling religion; Christianity or otherwise."

January 22, 1986

Dear Programmer:

I believe in God, the Father almighty,
   creator of heaven and earth.

I believe in Jesus Christ, his only Son, our Lord.
   He was conceived by the power of the Holy Spirit
      and born of the virgin Mary.
   He suffered under Pontius Pilate,
      was crucified, died, and was buried.
   He descended into hell.
   On the third day he rose again.
   He ascended into heaven,
      and is seated at the right hand of the Father.
   He will come again to judge the living and the dead.

I believe in the Holy Spirit,
   the holy catholic Church,
   the communion of saints,
   the forgiveness of sins,
   the resurrection of the body,
   and the life everlasting. Amen.

Sincerely,

Michael Roe

THE CALL

Official letter sent from Michael to program directors at
Christian radio stations, declaring his beliefs in an effort
to get broader airplay.

Along that same vein...

Michael, in an article by former L.A. Times staff writer Mike Boehm, back in August of 1994, had more to say on the subject of religion and spirituality.

"Been is thoughtful about the spiritual element in his music, which for a time even won The Call some attention in Christian-rock circles. Been said a good deal of that following fell away, however, after he took an acting role as one of Jesus' disciples in "The Last Temptation of Christ." Director Martin Scorsese's controversial merger of deep spirituality and imaginative speculation made for an excellent film, but it found no friends in conservative religious quarters where anything but a literal reading of the Bible was shunned as blasphemy."

"I was raised in the South, and (Christianity) permeates your life pretty seriously down there," Been said. "When I was younger, I rejected it all because of the obvious hypocrisies and obvious pettiness and orthodoxies. As you grow older, some of the things that weren't so obvious kind of stay with you. It's a struggle to figure out what was a lie about it, and what was true about it."

"My particular spirituality isn't too much based on some kind of cosmic relationship. It isn't all walking on air, up in the clouds and looking for answers or inspiration in some kind of otherworldly thing. The spiritual aspect of life usually comes to me through people. It's pretty much acted out in relation with other people. I think there's a point to it all. I can't really figure out what it is, but as corny as it is, I know it has something to do with love, something to do with (reaching) outside ourselves."

Michael went on in the same article to say...

"That in some way the greatness of the times we live in [is...] It isn't possible to be ignorant any more. Now we have to take some kind of responsibility [accountability for ourselves]."

"Perhaps the television network's satellite dish [this was pre-internet] is the new tree of knowledge, claiming the innocence of beholders who are forced into numbness in the face of horror."

Mike Boehm went on to say about Michael, "Been sees possibility and challenge in our current state."

The numerous articles through the years, interviews and this intriguing document, tell a mixed tale of Michael's inner conflict and turmoil, his non-traditional spirituality, and views of Christianity that were not your normal Sunday morning traditions and flavor.

The next document I have is from the collection of David Sallinger who was friends with Gary Heaton.

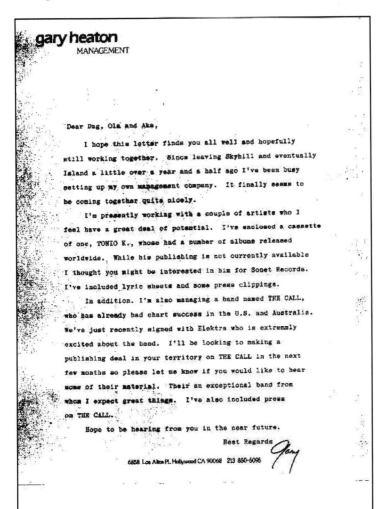

gary heaton
MANAGEMENT

Dear Dag, Ola and Ake,

    I hope this letter finds you all well and hopefully still working together. Since leaving Skyhill and eventually Island a little over a year and a half ago I've been busy setting up my own management company. It finally seems to be coming together quite nicely.

    I'm presently working with a couple of artists who I feel have a great deal of potential. I've enclosed a cassette of one, TONIO K., whose had a number of albums released worldwide. While his publishing is not currently available I thought you might be interested in him for Sonet Records. I've included lyric sheets and some press clippings.

    In addition. I'm also managing a band named THE CALL, who has already had chart success in the U.S. and Australia. We've just recently signed with Elektra who is extremmly excited about the band. I'll be looking to making a publishing deal in your territory on THE CALL in the next few months so please let me know if you would like to hear some of their material. Their an exceptional band from whom I expect great things. I've also included press on THE CALL.

    Hope to be hearing from you in the near future.

                Best Regards

       6858 Los Altos Pl. Hollywood CA 90068 213 850-5095

Just after The Call transitioned to Elektra from Mercury.

Here are a couple of great documents regarding Scott's drums and cymbals he used - as well as, an endorsement deal for Sabian Ltd. (Mar 14th, 1986) and obviously, Pearl supplying his drums (Dec 22nd, 1987).

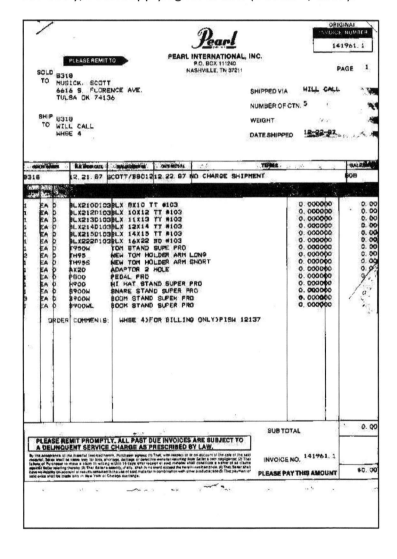

SABIAN Ltd.

CYMBAL MAKERS

SALES OFFICE 4800 SHEPPARD AVE EAST #115, SCARBOROUGH, ONTARIO M1S 4N5, CANADA 416-298-9551 TELEX 065-26227

ENDORSEE AGREEMENT

I, the undersigned, hereby authorize SABIAN CYMBALS and their advertising agency to use my name, photograph and endorsement in the advertising and publicity of SABIAN PRODUCTS, until such time as I cancel the arrangement. It is understood that during the tenure of this my authorization I will not endorse other makes of cymbals. I further understand that after termination of this arrangement my name and photograph might continue to appear for as long as the relative publications are in circulation.

(please print)

Name. Scott Musick

Group/Band. The Call

Address. 6858 Los Altos Pl. Los Angeles, CALIF.

Type of Group, etc. Rock

Telephone No. (213) 850-5095

My Sabian set up consists of:
14" Rock Hats - 17" Extrathin Crash - 18" med. Crash
20" Minibell ride - 18" Thin Crash - 20" Chinese.

SCOTT SIGN HERE

Signed.......

Signed.......

Roy Edmunds.
Sabian Ltd.

Date. 3/14/86

The above document provided from the collection of David Sallinger. March 1986 during the *Reconciled* era.

****

The next document is a hand written note by Scott about why he wants to use Pearl Drums. Probably leading up to an endorsement based on the previous receipt for Pearl drums shipped to Scott.

Decision to use Pearl?

I think Pearl drums & hardware are very high quality products. They sound especially great when played by Chester Thompson or Narada Michael Walden. I was impressed when I found that they use Pearl equipment. However, the decision was made when Ken Austin expressed a sincere interest in The Calls' music and helped out by supplying the equipment needed for our "Into the Woods" (The Calls' latest LP) sessions. His interest and attitude convinced me that Pearl would always + would provide the kind of support we need.

"Decision to use Pearl? I think Pearl drums & hardware are very high quality products. They sound especially great when played by Chester Thompson or Narada Michael Walden. I was impressed when I found that they use Pearl equipment. However, the decision was made when Ken Austin expressed a sincere interest in The Call's music and helped out by supplying the equipment needed for our "Into the Woods" (The Call's latest LP) sessions. His interest and attitude convinced me that Pearl had the best (?) drums & would provide the kind of support we need.

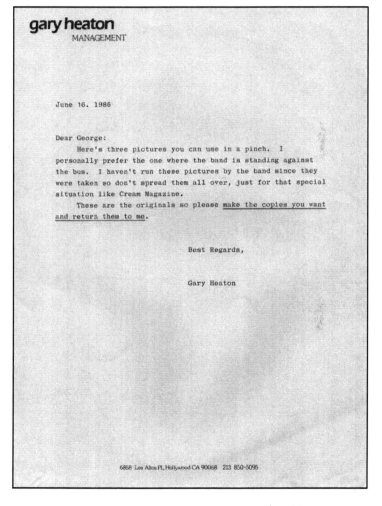

gary heaton
MANAGEMENT

June 16. 1986

Dear George:
   Here's three pictures you can use in a pinch. I personally prefer the one where the band is standing against the bus. I haven't run these pictures by the band since they were taken so don't spread them all over, just for that special situation like Cream Magazine.
   These are the originals so please make the copies you want and return them to me.

                    Best Regards,

                    Gary Heaton

6858 Los Altos Pl. Hollywood CA 90068   213 850-5095

Gary Heaton letter dated June 16th, 1986.

BEEN MUSIC *Red Music*
C/o Jerry Newton
6858 Pas Altas Pl.
Hollywood, Ca 90068

SONG TITLE	ROYALTY AMOUNT
ALL ABOUT YOU-F-M	75.49
ALL ABOUT YOU-F-P	7.05
BACK FROM FRONT-F-M	74.50
BANDITS-F-M	.06
DESTINATION-F-P	33.58
DESTINATION-F-M	76.13
DOUBT-F-M	.06
FACE TO FACE-F-M	74.70
FACE TO FACE-F-P	1.76
FULHOM BLUES-F-M	.06
MODERN ROMANS-F-P	47.73
MODERN ROMANS-F-M	72.52
THE WALLS DOWN-F-P	83.08
THE WALLS DOWN-F-M	18.22
TIME OF LIFE-F-M	72.68
TIME OF LIFE-F-P	31.83
TURN A BLIND EYE-F-M	73.79
TURN A BLIND EYE-F-P	53.03
VIOLENT TIMES-F-M	61.67
VIOLENT TIMES-F-P	8.84
UPPERBIRTH-F-M	4.84
VIOLENT TIMES-F-M	14.25
WHOS THAT MAN-F-M	.06
TOTAL ROYALTY AMOUNT	885.93

11 EAST 71ST STREET   -   NEW YORK, NEW YORK 10021

This document and the next one are a prime example why musicians, to this day, struggle to live on royalties. The artists do all the work, writing, and performing songs, and get very little in ongoing royalties.

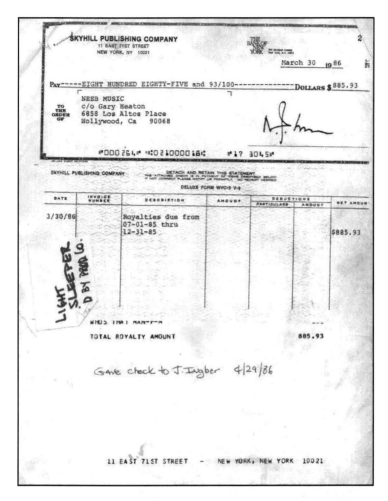

SKYHILL PUBLISHING COMPANY
11 EAST 71ST STREET
NEW YORK, NY 10021

THE BANK OF NEW YORK

March 30 19 86

Pay------EIGHT HUNDRED EIGHTY-FIVE and 93/100-------------DOLLARS $ 885.93

TO THE ORDER OF
NEEB MUSIC
c/o Gary Heaton
6858 Los Altos Place
Hollywood, Ca   90068

⑆000264⑆ ⑆021000018⑆ ⑈17 3045⑈

SKYHILL PUBLISHING COMPANY

DETACH AND RETAIN THIS STATEMENT
THE ATTACHED CHECK IS IN PAYMENT OF ITEMS DESCRIBED BELOW.
IF NOT CORRECT PLEASE NOTIFY US PROMPTLY. NO RECEIPT DESIRED.

DELUXE FORM WVO-3 V-9

DATE	INVOICE NUMBER	DESCRIPTION	AMOUNT	DEDUCTIONS PARTICULARS	AMOUNT	NET AMOUNT
3/30/86		Royalties due from 07-01-85 thru 12-31-85				$885.93

WHO'S THAT MAN???

TOTAL ROYALTY AMOUNT   885.93

(handwritten left margin) LIGHT SLEEPER D BY PROD CO.

(handwritten) Gave check to J. Ingber 4/29/86

11 EAST 71ST STREET   -   NEW YORK, NEW YORK 10021

Obviously, the royalties this was for was pre-*Reconciled* and a four-month period, during the transitional time between record labels and the new albums release.

(Not sure why there is a Light Sleeper post-it stuck to this, as that project came 6 years later.)

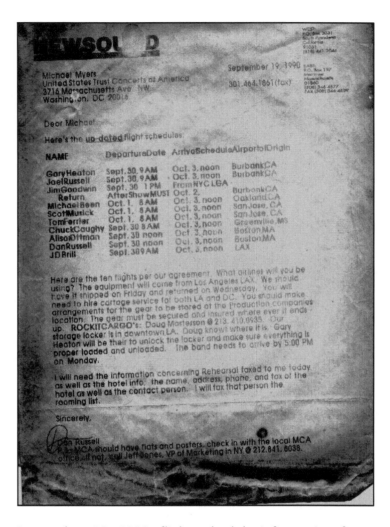

September 19, 1990, flight schedule information from Dan Russell, courtesy of the David Sallinger collection.

Here is a somewhat amusing look at merchandise sales on the road at shows.

The Call
T-shirt Journal

Rules

① Before you settle out w/ hall determine crew/employee comps. If hall gets a %, sell them at $10 per. If hall does not get a %, then the band will by for ≈ cost. Check w/ Road manager.

② Find/meet house, money person. (not always promoter) do a minimum inventory.

③ Beg Bal #50. (take it out during night — so your just left w/ sales.)

④ Make sure you won't run out of general inventory, call Gary to order more.

⑤ Cash out around 1000. leave money for float, crew ↑s

⑥ check wardrobe before Band Leaves.

Merchandise was so much cheaper back in the 80's.

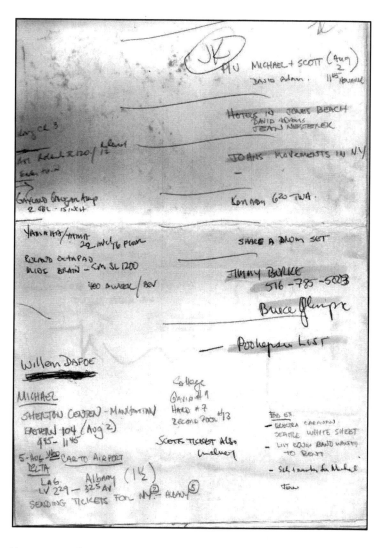

Here we have some hand written notes regarding Michael and Scott. The note also mentions Willem Dafoe so it is likely from around Oct. 1987 when Michael was filming Last Temptation of Christ with Dafoe.

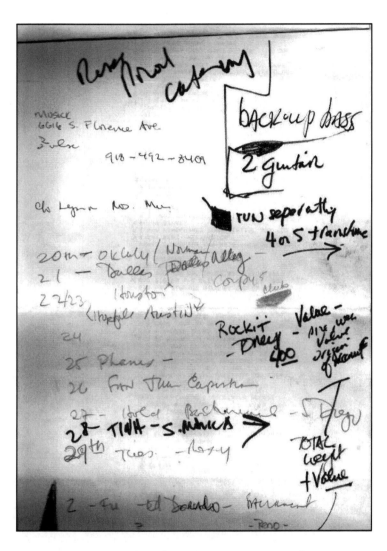

Some interesting hand written tour notes relevant to
Scott and possible tour dates and locations.

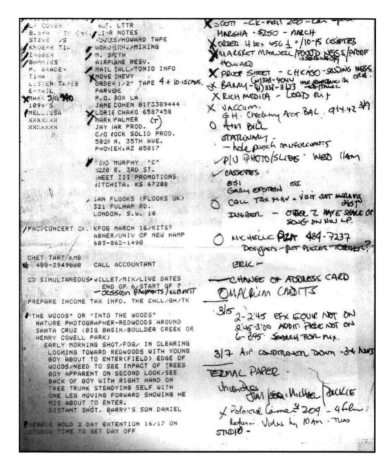

Lower left corner of document has an interesting note regarding taking the photo for the cover of *Into the Woods* describing when, where, and how it will be taken, and of whom... "Barry's son, Daniel"

Lower right corner is about Jim, Michael, and "Dickie" [Dicky], and a Polaroid camera and returning a video by 10 a.m. Tuesday.

A:RP841

THIS AGREEMENT is made the 18th day of
April One thousand nine hundred and
ninety-one BETWEEN MICHAEL BEEN SCOTT MUSICK and
TOM FERRIER all care of Jeffrey C. Ingber, Suite 1100,
1901 Avenue of The Stars, Los Angeles, California 90067,
USA (presently professionally known as THE CALL and
hereinafter called "Artist") of the one part and RED DOT
RECORDS LIMITED of Broadway House, 35 Harwood Road,
London SW6 (hereinafter called "Company") of the other
part

NOW IT IS HEREBY AGREED as follows :-

ONE: Definitions
The words and phrases defined below shall have the
meaning there attributed to them :-
A.   "the Act" means the Copyright Designs and
Patents Act 1988 as the same may from time to time be
amended or re-enacted
B.   "sound recording" and "film" shall have the
meanings respectively attributed to them in the Act
C.   "phonograph record", the noun "record" and/or
their equivalent means any kind of device, contrivance,
conception or material or non-material means whether
known unknown, invented or to be invented in the future
including without limitation vinyl discs, laser read
discs, tape and film by or through which sound may be
reproduced or transmitted either alone or in conjunction
with visual images or other sensory stimuli
D.   "audio visual device" means a record by or
through which sound may be reproduced or transmitted in
conjunction with visual images or other sensory stimuli
E.   "Artist Master" means, subject to the
provisions of sub-clause Seven E the original sound
recording or film or combination of sound recordings or

1

Recording contract between Red Dot records, and The Call signed April 18th, 1991. Entered into by Michael Been, Scott Musick, and Tom Ferrier, professionally known as The Call.

Retail Price used by Company or its licensees for top
line records of performances by popular artists

T.   "Artist's Name" means THE CALL and/or such
other professional name as Artist or any one or more of
them collectively or individually may from time to time
use

U.   "Recording Budget" means a written budget for
the anticipated Recording Costs to be expended in
recording Artist Masters

V.   "Recording Costs" means all costs of and
incidental to the recording and production of Artist
Masters including without limitation the cost of "demo"
recordings, rehearsals, pre-production, instrumental
musicians, vocalists, conductors, arrangers,
orchestrators, copyists etc., payments to a trustee or
fund to the extent required by any agreement with any
labour organisation or trustee, payment of any fee or
advance in relation to the services of a producer or
engineer, travel, accommodation and subsistence expenses
in relation to recording, studio, tape, editing, mixing,
re-mixing and re-recording and other similar costs
whenever the same are incurred in connection with the
production of the completed Artist Masters up to and
including the cost of mastering and "cutting" the
production master and also including the cost of
recording backing tracks for promotional use

W.   "Recording Fund" means that percentage of the
advances payable to Artist pursuant to sub-clause A of
the Third Schedule hereto during each Contract Period in
relation to Minimum Commitment Masters (or Call Masters
as the case may be) as may be expended by way of
Recording Costs during that Contract Period in recording
such Minimum Commitment Masters (or Call Masters as the
case may be)

X.   "Minimum Commitment Masters" means Artist
Masters specified in sub-clauses A and B of the Second
Schedule hereto

4

The Call never released a record on Red Dot records label. However, the date and label do seem to correspond to the *Michael Been: Light Sleeper Album.* Most likely this contract was ultimately *Light Sleeper.*

may be). The Recording Fund available for Minimum Commitment Masters to be recorded during each Contract Period shall be as follows:-

(i) Initial Period
Two hundred thousand United States dollars ($200,000)

(ii) First Option Period (if applicable)
Two hundred thousand United States dollars ($200,000)

(iii) Second Option Period (if applicable)
Two hundred and fifty thousand United States dollars ($250,000)

(iv) Third Option Period (if applicable)
Three hundred thousand United States dollars ($300,000)

(v) Fourth Option Period (if applicable)
Three hundred and fifty thousand United States dollars ($350,000)

(vi) Fifth Option Period (if applicable)
Four hundred and fifty thousand United States dollars ($450,000)

Further, unless Company agrees to the contrary Artist shall not be entitled to expend more than the Applicable Fraction of the Recording Fund available during any Contract Period in recording each Artist Master to be recorded during that Contract Period. For the purposes of this sub-clause B the expression "the Applicable Fraction" means a fraction the numerator of which is one (1) and the denominator of which is ten (10) where Minimum Commitment Masters (or Call Masters as the case may be) to be recorded pursuant to the Recording Fund available during any Contract Period comprise an Album and the denominator of which is two (2) multiplied by the number of Singles where Minimum Commitment Masters (or Call Masters as the case may be) to be recorded pursuant to the Recording Fund available during any Contract Period comprise Single(s). Company shall supply Artist with a copy of the Recording Budget and any revisions thereto. If Artist has any objections to or queries arising from the Recording Budget or revisions thereto

19

Page #19 of the 53-page contract specifies fund amounts for recording / masters in different periods of the contract.

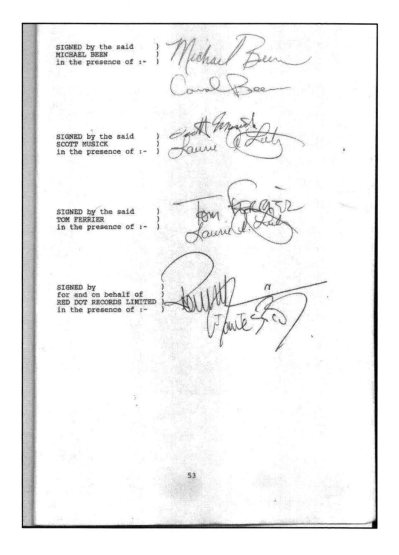

SIGNED by the said)
MICHAEL BEEN)
in the presence of :-)

SIGNED by the said)
SCOTT MUSICK)
in the presence of :-)

SIGNED by the said)
TOM FERRIER)
in the presence of :-)

SIGNED by)
for and on behalf of)
RED DOT RECORDS LIMITED)
in the presence of :-)

53

Final page (Page 53), signature page of recording contract. Signed by Michael Been, with Carol Been as witness, Scott Musick, and Tom Ferrier.

(Courtesy of: The Knoel and Wendy Honn collection.)

Chapter Sixteen:
In My Memory – Recalling The Call

"I had been a fan of The Call for several years when I got to see them live for the first time. I was blown away. The concert was a spiritual experience." – Knoel Honn

****

"Red Moon tour, Cincinnati, Bogart's.

A band called Hopscotch Army opens, and it's clear something isn't right. The singer/guitarist and the bass player are glaring at each other from the outset. Three or four songs in, the bassist sets his instrument down and stalks off of the stage. Singer runs after him. The drummer throws his sticks down and leaves. Screaming voices from backstage. Curtain closes.

The band broke up WHILE ON STAGE.

After a few minutes, Michael [Been] sticks his head out, laughing, and says "we're going to make it up to you".

They played for almost three hours." – Brian A. Smith

****

"What I loved was the passion in Michael's voice and lyrics, he could bring the emotional intensity up and down in an almost operatic way." – Peter Gabriel

"The Call was not your typical band in the 80s and 90s.. They wore their hearts on their sleeves. They played music that challenged the core of your being, your emotions and what you believe. They did not have the typical love songs. I still listen to various songs from Reconciled daily. I think Michael said it best about their music, "the song, "With or Without Reason", seems to be about the inability of the intellect or reasoning mind to understand certain basic truths about life" I was fortunate to see them five times in concert. The energy at their concerts was incredible. Michael's voice filled the hall along with his unique bass playing. Thank you Michael, Scott, Tom and Jim for your music. It still lives today in my heart and soul." - R. George Inness, III

****

"I got to know The Call via my love for Bruce Cockburn and Mark Heard. I read a review of LET THE DAY BEGIN and asked my father to buy me the album when he visited Europe. My three brothers and I were making CCM music in our home country of South Africa in Afrikaans. We were called THE MULDER BROTHERS (Francois, Frikkie, Ferdie and Fanie) and recorded an album with USA CCM artist Bobby Michaels in 1987. I loved the song UNCOVERED and we got the rights to translate and record the song on our lp. It came out in

1990 on our debut with Maranatha Record Company in South Africa - we changed our name to ELEISON."

- Francois Mulder

****

"I have been blessed with multiple years of addiction recovery. The Call have provided a soundtrack for my mental and spiritual well being. After a show in Seattle, Jim [Goodwin] and I were hanging out and I told him how emotional I had gotten during many of the songs that night. I found myself standing singing along with tears of joy running down my cheeks. I also told him that I saw others doing the same in the audience. He was quite surprised and later told me he began noticing more and more people doing the same at shows. "For people like us ~ in places like this ~ we need all the hope that we can get." - Mark Brittell

****

"The Call Cain's [Ballroom Tulsa, OK] show was and is still a favorite show of mine. Troubadour reunion show was special too." - Tate Wittenberg

****

The next message is from Ken Drew the keeper of *The Call* Website [For many, many, years now.]

"I became a Call fan back when I was in college. I had heard "The Walls Came Down" and liked it but never went to find their albums until I heard "Reconciled" in 1986. I thought that this album was amazing. Hearing Everywhere I Go, I Still Believe (Great Design), Blood Red, The Morning, Oklahoma, etc.....I was hooked. Thus we backtrack the first 3 albums and away we go."

"Now it was time to see them live. My first show was at UOP in Stockton during the Into The Woods tour. I have the set list which was awesome. As I was working the show for college, I was able to see how accessible the band was before the show as they were kind enough to sign my CD inserts for "Reconciled" and "Into the Woods" and Michael asked me my name and signed it "For Ken" on one and "To Ken" on the other. His presence was surreal. The best part of the show, which was billed as a Progressive Dance Party, was watching Michael look at the band singing "For people like us, in places like this" and rolling his eyes. I had to laugh as the crowded just didn't get it. It was a show that was poorly advertised and on a Thursday night in a venue not suited for such a show. That said, the band was super tight and sounded great."

"My next chance to see the band was in '89 at the Crest Theater in Sacramento during the "Let the Day Begin" tour. It was another great set as proven by the set list I

also have. They graciously signed my "Let the Day Begin" poster that I was able to get from a local record store. Once again, personalized. Four days later, I saw them at the Fillmore in SF. A fantastic concert experience once again. It's too bad that MCA ("Musicians Cemetery of America") dropped the ball on the band by not having product for potential fans to buy but I digress........."

"Then came the end of days....the release of "Red Moon" and the lack of a hit single meant the show in SF at Slims Dec. 13, 1990 would be the last chance to see the band all together again. The show had a strange vibe. It was as if the band knew that the end was near. Nonetheless, the music flowed and the fans went crazy."

"As I was off to post-doc in the mid-west, I taught myself how to make remedial websites and started the Call website as a billboard on the internet for the band. Little did I know that I was going to move to the Boston area and eventually get to meet Dan Russell who managed the band. I continue to help support the band and promote the Call on the internet. I was fortunate to be at the reunion shows with Robert Levon Been taking the helm for his father. The Troubadour show was amazing and I was able to provide a few glimpses of the sound-check on YouTube for fans to enjoy."

"I have conversed with Jim and Scott over the years and appreciate those conversations whether via email or

phone. As I sit back and listen to the body of CALL work, I am thankful that I had the chance to see them at their peak powers. It is an experience I treasure to this day. #LetTheDayBegin #IStillBeleive" - Ken Drew

****

"The truth can change a man / In the wisdom of his days / It whispers soft but constantly / You cannot live this way" Michael Been, The Call. When I first heard "The Walls Came Down" as a Senior in High School via MTV. I was mesmerized by such a cool band with what sounded like cool lyrics, the power struck me, but I was busy. I had serious socializing to do, drinking parties to host and girls to meet. After hitting bottom living in Florida, spending my nights as a DJ as a dance pub getting free beer as most of my pay, I moved from Florida to Texas in 1985. A roommate from California had a killer Album collection with "Modern Romans" and the Call's first album. The first self titled first album sank deep and the messages whispered soft but constantly, I couldn't live the way I was living. Truth began to appear in my life and I began to change, leaving behind the alcohol and casual relationships. I converted to life changing Christianity. Reconciled came out and was played constantly on my local College Radio Station, FM90 Amarillo. "Everywhere I Go" was a mantra of mine. I served a two year mission in Belize and Honduras. I

returned home found a wonderful woman. We've now been married over 27 years. I found "Let the Day Begin" listened to "When" and realized, truly, the Truth did change a man, me, whispering soft but constantly, I couldn't live that way and the Call had planted the seed and softened my heart. I once wrote a letter to The Call, praising their music as what I always came back to. I got a letter, telling me that "To Heaven and Back" would soon be released. I found that symbolic, found the CD, still have it. I still regularly listen and feel all of the Call discography, knowing how the lyrics and driving music changed me."- Joe Lockwood, Los Alamos, New Mexico

****

"When I first saw them in concert, which I believe was at the Cain's Ballroom, around 1988 I think, they were amazing, just mesmerizing to hear and see. It was almost like a religious experience! It was four incredibly talented musicians, totally in the zone, completely immersed in their music and the moment."

"It felt like the entire building was moving and the crowd right along with it to their songs. Everybody was singing along and jumping to songs like the spiritual sounding "I Still Believe", to the commanding "Everywhere I Go". They were able, like all great bands, to just kind of pull you into the music, as if time had stopped and we were just completely absorbed into the raw emotion of the songs. You could feel the energy in the air, as if a ball of electricity had entered the room and set the crowd on fire!"

"The entire band was amazing, from Dicky's skillful, soulful guitar licks to Scott Musick's floor pounding, eternally in the pocket drums, I had rarely before or since seen or heard such a passionate powerful performance by a band. All that being said, the night belonged to Michael Been. He played and sang like a man possessed! That night he was like a minister preaching the Gospel of Rock and Roll, and the stage was his pulpit. People always talk about a performer having the "It" factor, that undefinable quantity that puts them in a league of their own. Well, whatever "It" is Michael Been had and [he] had it in spades! He sang with a mix of fire, passion, and conviction that all great charismatic singers have, and he did it with flair and a mind for showmanship. During one song, which was "Everywhere I Go", I think, he's going along singing and playing the bass, and then just totally impromptu (and probably unexpected, even to the other members in the band) he picks up a Telecaster and just starts bustin' out a solo like he's Carl Perkins! It was an incredible time to be alive and an amazing night of music."

"I think the consensus is that like a lot of other bands in that period, The Call really didn't get all the accolades *and attention that they truly deserved, and I think that's true. I think that their songwriting and performing was on par with many other great bands of that time like, U2, The Police, REM, Smithereens, Tom Petty and the Heartbreakers, and all the other great singer/songwriter, power pop type of bands that were around then."*

"On a personal note, it has been a great pleasure to get to meet and know Scott Musick and some of the other members in the band. As well as being world class musicians, they are also good, genuinely nice, cool, humble down to earth people who don't mind taking time out for the local musicians and their fans."

"I am very grateful that this book is being written about The Call. They were definitely one of the greatest bands of the 80's, and put out some of the best songs and live performances of any band I've ever seen or heard. I hope that it draws more attention, and hopefully a new generation of fans to the band, and their amazing, passionate, soul-inspiring music!"

- Philip Johnson, local [Oklahoma] musician, and friend of Knoel Honn, author, and Scott Musick, drummer for The Call.

****

"I was at a sound-check of The Call's on the Into the Woods tour. The song that Michael used to check levels was 'Alive and Kicking.' When the bass and drum break hit, (at the level Michael wanted), I could feel it in my chest at fifty feet!" – Ken Hawkins

****

"My first wake up-Call happened in a record store in 86. The cover of Modern Romans and the presence of Garth Hudson caught my attention. Since then they have been a big part of the soundtrack of my life: The post-punk Joy Division-inspired first two releases, the spiritual lyrics giving me hope during my theological study and work in addiction therapy and rehabilitation, and the once in a lifetime concert experience in my hometown Stavanger, Norway, in 88: They were touring all over Norway that summer, from Kristiansand in the south to Tromsoe in the far north. The concert took place in a small venue in the attic of an old wooden fish factory. They were rocking really loud that evening. A band of young Norwegians named Uncle Sam`s Wig Wam Party opened for them on the whole tour. I guess this tour gave a good start for Kyrre S Fritznes who is a well known musician and producer. I remember that Tom Ferrier came onstage during their set bringing drinks to the hard working young men. It was a hot and crowded evening that I always will remember." - Per Arne Tengesdal

****

"On two separate occasions, Two times I got to talk to him [Michael Been] in person. Both of the times I talked with him was after concerts at a venue in Norfolk, Virginia called the Boathouse. It is no longer standing due to a hurricane. [Then] I saw him again, that time at a place called Alley Katz in Richmond, Virginia. So I had seen the band three times total. Once for Let The Day Begin. The second for Red Moon and The third in support his solo album. All great shows. Great memories! … [and] that is how I got to meet Michael Been." – Robert Long

****

"When I first saw the video for "The Walls Came Down" on MTV it hit me right in the gut. It just had more meat to it than most of the stuff out in the early 80's. That took me down a rabbit hole, soon I discovered there were two Okies in the band and that cemented the deal for me. Discovering Garth Hudson on keyboards lead me to The Band, this became another lifelong love. The Call is a band that I always have on hand for those days when you just need to hear "I still believe", "Let the day begin" or "Us". Michael Been wrote such emotional and spiritual lyrics." - Dr. Rick Huskey

****

Thank you for all you've given us – We Still Believe!

"As one of Scott's protégés maybe I'm a little bit biased but I've never met anyone kinder. With my time as a student at his music school he taught me more about appreciating music and playing [guitar and drums] than anyone else. Truly a life experience I will forever be grateful for. Thanks for all you do." – Caleb Nelms

"We all talk about our roots. I believe that Mike's roots, where his performing is concerned, started in the mid 60's in the small town of Park Forest, IL. He was in a band with 4 friends called The Saints. They were akin to The Beatles in popularity at the time and if you had the chance to actually meet them it was a big deal. I was 14 at the time and totally infatuated with the band. I never missed them performing at the tennis court dances. Due to an ironic set of circumstances I not only met them but they ended up practicing in our basement, became part of the family and were a huge influence on my life. Mike (he wasn't Michael yet) was the most serious of the guys and looking back, it was inevitable that he would stay in the world of music. I remember how excited they all were when they were about to record "Please Don't Leave Me" and "Out In the Streets" the two songs they wrote together. Mike was the one that insisted they do it until it was perfect. His "big brother" advice to me was that whatever I am doing, do it as many times as it takes to be proud of it and then let it be. I've always had an affectionate admiration for our "basement band" and the time we all had together. I believe my folks "Ma and Pa" Wilson's enthusiasm and encouragement at a time when "long hairs" were looked down upon contributed to Mike's confidence to go out into the world and make the amazing music that he did. You are loved and missed, my friend." – Pam Wilson Wetzel – Friend

Through all of the memories and stories you can still feel the impact The Call had back then and even now. If there is any question of the veracity after the previous memories and stories you only have to look to the new OKPOP museum in downtown Tulsa, Oklahoma. Like with many others Executive Director of OKPOP, Jeff Moore, explains how The Call influenced him and will continue to influence Pop culture and music for many more generations to come via OKPOP.

"In 2007 the Oklahoma Historical Society launched an effort to document the history of Rock and Roll in Oklahoma. The work entailed acquiring new artifact and archive collections, conducting more than two hundred oral history interviews, and creating 6,000 square foot of exhibit space. As the curators began the research for a theme to tie all of the different pieces together, they looked into the careers of Wanda Jackson, The Collins Kids, Leon Russell, JJ Cale, The GAP Band, and many more, looking for the perfect title. Being fans of 80s college radio, the staff were also very aware of The Call.

Though The Call was not formed in Oklahoma, founding members Michael Been, from Oklahoma City and Scott Musick, from Tulsa had to be included in the project. The band embraced their Oklahoma roots for the album cover art on their 1986 release Reconciled, which included two images from the University of Oklahoma's Western History Collection. The now iconic purple-toned photograph of the baby sitting in an early 1900's doctor's bag was on the cover and an image of an Oklahoma tornado on the back side.

The fifth song on the album was titled "Oklahoma." The lyrics combine the nervous anticipation of an impending thunderstorm and tornado with the heat and energy of an old-time tent revival. Both concepts are very real in Oklahoma. The line: "Another Hot Oklahoma Night" would serve as the title for the project and an allegory for the heat and energy of Rock and Roll. Oklahoma Rock and Roll can be very hot and very humid, whether you're watching Leon Russell play "Jumping Jack Flash" during George Harrison's Concert for Bangladesh, sitting in a car making out to Eddie Cochran with your high school sweetheart, or dancing to the GAP Band at the Rose Room in North Tulsa.

After picking the project title, Michael and Scott had to be involved. The staff met with Michael and his son Robert at a Black Rebel Motorcycle Club show in Oklahoma City, appropriately on Father's Day; and connected with Scott via MySpace (remember it was 2007). Michael was flattered that the title was a tribute to him and The Call. Scott was also very enthusiastic and worked with the exhibit team to arrange for him and Michael to be interviewed in August 2008.

Michael discussed growing up in Oklahoma and performing as "Little Elvis" during the Oklahoma semi-centennial in 1957. Michael and Scott told the story of how their grandfathers were classmates at the University of Oklahoma in the School of Pharmacy. And when asked about the significance of the song Oklahoma, Michael replied, "you write what you know."

Another Hot Oklahoma Night became an award-winning exhibit that opened at the Oklahoma History Center in May 2009, followed later that year by a book including articles written by Oklahoma music legends Steve Ripley, Jimmy LaFave, and Wayne Coyne. The success of Another Hot Oklahoma Night: A Rock and Roll Exhibit prompted an effort by the Oklahoma Historical Society to build a museum, called OKPOP, in downtown Tulsa across the street from historic Cain's Ballroom. OKPOP is dedicated to Oklahoma's influence on music and all forms of popular culture, and it all began with The Call."

****

Clearly The Call, that little band from Santa Cruz, CA helmed by the Okie with the big voice and powerful message has made a lasting impact in our hearts, our memory and our music culture. Whether getting us through tough times, uplifting us with their spiritualism or just telling us we will be okay, they made a difference. Underrated. Underestimated... Yet their songs endure as relevant as ever, forever in our hearts and souls.

Thank you, Michael, Scott, Dicky, Greg, Steve, and Jim. Through all of the trials, and tribulations in life, your music, and message rings clear and true.

Thank you for sharing your music and memories.

- Knoel

Dicky, Michael, (with Unknown), Jim, and Scott on tour in Norway.
Photo used with permission from Jim Goodwin collection.

Club Lingerie w/ Harry Dean Stanton – Photo courtesy Jim Goodwin

Wendy (my wife), with Dicky in April 2018. She rescued his black 1971 lefty Gibson Les Paul, after the airline lost it. The guitar he toured with for many years with The Call. This was the second time Dicky almost lost his Les Paul for good. It was missing, this time, for 5 days.

Thank you, to everyone who contributed to this book. It wouldn't have been possible without a lot of people going above and beyond to dig out and send me old photos, rare items, special memories and so much more.

Thank you to **The Call** for trusting me to put this together. I have never done anything like this before. It was quite the task but a rewarding one in the end. Thanks for all of the great music and for being my friends.

Finally thank you to everyone who supported this effort and bought the book. Thank you for continuing to support The Call after 40+ years. I hope you enjoyed the book, the stories, the pictures, the memories and so much more.

Thank You!

Knoel

Acknowledgements

All lyrics / photos / album art and promotional items used with the knowledge of and permission from The Call.

All original photo's from New Orleans, 2017, and Tulsa, 2018, taken by Knoel C. Honn.

Most rare items pictured are part of the Knoel & Wendy Honn music collection including original vinyl test pressings, and record contract signed by the band, unless otherwise noted.

All information is collected from the band, band members, first hand interviews, friends, cited articles, and other cited reliable sources. The information has been verified to the best of our ability for accuracy. All information, data, and photographs are reproduced, and used with permission of The Call and copyright owners, no infringement is intended. Corrections and updates will be added to future printings of this book.

Lyrics/Images/Album Covers: Used with permission from The Call. All rights reserved on lyrics by: Neeb/Tarka/Tileface Music and Michael Been, Jim Goodwin, Scott Musick, Tom Ferrier and The Call.

No part of this book can be reproduced without written permission from Knoel Honn / Exotic Okie Productions.

Special Thanks To:

Scott Musick, Tom Ferrier, Greg Freeman, Jim Goodwin, Steve Huddleston, Carol Been, Robert Been, Dan Russell, Barry Albright, Ralph Patlan, Joe Read, Jim Kerr, Simple Minds, Peter Gabriel, Bruce Cockburn, Pat Johnson , Joe Piccorossi, R. George Inness III, Rick Malcomson, Jeff Moore, OKPOP Museum, Rick Huskey, Tate Wittenberg, Tim Spence, Ken Drew, Wendy Honn, Ken Hawkins, Philip Johnson, Mark Brittell, Lydia Bracken Musick, Gayles Mullen, Carla Olson & The Textones, David Salinger, Mikel Lomsky, Patty Ferry, Paul Goeltz, Pam Wilson Wetzel, Wood Mason, Phil & Debra Honn.

https://the-call-band.com/

https://www.facebook.com/groups/206565563474061

The Call – Like You've Never Been Loved FB Group
https://www.facebook.com/groups/206565563474061

https://www.facebook.com/TheCallBandOfficial

https://www.thecall40.com

https://www.facebook.com/The-Call-40-100999351861797

https://www.facebook.com/The-Call-Reconciled-103607294925227

Index:

Photos / Credit / References

April 21st, 2017 – New Orleans, LA with The Call

Tom Ferrier, Jim Goodwin, Me (Knoel Honn) and Scott Musick

Photo Courtesy of Wendy Honn – Photographer

This book was the culmination of listening to The Call for 38 years, collecting their albums and rarities, becoming friends with Scott, Dicky, Jim, Greg, and Steve, and spending way too much money on stuff, according to my wife. Finally, I pulled it all together during a pandemic, with a lot of help, after years of talking about it, and planning it. Again, on behalf of my wife, me, and The Call, we thank you for buying this book and your continued interest and support after 40 years.

Love notes:

"*Into the Woods* is their most complete artistic statement, but every album they put out was great. However, 'I Don't Wanna' is transcendent." – Matt Tomich

"*Reconciled* was the 1st CD I bought of The Call. The songs hit me so hard, and still do to this day." – Sal Espinoza

"It was hard for me to choose between *Reconciled*, *Into the Woods*, and *Let the Day Begin*. All three [albums] are strong throughout. But I chose *Reconciled* because it was my first Call album, and it gets the edge in terms of cover art (front and back)." – Tom Miles

"SO difficult because each [album] is strong in its own way; *Let the Day Begin* for me [is my favorite] because of the cohesiveness and themes." – Chris Collins

"*Reconciled* was my first cassette by The Call. Amazing album but once I heard *Into the Woods*, it became my favorite. 'I Don't Wanna' just hit me so hard and when I heard the rest of the album, it wasn't just music I was hearing, it was poetry from the soul. Brilliant body of music from The Call but *Into the Woods* remains my favorite to this day." – Jeff Reese

"*Reconciled* is the album that took me from being a casual fan of the band to a devoted follower. It has the perfect blend of righteous rage tempered by a sense of hope. It remains one of my top ten favorite albums. Not a weak song in the lot." – Brad Duren

"*To Heaven and Back*. It is the ultimate example of a mature Michael Been as songwriter supreme and a tight band flexing its musical muscles in the studio." – Steve Fekete

"*Reconciled* was my first. 'Everywhere I Go', and 'I Still Believe' hooked me for life. 'Blood Red', and 'With Or Without Reason' helped prove that spiritual lyrics could actually be done without losing musical quality. The Call, The Alarm, and U2 were my entry into that world." – Brian A. Smith

"*Modern Romans*, [is my favorite The Call album] because of the post-punk energy and the strong set of songs, and It was my first Call-LP!" – Per Arne Tengesdal

"I always thought 'Memory' would be special to me when I might lose my mother. She passed 5 years ago. I was right." – Randy Chamberlain

"The passion in Michael's voice in 'I Don't Wanna' is unbelievable. It still gives me chills." – Gary Banton

"Saw The Call at the paradise in Boston. It was the *Reconciled* tour. Michael sang 'I Don't Wanna' and it blew me away. Got to speak to him after the show and questioned him about the song. Told me he wrote it the night before the show in the hotel room. My all time favorite!" – Rick Malcolmson

"'Turn a Blind Eye' [is my favorite song] - for the energy and the desperate importantness of the signing and the lyrics! For being blown away as a teenager and discovering the raw social committed side of Christianity." – Per Arne Tengesdal

"'Uncovered' - Simplistic beauty of the song; keyboard, Michael's deep voice. They finished their set with that in Chicago on *Let the Day Begin* tour. Powerful!" – Chris Collins

"Have to go with *Let the Day Begin* [album]. John Beaumont in architecture school let me borrow the CD in 1989. I credit the album with a) leading me to a relationship with Jesus Christ, and b)

opening my eyes to all the other Call albums. (Scene Beyond Dreams is the best, tho.)" - Robert Nesmith

"'I Still Believe (Great Design)'. That song still gives me chills hearing the very first bass note. And it has helped get me through so many rough patches of life. It is like a booster shot of faith that I so need every now & then!!" – Ron Shockley

"'What's Happened to You?' - Every other group would have made this a negative, but the change that comes on people when they are spiritually born again is what is really important in life. ...Now there is a spring in your step and your words are on fire... Beautiful. Comes from a place of knowing." – Joe Lockwood

"*The Call* debut album. The power, raw feeling, energy, you can feel the years of thinking, stewing, working to emerge with the most powerful of debuts. There is a Heart Here!" – Joe Lockwood

"'Red Moon' has such a moody and stark mix to it. A most emotional album for me." – Kevin Rogers

"*Reconciled* [is my favorite album]. Love the faith based messages in its songs." – Greg Netter

"The truth is, I return to *Red Moon* more than any of the others. I get nostalgic when I listen to it. It just sucks me in. I wonder if the reason we lean towards a particular piece of music doesn't have to do with genre or a hook, but maybe has more to do about what your life was all about when you first listened and then re-listened to that piece of music. I really loved that stretch of my life when *Red Moon* first came out. I love my life now too but the sheer joy of holding my giggling daughter in my arms while singing 'Like You Never Been Loved' is a high point." – Cal Walker

"I can't even imagine my early life without The Call - and I am a lifelong atheist. You don't have to be Christian to love the music, passion, honesty, sheer singing and writing ability of Michael and the band. And it was Red Moon that got me totally hooked. Honestly, I never even thought the band was 'Christian Rock,' I just thought they were amazing and that Michael was one of the best vocalists out there." – Tara Foss

[Favorite album] "It would be *Reconciled* for me. Though *Modern Romans* was my first purchase after hearing "The Walls Came Down" on radio in 1983, and I became a big fan because of it ("Turn a Blind Eye" is still a Top 5 track of theirs for me). It was *Reconciled* as THE Call album that really cemented their all-time legend status with me. Side one is quite the opening salvo of first 5 tracks! Besides the subtle yet powerful faith strength of "Everywhere I Go" and "I Still Believe", it was the fury and lyrical rich imagery of songs like "Oklahoma" that hooked me ever more. Of course to be fair when *Reconciled* came out I had moved to my parent's home state of Oklahoma and was attending college there. So, hot summers, tornados, and fiery preachers were part and parcel of my mid 80's experience also being there in Michael and Scott's home state! The historical photograph cover in that cool purplish hue is a favorite all-time image as well. Additionally, in later years, I named my DFW church group startup "Reconciled" because of this album and its biblical meaning both. That said *Into the Woods, Let the Day Begin,* & *Red Moon* are all special in their own right and make up different vital music history in my life. Especially the latter two, when I was running record stores and promoting those two for MCA."
– Ron Shockley

"'I Don't Wanna,' to me, is one of the most powerful songs ever recorded. I still get chills when I listen to it."
- David Abe Abrahamson

Published by: Exotic Okie Production for Knoel C. Honn 2021

Made in the USA
Middletown, DE
28 August 2023